Rethinking Political Risk

Political risk was first introduced as a component for assessing risk not directly linked to economic factors following the flow of capital from the US to Europe after the Second World War. However, the concept has rapidly gained relevance since, with both public and private institutions developing complex methodologies designed to evaluate political risk factors and keep pace with the internationalization of trade and investment. Continued global and regional economic and political instability means a plethora of different actors today conduct a diverse range of political risk analyses and assessments. Starting from the epistemological foundations of political risk, this books bridges the gap between theory and practice, exploring operationalization and measurement issues with the support of an empirical case study on the Arab uprisings, discussing the role of expert judgment in political forecasting, and highlighting the main challenges and opportunities political risk analysts face in the wake of the digital revolution.

Cecilia Emma Sottilotta is currently a post-doctoral research fellow in political science at LUISS Guido Carli, Rome, and an adjunct faculty member at the American University of Rome and at the University of Calabria, Italy.

Rethinking Political Risk

Concepts, Theories, Challenges

Cecilia Emma Sottilotta

Routledge
Taylor & Francis Group

LONDON AND NEW YORK

First published 2017 by Routledge

2 Park Square, Milton Park, Abingdon, Oxfordshire OX14 4RN
711 Third Avenue, New York, NY 10017

Routledge is an imprint of the Taylor & Francis Group, an informa business

First issued in paperback 2018

British Library Cataloguing in Publication Data
A catalogue record for this book is available from the British Library

Library of Congress Cataloging in Publication Data
A catalog record for this title has been requested

ISBN: 978-1-4724-7751-4 (hbk)
ISBN: 978-1-138-36137-9 (pbk)

Typeset in Times New Roman
by Apex CoVantage, LLC

To my grandfather Angelo Sottilotta

Contents

Tables

Figures

Preface

Political risk analysis and assessment (PRA) can be described as a practice-driven, forward-looking set of activities performed every day by a plethora of corporate and governmental actors to provide investors with insights into questions that escape the realm of conventional business risks, as they pertain instead to the magmatic and sometimes indecipherable world of sociopolitical events.

From the point of view of a political scientist, PRA is an elusive, yet extremely fascinating, subject of study. Perhaps the most interesting aspect of this multi-faceted field of inquiry is the fact that any scholar venturing into it is confronted with virtually all of the big questions that have haunted political thinkers since the dawn of time, from the determinants and dynamics of social change to the relationship between the government and the individual, from the shifting nature of statehood to the possible (dis)equilibria underpinning the functioning of different types of political regimes – this, however, with a specific point of view in mind, that of international businesses engaging in foreign direct investment (FDI). In the information age more than ever before, the availability of reliable sources of intelligence – but also of intellectual tools to discriminate among them – is key to any business venture: businesses worldwide are becoming (often at their own expense) increasingly more aware of the costs implied by the dismissal of political considerations when making medium- and long-term investment decisions.

This book is the fruit of long reflection on how to make political knowledge genuinely relevant and intelligible for corporate actors whose jargon, conceptual categories and perspectives are profoundly different from those of scholars of politics. In this sense, one of the key themes of the book is precisely this inextricable connection between theory and practice, as the inaccurate conceptualization and translation of political hazards into actionable risk thresholds can result in serious damage – in the worst case scenario, even in the loss of human lives, as was the case in the 2013 In Amenas terrorist attack discussed in Chapter 3.

In spite of the many claims – by scholars and practitioners alike – about its theoretical underdevelopment, research into political risk as such has languished in the last few years. Thus, this book also aims to reorganize the research agenda on political risk as an autonomous field of inquiry by enlarging its scope to incorporate a number of other issues which are sometimes overlooked in the context of PRA, such as its epistemological affinities with futures studies, the dominant yet controversial role of expert judgment, and the political impact of the digital revolution. An important, preliminary disclaimer to be made is that this study deals with the *analysis* (that is, singling out the causes) and the *assessment* (which is about the modeling and measurement) of political risk, while the *management* of political risk (that is, the strategies for risk mitigation that can be implemented by the international investor) falls beyond the scope of this book. Closely linked as they are, these three phases are to be kept separate, as they constitute different steps of a process: there cannot be political risk management without political risk assessment, and equally there cannot be a risk assessment without prior analysis.

The book is ideally aimed at a threefold audience: (1) practitioners, including but not limited to those with an academic background and/or those working in the field of business intelligence and political risk analysis; (2) students taking – and lecturers teaching – postgraduate courses on country and political risk analysis or on international political economy with a special focus on multinational enterprises; and (3) scholars and lecturers of either political science or business studies wishing to deepen their understanding of the theoretical and practical challenges posed by the analysis and assessment of political risk for FDI.

Rome, April 2016

Acknowledgments

This book would never have been written without the help and support of many people.

First of all, I owe my deepest gratitude to Professor Leonardo Morlino, who patiently introduced me to the world of comparative research and encouraged me to research political risk when I started my Ph.D. at LUISS Guido Carli, Rome.

Special thanks go to Giulia Tufo, for her patience and understanding in the last year of hard work. I am also extremely grateful to Chiara Labate, Marika Gangemi, Antonino Ciancia, Lucia Mammì, Federica M. Canale, Mario Meliadò, Giuseppe Loddo and Paolo Catalano. Warm thanks also go to Jelena Pavicevic, Enma Andrés Sierra, Mely Cortés Verdón and Paolo Swuec for their support during my research stays in Belgrade, Berlin and London, and to Lucia De Cicco, Lucia Mencaroni and Alessandro Toppi for the indispensable laughter we shared in the last couple of years.

My deepest appreciation goes to Marco Giorgetti, who (among the other things) generously shared his insights as an IT specialist.

My thanks also go to Carlo Gallo (Director of Enquirisk) and Julian Campisi (from York University, Ca.), who both share my insane curiosity about political risk – thanks for the great discussions we had. Equally, I would like to thank Andreea Iancu, Managing Director of the Search Group (Global) Limited, for the useful comments she kindly provided, and Professor Llewellyn Howell, who in the wake of a LUISS School of Government 2012 conference on 'Investing in the age of political risks' provided precious suggestions and insights.

I am also indebted to all of my colleagues for support, advice and debates – particularly to Chiara Vania, Andrea Fumarola, Mohammed Hashas, Lorenzo Kihlgren Grandi, Manohar Kumar, Federica Liveriero, Domenico Melidoro, Sandro Romano, Valerio Scalone, Noemi Trino, Giovanni Vezzani and Fabienne Zwagemakers. A loving thought goes to Serena Percuoco, who left us prematurely in 2012.

I would never have taken the path that eventually lead to the publication of this book if it hadn't been for Katia Incandela. I am also grateful to Francesco Raniolo for his support when organizing my teaching schedule at the University of Calabria during the last months of writing, and to Raffaele Marchetti and Lorenzo Valeri, who provided useful advice at different stages of my research on political risk.

I wish to extend my thanks to the anonymous reviewer whose comments have been very helpful in shaping the volume as a whole, to the ten interviewees who kindly offered their insights and firsthand experience, and to my students at the University of Calabria and at the American University of Rome. I would also like to express my gratitude to Rob Sorsby for patiently answering my numerous questions.

Finally, I would like to thank my family: Elena, Silvana and Pasquale, Salvatore, Francesca, Sonia, Simona, my grandmother Emma and, last but not least, my grandfather Angelo, to whom this book is dedicated.

Abbreviations

ACLED	Armed Conflict Location & Event Dataset
ARIMA	Auto-Regressive Integrated Moving Average
ARPA	US Advanced Research Projects Agency
ARPANET	Advanced Research Projects Agency Network
BIT	Bilateral Investment Treaty
CIA	US Central Intelligence Agency
CRAM	Country Risk Assessment Model
DARPA	US Defense Advanced Research Projects Agency
DDoS	Distributed Denial of Service
ECA	Export Credit Agency
EIU	Economist Intelligence Unit
EU	European Union
EUT	Expected Utility Theory
FCPA	US Foreign Corrupt Practices Act
FDI	Foreign Direct Investment
FPP	Forecasting Principles Project
GDELT	Global Database of Events, Language, and Tone
GBN	Global Business Network
GJP	Good Judgment Project
GPRI	Global Political Risk Index
HB	Heuristics and Biases
IARPA	Intelligence Advanced Research Projects Activity
ICEWS	Integrated Crisis Early Warning System
ICJ	International Court of Justice
ICRG	International Country Risk Guide
ICSID	International Centre for Settlement of Investment Disputes
ICT	Information and Communication Technology
IEM	Iowa Electronic Market
IoT	Internet of Things
IP	Internet Protocol
IPCC	Intergovernmental Panel on Climate Change
IPE	International Political Economy
IQ	Intelligence Quotient

ISIS	Islamic State of Iraq and Syria
IT	Information Technology
ITCs	Information and Telecommunication Technologies
ITU	International Telecommunication Union
JV	Joint Venture
LDC	Least Developed Country
MENA	Middle East and North Africa
MIGA	Multilateral Investment Guarantee Agency
MNE	Multinational Enterprise
NDM	Naturalistic Decision Making
NGT	Nominal Group Technique
NSA	US National Security Agency
OECD	Organization for Economic Cooperation and Development
ONDD	Belgian Office National du Ducroire
OPEC	Organization of the Petroleum Exporting Countries
OPIC	Overseas Private Investment Corporation
PAM	Policy Analysis Market
PITF	Political Instability Task Force
PR	Political Risk
PRA	Political Risk Analysis & Assessment
PRS	Political Risk Services
PTA	Preferential Trade Agreement
SWOT	Strengths, Weaknesses, Opportunities, Threats
UNCTAD	United Nations Conference on Trade and Development
US	United States of America
USAID	United States Agency for International Development
WEF	World Economic Forum
WFSF	World Futures Studies Federation

Introduction

Whether dealing with debt issues in the Euro-zone, geopolitical developments in the Middle East, fast-changing investment prospects in emerging markets, or potential disruptions in patterns of global trade, the identification, assessment and measurement of political risk (PR) are recurring issues for businesses and governments today. According to the most recent World Investment Report, although total global foreign direct investment (FDI) in 2014 slightly declined vis-à-vis the previous year, it still amounts to $1.2 trillion and, most importantly, accounts for over 40 percent of external development finance in developing and in transition economies (UNCTAD, 2015). The role and impact of multinational enterprises (MNEs) in today's globalized economy remain highly controversial (Oatley, 2011), yet considering that FDI can have beneficial effects on host countries going beyond the mere inflow of financial capital – for instance, in terms of employment, accumulation of human capital and technology transfer – it comes as no surprise that countries from both the developing and the developed world compete to attract it (see for instance Barros & Cabral, 2000; Vukšić, 2013; Campisi & Sottilotta, 2015). On the other hand, when making long-term investment decisions, MNEs face a number of risks deriving from multiple sources – many of which fall outside the scope of ordinary business risks but are connected rather to changes in government policies after up-front investments have been made (Shotts, 2015), or to regional economic and political instability which may negatively affect an expected upturn in FDI. In fact, broadly speaking, political risk to foreign direct investment can be defined as "the probability that political decisions, events, or conditions will significantly affect the profitability of a business actor or the expected value of a given economic action" (Matthee, 2011, p. 2010).

Although risk calculation has always been part of any business venture, it was only after the Second World War – especially in relation to the substantial outflow of capital from the US to Europe – that political risk analysis, assessment and management began to be developed as such. The concept of political risk was initially introduced as a component of country risk, in order to account for the causes of insolvency within a country, and was directly linked neither to financial nor to economic factors. Political risk started to draw increasing attention in the following decades, as several institutions began to develop specific methodologies to evaluate it, trying to keep pace with the fast-changing dynamics of trade and investment internationalization. In today's world, characterized by complex and intertwined phenomena such as the proliferation of low-intensity conflicts, an increasing flow of forced migration, and transnational terrorism, downplaying or ignoring political risks may come at a very high price for MNEs (Primo Braga, 2015). In spite of its growing practical relevance, political risk analysis and assessment (PRA) as a field of inquiry has been systematically overlooked by political scientists; scholars of political risk converge in highlighting the theoretical underdevelopment of this concept.[1] Such 'theory gap' can be attributed to a number of circumstances: for one thing, PRA is a practice-driven field of inquiry, meaning that MNEs by and large demand – and political risk consultancies are bound to supply – real-time actionable intelligence rather than speculative analyses. On the other hand, PR is intrinsically multidisciplinary – practitioners are typically area or subject matter specialists – so that identifying overarching, universal epistemological categories for PRA is a formidable task.

After taking stock of what PRA is today in practice, the objective of this study is to bring together under a unified framework a number of theoretically relevant issues which traditionally have been either overlooked or treated sparsely in the context of diverse disciplines. Rather than chasing the elusive objective of devising a 'grand theory' for PRA, this book proposes a reflection on its conceptual and epistemological foundations, subsequently moving to explore operationalization and measurement issues with the support of an empirical case study. In addition, three cross-cutting aspects are comprehensively discussed: the role of political forecasting, the meaning of expert judgment and the impact of the digital revolution on political risks in general and on PRA in particular. In light of the practice-oriented nature of the subject of inquiry, complementing the use of secondary data sources, ten semi-structured interviews with PR practitioners and analysts based in Germany, Hong Kong, Italy, Serbia and the UK were conducted between July and December 2015.[2] Along with suggestions and useful remarks on the research, they provided precious firsthand insights into the actual functioning of the PRA industry.

Chapter 1 sets the stage for the rest of the book by reviewing the extant literature and providing an overview of political risk as a social science concept. A reappraisal of the existing, diverging definitions of PR is proposed; the most common approaches to micro and macro political risk assessment are presented, also hinting at the role of expert judgment in PRA, an issue that is further discussed in Chapter 5; a conceptual analysis is carried out, and a number of explicit rules are developed for concept building in political risk in order to lay the logical foundations for its assessment. Chapter 2 focuses on the epistemological and heuristic problems raised by political risk as an interdisciplinary field of inquiry. As far as the first set of problems is concerned, in rejecting the sheer positivism characterizing current approaches to PRA, the chapter suggests a critical realist approach based on a falsificationist logic; as regards the heuristic aspect, the chapter proposes an alternative to the traditional micro-macro political risk divide based on the concept of 'level of analysis' whereby it is possible to combine impacts and sources of political risk. Chapter 3 substantiates the claims made by the previous chapters with empirical data, showing how PR has been operationalized and measured by five different organizations whose (poor) predictive performance is discussed vis-à-vis the Arab uprisings beginning in 2010–11. While careful attention is devoted to the shortcomings of the approaches discussed, some possible improvements are also suggested, including a more nuanced understanding of the relationship between political risk and different political and institutional settings at the country level. Chapter 4 deals with another crucial issue in PRA – that is, the forecasting of sociopolitical events. Starting with a discussion of the past and present relevance of political forecasting, from the Delphi Oracle in ancient Greece to today's TV 'pundits', the chapter explores the strengths and weaknesses of seven categories of techniques: statistical extrapolation, game theory and simulations, expert opinion, the Delphi technique, opinion polls, prediction markets, and scenario analysis. Chapter 5 is devoted to the cross-cutting role of expert political judgment. The chapter opens with a discussion of the meaning of expertise which exposes the confusion still prevailing in the literature on this subject. Subsequently, two different perspectives on expert judgment in PRA are proposed and analyzed: in a first sense, expertise is equated with subject matter knowledge, while in a second sense expertise is associated with the capability to provide accurate probability estimations about the possible occurrence of political events. The chapter concludes with a call for increased accountability as a way to improve expert-based political risk assessments. A book aiming to provide a bird's-eye view of political risk analysis and assessment today would not be complete without a careful review of the practical and theoretical implications of the use of information technologies within PRA – including, but not limited to, big data, the Internet of Things (IoT), data mining technologies, early warning modeling, and the use of open source intelligence. Chapter 6 elaborates on how, on the one hand, the digital revolution has generated new forms of hybrid political risks, such as politically motivated cyberattacks, hacktivism, cyberterrorism; on the other hand, the chapter shows how – while raising important issues relating to the relationship between surveillance, security and privacy – the new technologies available can be used to track developments in the political world, crucially influencing the modes, speed and accuracy of political knowledge being collected and disseminated.

Notes

1 On this point, see Chapters 1 and 2.
2 The interviewees were guaranteed anonymity at the time of the interview; therefore, their personal information is not disclosed in the book.

References

Barros, P.P. & Cabral, L. (2000). Competing for foreign direct investment. *Review of International Economics*, 8(2), 360–371.
Campisi, J. & Sottilotta, C.E. (2015, August 27). *Unfriendly or unwanted? Inward-investment and political risk in Italy*. Paper presented at the ECPR General Conference, Montréal.

Matthee, H. (2011). Political risk analysis. In Badie, B., Berg-Schlosser, D. & Morlino, L. (Eds.), *International encyclopedia of political science* (pp. 2011–2014). Thousand Oaks: SAGE Publications, Inc.

Oatley, T. (2011). *International political economy*. Oxon & New York: Pearson.

Primo Braga, C.A. (2015). Strategy and geopolitics: Games countries play and implications for business. *IMD Blog*. Available at http://www.imd.org/research/challenges/TC025-15-geopolitics-and-strategy-carlos-braga.cfm [Accessed on 10 April 2016].

Shotts, K. (2015). Political risk as a hold-up problem: Implications for integrated strategy. *Stanford Graduate School of Business, Working Paper No. 3254*. Available at https://www.gsb.stanford.edu/faculty-research/working-papers/political-risk-hold-problem-implications-integrated-strategy [Accessed on 10 April 2016].

UNCTAD (2015). *World investment report 2015: Reforming international investment governance*. Available at http://unctad.org/en/PublicationsLibrary/wir2015_en.pdf [Accessed on 10 April 2016].

Vukšić, G. (2013). Developing countries in competition for foreign investment. *The Journal of International Trade & Economic Development*, 22(3), 351–376.

1 Political risk as a social science concept

> There is nothing worse than a sharp image of a fuzzy concept.
> (A. Adams, quoted by Hoffmann, 2014, p. 84)

1. A fuzzy concept

Even more than portfolio investment, FDI – especially when taking the form of greenfield investment – entails careful consideration of the possible political scenarios pertaining to a given host country: it therefore comes as no surprise that in recent years the analysis and assessment of political risk have become essential tools for executive decision-making for businesses of all sizes.[1] Today, a plethora of different actors carry out PRA for investment-related purposes, from consulting firms to export credit agencies, from rating agencies to insurance companies. The diverse nature of the actors performing political risk analysis is mirrored by the diverse meanings attributed to this catchall term. Partly due to its intrinsically interdisciplinary nature, political risk as such has been neglected as a subject for study within the academic framework of political science and international relations, despite the tradition of study into the disparately defined concept of 'political instability'. When data on political risk is gathered, elaborated and provided to multinational investors in the context of the political insurance industry, comparisons between the different political risk assessment approaches and relative indexes cannot be carried out easily for obvious reasons of competition. This explains the lack of transparency in the field, which raises questions about the logic and practice underpinning existing approaches to PRA. It must be acknowledged that, for instance, despite some interesting contributions in the last few years (see in particular Jensen, 2003, 2008), the relationship between political regimes proper and political risk remains largely unexplored.

Although risk assessment in terms of political environment has always been part of any business venture,[2] the acknowledgement of political risk in economic and financial literature only dates back to the 1960s. The conceptual boundaries of political risk have always been hazy, as is corroborated by the fact that since the 1970s, the scholarship on PR has been beset by literature reviews trying to bring this ambiguous concept into focus (see for instance

Kobrin, 1978; Fitzpatrick, 1983; Simon, 1984; Friedman & Kim, 1988; Chermack, 1992; Jarvis, 2008). Yet, as a first step in trying to achieve more clarity in this field, it is possible – indeed useful – to analyze the use of the term in its historical evolution. In the 1960s, when financial and economic actors began to develop country risk analysis, the political scenario worldwide was shaped by two complex and intertwining processes: the Cold War, with its inherent ideological contraposition between capitalism and socialism – that is, between free market and planned economies – and the beginning of decolonization. The likelihood of events such as the 1956 Suez crisis or the 1960 Congolese upheaval that could suddenly and drastically change the political as well as the business environment considerably increased. Political risk, however, sometimes also referred to as 'non-economic risk',[3] was predominantly considered to be a feature of 'underdeveloped' or 'modernizing' countries (Zink, 1973; Green, 1974; Green & Korth, 1974): as Jodice puts it, first-generation political risk analysts were mostly concerned about investment disputes deriving from so-called 'economic nationalism': the trend, typical of developing countries, to confiscate or expropriate foreign property in the name of public interest (Jodice, 1985, p. 9). The 1970s were marked by two events, both – unsurprisingly – with a relevant impact on the business world's perception of political risk: the 1973 oil-shock and the 1979 Iranian revolution. The occurrence of such grand-scale events highlighted the importance of political risk assessment and management, and the political risk industry began to flourish, with the proliferation of consulting firms as well as of applications for political risk coverage, provided both by public and by private insurers (Simon, 1984). The 1980s saw another shift in the implications of political risk, with a new focus on the problem of debt management by host countries.[4] Since the 1990s, however, and particularly after the attacks on the World Trade Center in New York City, terrorism has become a major source of concern for international investors and has emerged as a significant form of political risk (Berry, 2010). The scope and breadth of political risk analysis has also evolved in geopolitical terms from being mostly performed by and in the interest of Western (largely American) MNEs, to becoming a truly global activity. Firms in emerging economies invest in risky markets more than their global counterparts (Satyanand, 2011), and in light of the financial (and political-economic) crisis which began in 2008, developed countries do not look as devoid of risk to foreign investors as they had in the past. Thus, political risk is no longer seen as an exclusive attribute of least developed countries (LDCs). Generally speaking, it can be said that the term political risk has come to designate a component of country risk, the latter being defined as "the ability and willingness of a country to service its financial obligations" (Hoti & McAleer, 2004, p. 1). However, it should also be noted that 'country risk' today commonly refers to a wider array of risks, not only financial but also operational in nature: "country risk is of a larger scale, incorporating economic and financial characteristics of the system, along with the political and social, in the same effort to forecast situations in which foreign investors will find problems in specific national environments" (Howell, 2007, p. 7).

2. Definitions

2.1 A review

In an attempt to classify the alternative technical meanings that have been attached to political risk over time, the following definitions can be identified: (1) political risk as *non-economic* risk (Ciarrapico, 1992; Mayer, 1985); (2) political risk as unwanted *government interference* with business operations (Eiteman & Stonehill, 1973; Aliber, 1975; Henisz & Zelner, 2010); (3) political risk as the *probability of disruption* of the operations of MNEs by political forces or events (Root, 1972; Brewers, 1981; Jodice, 1984; MIGA, 2010); (4) political risk as *discontinuities* in the business environment deriving from political change and which have the potential to affect the profits or the objectives of a firm (Robock, 1971; Thunell, 1977; Micallef, 1982); (5) political risk substantially equated to *political instability* and *radical political change* in the host country (Green, 1974; Thunell, 1977).[5]

The first definition is typical of an initial phase in which firms and banks began to address the problem of assessing risks that could not be classified as mere business risks or be evaluated by simply looking at the economic fundamentals of a country. The second definition is quite restrictive and, as noted by Kobrin (1979), has relevant normative implications because it assumes that government intervention is necessarily harmful – in other words, that host government restrictions on FDI involve economic inefficiency. This is not always true, and in PRA the objectives of companies and host governments – which may diverge as well as coincide – should be analyzed accordingly, in order not to be misled by preconception. It could be added that, in light of the debacle of the 'Washington consensus', and also considering the financial and economic crisis beginning in 2008 – which exposed the implicit risks in the under-regulation of markets – the concept of *laissez-faire* government has lost much of its appeal to business theory and practice.

The third definition is perhaps the most precise from the semantic point of view, because it rightly considers political risk not simply in terms of *events* but rather in terms of the *likelihood* of events (harmful to an MNE's operations). If the aspect of probability calculation is overlooked, by conceptualizing political risk in terms of mere 'events' which can have an impact on a firm,[6] one might end up behaving like the proverbial fool who, when a finger is being pointed at the moon, only looks at the finger. Political risk calculation is an intrinsically forward-looking task (on this point, see Chapter 2), and political risk may well be structurally high, and be perceived as such by a firm, even in the current absence of possibly harmful events.

The fourth category of definitions is broader, since it focuses on the business environment rather than on the individual firm. The influential definition provided by Robock (1971) deserves a closer look:

Political risk in international business exists (1) when discontinuities occur in the business environment, (2) when they are difficult to anticipate, (3) when they result from political change. To constitute a risk these changes in the business environment must have a potential for significantly affecting the profit or other goals of a particular enterprise

(p. 7)

The idea of an existing, observable discontinuity in the business environment is quite common in definitions of political risk. Once again, it is important to underscore a point: even situations which apparently look stable – and that have been so for a relatively long time – may in fact be extremely risky. The notion of latent variables in statistics effectively illustrates this concept.[7] Risk can be thought of as the likelihood of a certain event taking place. What is subsequently observed is, in fact, a binary outcome: either the event does take place or it does not. The idea behind latent variables is that they are generated by an underlying propensity for a particular event (say, a general strike, a revolution or a mere act of expropriation) to occur. The political scenario in a country may look stable because it *actually* is stable, or, paradoxically, it can look stable in a given moment *notwithstanding* the fact that the political regime in force is about to collapse. A quite effective example thereof can be provided by recalling that, on December 31, 1977, President Carter famously toasted the Shah of Iran for representing "an island of stability in one of the more troubled areas of the world" (Carter, 1977). In the wake of the subsequent and unforeseen Iranian revolution and of the Soviet invasion of Afghanistan, however, PR analysts and scholars such as Brewers had to acknowledge the fact that "the past stability of an authoritarian regime should not be taken as a predictor of future stability" (Brewers, 1981, p. 8). This lesson has proved valid also for the Middle East and North Africa (MENA) countries which experienced drastic political change in the form of revolution in early 2011 (on the Arab Spring as a PR case study, see Chapter 3).

Robock also introduced a distinction that is particularly salient to this inquiry – that is, the distinction between 'macro' political risk (when political changes are directed at all foreign enterprises) and 'micro' political risk (when changes are selectively directed toward specific fields of business activity). Evidently, micro political risk assessment should be performed at industry – or even at firm – level, while, as can be seen from the present analysis, when writing about political risk in general, most authors are referring to macro political risk.

The fifth group of definitions was basically developed by authors who aimed to bridge the gap between political science and business studies, building on the extant scholarship on political change. Green's contribution is the first to focus on the relationship between the type of political regime and political risk (Green, 1972, 1974). Seven types of regime are individuated, with an increasing level of risk (Table 1.1): Instrumental Adaptive (such as the US and UK) and Instrumental Non-adaptive (such as France and Italy), which are labeled as 'modernized nation-states'; Quasi-instrumental (such as India and Turkey), Modernizing Autocracies (such as Syria and Jordan), Military Dictatorships (such as Burma and Libya), Mobilization Systems (such as China, Vietnam, Cuba and North Korea) and Newly Independent (such as Indonesia and Ghana), which are defined as

Table 1.1 Governmental forms and risk of radical political change

Modernized Nation-States (lower risk)		Modernizing Nation-States (higher risk)				
Instrumental Adaptive	Instrumental Non-adaptive	Quasi-instrumental	Modernizing Autocracies	Military Dictatorships	Mobilization Systems	Newly Independent

Source: Author's elaboration based on Green (1974).

'modernizing nation-states'. Green's approach rests on a number of assumptions. The first is that radical political change is intrinsically detrimental to the activity of MNEs. The second is that the younger the political system, the less it is 'adaptive' to change, and thus the higher the risk of radical political change. The third is that economic modernization inevitably puts the political system under stress, and that political institutions in modernizing states must either change or be replaced. Although, as already pointed out, this analysis does focus on the origins of political risk in terms of political regime 'structures'; it is not overly concerned with the empirical foundations of the claims made and does not delve into the specific mechanisms linking different kinds of political regime with political risk.

Today, more so than in the past, the task of political risk conceptualization and assessment is performed by private or public agencies (Business Environment Risk Intelligence, Control Risks, Eurasia Group, the Multilateral Investment Guarantee Agency in the World Bank Group, Oxford Analytica, Political Risk Services Group, to name but a few). As a matter of fact, most of them do not disclose – except to a very limited extent – their methodology for risk assessment, nor do they seem to agree on a precise definition of what a political risk is to the purposes of their activities. This aspect is particularly relevant because the lack of transparency in definitions and criteria for measurement is one of the reasons why the realm of political risk assessment is often hastily dismissed as a 'soft' science.

It is possible to draw some provisional conclusions from what has been said so far. First, despite several decades of scholarly endeavors, political risk in international business and political science seems to be affected by conceptual confusion. Second, in light of the renewed interest of scholars and practitioners of the subject, a reappraisal of political risk from the conceptual point of view seems timely. Third, no author, except Green (1974) and more recently Jensen (2003, 2008) has specifically analyzed political risk in relation to political regimes. As Sethi and Luther (1986) point out, "It seems that in much of the research effort on political risk, not enough attention has been paid to the development of concepts and definitions that capture the breadth of the problem. Unless the definitions are clear, other methodological issues are not likely to be resolved" (p.58). As Jarvis and Griffiths (2007) put it, the 1980s marked a renunciation by political risk analysts of such a 'systemic' approach, mostly because it seemed to be inevitably plagued by circular logic: "Low political risk and high political stability are manifest in systems that are developed, predominantly Western, liberal democratic, and capitalist. By definition, any state that displays dissimilar characteristics represents a political risk and the possibility of instability" (p.15). Nonetheless, the political and economic upheaval that has followed the 2008 financial crisis has proven not only that Western, liberal democratic and capitalist countries are not free from political risks to foreign investors, but, on the contrary, that they can indeed generate such risks – for instance, failing to introduce and enforce effective mechanisms for financial governance.

In sum, political risk could be defined as the probability that the profitability of an investment may be negatively affected by circumstances ascribable either to *adverse* unforeseen changes (such as revolutions, even when linked to democratization processes, or the outbreak of tribal/ethnic conflict) in the domestic or international political arena, or to governmental policy choices affecting an international investor's property rights. In both cases, risk analysis would need to be conducted by carefully looking through the twin lenses of domestic political regimes on the one hand and of international factors on the other. In particular, the role and operationalization of the second aspect deserve a closer look. As explained in more detail below (see Chapter 3), while some have conceptualized the 'external' or international dimension of PR in terms of 'bad neighborhood',[8] further reflection is certainly needed in order to reach a more refined understanding of such a dimension.

2.2 Open questions

Although they largely reflect the extant literature on the subject, none of the five groups of definitions listed above explicitly elaborates on the dyadic nature of political risk. Table 1.2 illustrates the idea that PR arises from the interaction of the specificities of an international firm with the specificities of a host country.[9] Elements such as the industry[10] within which a company operates or its size have an obvious impact on risk calculations. While a manufacturing firm on the lookout for new opportunities may have numerous options in terms of target markets, in other cases the freedom to choose a less, rather than a more, risky market might be limited (for instance non-renewable natural resources firms, whose choices in terms of location are normally constrained). Certain characteristics of the firm, such as its nationality, also deserve closer attention as 'country of origin' effects (Noorderhaven & Harzing, 2003) crucially influence the risk exposure of the firm itself. As one senior analyst puts it, the perception of risk of a company varies depending on where it wishes to invest: if the company aims to invest in a highly regulated market, the standpoint it adopts is likely to be the same as if the company were from that market. On the other hand, there would be a difference when an investor in a less regulated market invests in another under-regulated market as opposed to an investor from a highly regulated market investing in an under-regulated market (Interview, 2015l). As Pauly and Reich (1997, p. 4) point out, nationality does not necessarily derive from the location of corporate headquarters or the residence of principal shareholders but rather depends on historical experience and the institutional and ideological legacies thereof. In this regard, it should be noted that in international public law there also exists a trend toward the recognition of substantial criteria when it comes to determining the nationality of a firm (for instance the existence of a genuine connection between a given state

Table 1.2 MNE host country interaction and political risks

Relevant Dimensions – MNE		Relevant Dimensions – Host Country
Industry		Government attitude
Nationality		Political regime type
Business size		Level of corruption
Corporate governance	← Political Risks →	Contract enforcement
Core business location		Policy continuity
Overseas investment strategy		Factionalism
Intra-firm trading strategy		Political competition
. . .		. . .

Note: The lists on both sides of the table are illustrative.

and a firm), in addition to formal benchmarks – namely, the place of incorpora-tion of the firm.[11] In fact, although scholars belonging to the liberal tradition have argued that in the era of globalization the national identity of MNEs is losing relevance (see for instance Ohmae, 1990; Reich, 1990), the opposing literature suggests that, on the contrary, the national identity of the firm matters and has an impact both on its internal organizational choices and on investment strategies.[12]

Practical examples of how the nationality of a firm may constitute a source of political risk abound. The twenty-two members of the Arab League have been maintaining a boycott against Israeli companies and made-in-Israel goods since 1948. Although the actual enforcement of the boycott has been inconsistently applied over time, and despite the fact that its overall impact can be considered limited (Weiss, 2015, p. 2), there is little doubt that a potential venture with a partner residing in one of the Arab League countries would be much more risky for an Israeli firm than, say, an American or a British one. Similarly, following the annexation of Crimea by the Russian Federation in March 2014, the European Union (EU) has targeted Russian individuals and entities with economic sanc-tions meant to coerce the Russian authorities into desisting in their support of separatist rebels in the eastern provinces of Ukraine (Giumelli, 2015). In 2015, the newly elected leader of Sri Lanka, Matripala Sirisena, took a number of steps to counter the increasing influence of Chinese investors over the country's economy, including the suspension of works on a $1.5 billion port project being built by China Communications Construction Company (Kynge & Wildau, 2015). Again, a firm's nationality and business culture may constitute a factor of risk in itself even when the target market is seemingly stable and generally rid of 'macro' political hazards, but the same line of reasoning can apply to the full range of a company's features, as exemplified in the left column of Table 1.2.

In general terms, investors from highly regulated markets would be more risk conscious because its regulators are stricter in enforcing the rule of law and have higher expectations, in the sense that penalties imposed in highly regulated mar-kets are typically more severe and more likely to cause reputational damage to the investor. As highlighted by a senior analyst (Interview, 2015l), the US Foreign Corrupt Practices Act (FCPA) aims to prevent the corruption of public officials abroad, whereas corruption regulations in China, for example, would be focused on preventing corruption of officials within the country: in sum, the regulatory benchmark is much higher in a 'developed' economy, another example being the Ultimate Beneficial Ownership (UBO) principle whereby companies need to know the true ownership of the companies they are doing business with (Interview, 2015l). The point is to show that general definitions of political risk, as well as generalist approaches to PR modeling, by focusing on the host country inevitably tend to disregard the company's features and perceptions as risk determinants.[13] In this sense, generalist approaches to PRA make implicit assumptions about some features of the target locations which are likely to 'universally' affect investment, while practitioners and scholars alike should always remember that risk arises out of the interplay between different attributes of the firm and the host country's environment. Indeed, political circumstances that may harm a certain business or industry may at the same time constitute opportunities for another business or industry. While the Arab uprisings of 2010–11 produced considerable losses for foreign investors across virtually all the relevant sectors in the MENA region (see Chapter 3), they also provided new windows of opportunity for specific economic actors.[14] On the other hand, with this *caveat* in mind, it must also be recognized that generalist approaches to political risk retain an undeniably practical relevance, insomuch as they are indispensable to the production of cross-country comparisons. While, as further discussed in Chapter 2, Robock's micro-macro political risk distinction seems to be outdated and questionable today, it is still widely used in the prevalent literature. For this reason, it will be maintained in the next sections as a basic framework to describe the most used approaches to PR assessment.

3. Approaches to macro PR assessment

As already clarified, country risk refers to the analysis of the creditworthiness of a country. A number of well-established indicators and techniques have been developed over time to this purpose. Among the first, there are ratios such as capital inflows/debt service payments, debt service payments/external debt, external debt/GDP, as well as the default history of a country.[15] As far as the second are concerned, the methodologies used include logit/probit analysis, regression analysis, Monte Carlo simulations, value at risk and principal components analysis, and non-parametric methods such as neural networks.[16] A more detailed analysis of the forecasting techniques that can be used in PRA is carried out in Chapter 4 below; nonetheless, it should be stressed from the beginning that in most cases a purely quantitative approach is simply impossible to apply to the assessment of political risk. Events which are political in nature, such as revolutions, terrorist attacks, abrupt changes in tariffs or acts of expropriation, are generally much more difficult to predict than sovereign default. Therefore, human judgment – often referred to as 'expert' judgment – plays a central role in political risk analysis, as showed in Chapter 5 below. Looking at the historical evolution of political risk assessment and monitoring, after having surveyed a number of American MNEs, Rummel and Heenan (1978) found that four methods were mostly used for political risk analysis: 'grand tours', 'old hands', 'Delphi techniques' and 'quantitative methods'. The first category encompasses companies' efforts to get a sense of the political and business climate by recurring to company representatives' visits to a potential host country. The second basically consists in looking to unstructured advice from experts (such as diplomats, journalists, executives with country or area expertise). The third category comprises the Delphi techniques, developed by the RAND Corporation in the 1960s, used to elicit and aggregate expert opinion to obtain overall measures of political risk.[17] Finally, the fourth category embraces quantitative studies aiming to uncover political trends by resorting to multivariate data analysis (the authors recall how data on Soviet weaponry was useful to help predict the end of detente in the mid-1970s).

Although the techniques listed are still widely used today, the field of political risk has gone through remarkable changes and evolution over the last few decades. A fifth category of approaches can be added, with reference to efforts aimed at modeling risk on the basis of assumptions about the causal relationship linking certain features of the political environment to the likelihood of political risk events. Such models are used to perform scenario analysis and to provide aggregate measures of political risk. Building on the work of Robock (1971), for instance, Haner (1979), Simon (1982), Alon (1996) and Alon and Martin (1998) present a model of macro political risk assessment based on an overarching discrimination between internal and external sources of risk, and a further distinction between societal, governmental and economic factors (internal government-related factors, for instance, include 'degree of elite repression', 'degree of elite illegitimacy', 'likelihood that regime change will affect economic policy', each of which can be assigned a score ranging from '− 2' to '+2': the higher the score, the lower the risk). Brink (2004) proposes a model based on three main dimensions: 'political risk' (including thirty-seven indicators), 'economic risk' (forty-one indicators) and 'social risk' (twenty-five indicators), each of which can be dropped or weighted differently according to the user's needs. Many consulting firms use similar models. This is the case, for instance, of the model developed by Coplin and O'Leary, used by PRS Group to provide differentiated risk forecasts for three categories of investment: financial transactions, FDI and exports, with two different time horizons (eighteen months and five years), based on the estimation by country experts of the three most likely future regime scenarios (PRS Group, 2016). The PRS Group also produces the International Country Risk Guide (ICRG) country ratings based on three categories of risk: political, financial and economic. The Political Risk Rating, which accounts for 50 percent of the overall index, includes twelve weighted variables covering the following political and social attributes: government stability, socioeconomic conditions, investment profile, internal conflict, external conflict, corruption, level of military involvement in politics, religious tension, law and order, ethnic tensions, democratic accountability, bureaucracy quality. Variously designed political risk indexes and models developed by other bodies and consulting firms, such as Business Environment Risk Intelligence (BERI) Political Risk Index, the Economist Intelligence Unit's (EIU) Political Instability Index, and Eurasia's Global Political Risk Index, all share some basic features with the three models described above – namely, a reliance on the judgment of country experts, and the subjectivity of the weights assigned to risk factors and indicators. One of the most relevant problems associated with political risk ratings is that of their accuracy: how is it possible to 'assess the assessment techniques'? The question – which is further examined in Chapters 3 and 4 below – is thorny for a number of reasons. First of all, comparisons are not easy to carry out because of evident reasons of competition: most ratings are provided by private consultants or in the context of political risk insurance and as such are not open to scrutiny. Second, even when they are, it is not easy to quantify politically motivated losses incurred by companies, in order to place them directly in relation to past political risk ratings and test their predictive power against actual losses.

4. Approaches to micro PR assessment

Definitional confusion and lack of data affect macro political risk models, such as those described above, as well as sector-specific and even firm-specific models. In this respect, it is important to recall that distinctive approaches depend not only on the dimension of the firm but also on the business sector they belong to. For instance, political risk analysis has typically been a major concern for energy and natural resources companies, which are characterized by high sunk costs and which face unavoidable constraints as regards the choice of the countries in which they can operate. In this sector, risk avoidance is often not an option, and the only remaining possibility might be to try to build up an adequate risk mitigation strategy. Natural resources companies have always been exposed, in particular, to the risk of expropriations and nationalizations (as happened on a massive scale in the 1970s). Although losses related to expropriation episodes have declined over time (the World Bank reports 423 cases of expropriation of foreign assets in the 1970s, against seventeen during 1980–87 and zero between 1987 and 1992),[18] subtler forms of expropriation have witnessed a surge in the last few years, assuming the physiognomy of 'creeping expropriation', such as increasing tax rates on profits, which affect the profitability of the business over time.[19] The vulnerability of the energy sector to political risk is also well exemplified by the losses incurred by natural resources companies during the Arab Spring, which swept across the MENA region from January 2011.[20] Banks represent yet another crucial actor with a specific standpoint on the matter. Political risk in the banking context can be defined as "[t]he risk that cash flows accruing to a country's banks and bank investors will be adversely affected by changes in government policy that are independent of monetary policy considerations" (Simpson, 2007, p. 14). While also in this field political risk has often been assimilated to country or sovereign risk, there is a growing awareness that it deserves specific attention.[21] Moreover, although certain typologies of risk affect the business environment in general, there are specific risks which are likely to affect the financial sector in an almost exclusive fashion: in the case of the financial crisis that hit in 2008, in which big commercial banks were caught in the eye of the hurricane, political risk in the form of normative activity by governments aimed at regulating aspects such as capital adequacy requirements and bank reserves requirements (not to mention the much debated 'Tobin tax' proposals) witnessed a dramatic escalation. Specific risk models have been developed in the banking sector, such as the CAMEL model, based on the assessment of capital adequacy, asset quality, management quality, earnings, and liquidity; the Zonis model, based on three broad indexes (Political Stability Index, Policy Foundations Index, Institutional Strengths Index); and the Bank of America model, based on ten variables: GDP per capita, real GDP growth, nominal GDP, trade balance, current account balance, gold reserves, external debt, money growth, consumer price inflation, and exchange rate (Alon et al., 2006, pp. 629–630).

To sum up, the problem of the standpoint from which political risk assessment is performed is crucial (generalist versus firm-specific and even project-specific approaches), and it has an obvious impact on the techniques chosen. The methodological implications of the level at which the analysis is performed (depending on whether one is dealing with 'macro' or 'micro' political risk, to use Robock's taxonomy) are evident: while an index-based approach is indispensable to the provision of a cross-country risk overview, and is necessary, for instance, for insurers or ECAs to establishing within which class of risk a country belongs, at the lower extreme of this 'ladder of generality' lay micro-risk approaches focusing on individual projects. Micro political risk assessment also needs to take into account the stage of the investment-related decision-making process. The initial phase, for instance, might imply the need to choose the market in which to invest: in this case a general, cross-country approach might be the most appropriate. Once the decision has been made, and the operational phase of the investment begins, another approach is required, focusing on monitoring rather than rating countries. Nonetheless, it must also be stressed that both indexing widely used in macro PR assessment and more punctual, tailor-made evaluations typical of micro PR assessment share the same logic and the same theoretical and conceptual assumptions: they all have to face and solve definitional conundrums, and they equally require causal thinking and forecasting accuracy.

5. The role of human judgment: measuring the immeasurable?

An important observation has to be made at this point, although what follows is only an anticipation of the issue which will be treated in greater depth in Chapters 4 and 5. As previously hinted at, whether they be generalist or sector/firm/project specific, efforts aimed at measuring and modeling political risk cannot but rely on human judgment, which plays a crucial role both in designing models and in the concrete rating of 'soft' variables which cannot be measured otherwise. In the end, the probability of a harmful event derives from a judgment that "converts a political uncertainty into political risk" (Root, 1972, p. 57). Models for political event forecasting are only as good as the information they factor in – paradoxically, even the 'ideal' model, taking into account the truly relevant variables to devise the best risk mitigation strategy, would be completely useless if the raw data about those variables were flawed. Trying to circumvent the problem of forecasting political events which lay far ahead in the future, Clark (1997) for instance, develops a model aiming to measure the impact of PR in terms of value of an insurance policy reimbursing politically motivated losses. However, as the political risk parameters considered (such as the mean 'arrival rate' of political events generating explicit losses) are exogenous to the model, it is in fact virtually impossible to escape the necessity of defining what exactly constitutes political risk for the company, as well as trying to measure the level of risk in terms of the likelihood of political events occurring. In sum, although this issue is often forgotten or ignored by PR practitioners, political risk analysis and assessment epitomize the much-debated problem of measurement in social sciences.[22]

Translating abstract concepts into numbers, and doing so effectively, requires first of all a clarifying effort since "concept formation stands prior to quantification", to recall Sartori's famous warning (Sartori, 1970, p. 1038), and then, inevitably, a careful validity and reliability check (Jackman, 2008). Validity refers to the subject of measurement, and it is closely linked to the question of concept formation: when measuring political risk, what are we exactly measuring? In other words, which causal relations are we postulating between the abstract concept (for instance 'the risk of losses due to political causes') and the underlying indicators we choose to include in our model? A valid model is the one that 'hits the target' and therefore cannot exist without an unambiguous definition of the target itself. Reliability, on the other hand, refers to the variability of the measurement, its repeatability and consistency.

Indeed, it is not possible to ignore the limits of expert political judgment. However, it can be argued that political risk assessment techniques would greatly benefit from a general reflection on the process of judgmental data construction. Schedler effectively summarizes the terms of the question by calling for "common standards and operating procedures" in five crucial areas: expert selection, measurement comparability, transparency, convergence, and accountability (Schedler, 2012, p. 31). In the end, assuming that one of the most important issues in PRA is the quality of expert judgment, it has to be recognized that it depends heavily on (1) the background of the expert panel (what is meant exactly by 'expert'? Are criteria for expert selection thoroughly codified?); (2) the comparability of ratings (are there explicit, shared standards for such ratings? Are response-style adjustment techniques adopted?); (3) the overarching issue of transparency (the lack thereof in the field of political risk assessment has already been underscored); (4) convergence (how are final figures measuring risk components obtained?). As hinted at above, Delphi techniques are widely used, but other methods are also available, such as deliberative procedures to reach consensus, unstructured face-to-face meetings, the nominal group technique and so-called prediction markets);[23] (5) accountability, which as stressed in Chapter 5 necessarily entails efforts such as those prescribed by Tetlock, aimed at testing expert performance against "standardized baseline measures of forecasting accuracy and timeliness of belief updating" (Tetlock, 2006, p. 234).

6. What theory for political risk?

Apparently, not only does conceptual confusion still dominate the field of political risk analysis and assessment: the real problem is that such confusion is often not acknowledged. In addition, even the authors who recognize conceptual confusion mostly limit themselves to taking stock of the existing PR definitions, and they rarely 'get their hands dirty' by trying to point out which aspects of the model do not work and what could be done to improve them.[24] Thus, it is safe to say that the attempts made so far at bridging the gap between scholarship and practitioners are not completely satisfactory. In the attempt to show a way forward, this section reviews the extant endeavors aiming to reconstruct the theoretical foundations for political risk assessment exercises and suggests that PR is in fact a social science concept, and its study could draw useful lessons from political science subfields such as comparative politics and the study of the quality of democracy and institutions. In this sense, the main sources of conceptual confusion are explored and some rules for concept-building in PRA are proposed. As already pointed out, a relevant problem in PR analysis and assessment is that they are often carried out in an a-theoretical manner.[25] However, as theoretically unaware as they may be, all models necessarily factor in assumptions which are theoretical in nature. Howell (2007) for instance points out that

> [t]he theory determines what kind of predictive variables are examined, how they are measured, and how they are combined to generate an overall risk rating. Although theories are seldom explicated by the various ratings systems, they exist nevertheless and can usually be derived from an examination of the system or model utilized.
>
> (p. 13)

Although this is certainly true and is a realistic description of the state of the art, what is argued here is that in order to avoid conceptual and theoretical loopholes, theory – including epistemologies – behind models (and not just methodology) should always be made explicit and open to scrutiny.

What theory for political risk measurement then? Starting from this question, it is possible to point to at least two streams of literature in the social sciences intersecting the subfield of political risk analysis and assessment. The first explores the determinants of FDI in a broad sense. Such a stream could be referred to as a 'macro' approach to risk, because it looks at the interaction between two complex actors: the host government and the multinational enterprise. Vernon (1971) famously proposed an explanation of the activity of MNEs based on the obsolescing bargain theory, theorizing in this framework a competitive interplay between MNEs and host governments, in the context of a constantly shifting bargaining power. In this case, PR is mainly conceived of in terms of contract breach and risk of expropriation or nationalization. In proposing an eclectic approach to the activity of multinational enterprises, Dunning (1988) stresses the role of economic development as a major determinant of FDI, with little emphasis on the political setting of the host countries. Henisz (2000) finds that the institutional environments of countries matter when it comes to measuring 'contractual hazards' and 'political hazards'. However, also in this case, PR is conceived of as adverse government action. Thus, it can be said that the subject has been studied either from a micro point of view – that is, from the point of view of the individual enterprise – or from a macro point of view, or, rather, looking at the big picture but sometimes forgetting about the specific standpoint of the individual MNE. The attention of scholars of multinational enterprise has focused primarily on the determinants of FDI. Political hazards have generally been included among these determinants, but apparently interdisciplinary dialogue, for instance between theories on international production, political science, and IR, has been only limited.

The second stream of literature dealing with PR relates to decision theory. In one of the rare reflections on the theoretical grounding of PRA featured in the extant literature, Brink (2004) suggests that "where political risk analysis is a first step in decision making regarding foreign investment optimalization, political risk assessment focuses on problems that call for decisions concerning the implementation of actions (investment), and in a way, deals with decision problems" (p. 31). Therefore, the theoretical framework to which political risk analysis and assessment should be ascribed is that of problem-solving theory and decision theory. In this respect, risk is relevant in two different ways: first, in the assessment phase by the raters; second, when the rating is processed by decision makers. However, although decision theory certainly provides useful insights into how investors use information to decide "whether, when and where to invest" (Brink, 2004, p. 30) – in a nutshell, how PR ratings are *employed* – it does not seem to be equally salient to the *production* of those ratings. As a consequence, we should look elsewhere if our aim is to provide PR assessment with sounder theoretical bases. In this sense, it should be recalled that when building models to compare states across a number of dimensions associated to higher or lower risk for investors, many issues emerge that are similar to those encountered by political scientists when comparing political regimes for other purposes. In particular, the process and practice of measuring political risk seems to pose challenges which are similar to those faced when measuring the quality of democracy, for at least two orders of reasons. First of all, measuring risk and measuring democracy share all the problems related to measuring a latent variable. Those problems include providing unambiguous working definitions free from conceptual confusion and their operationalization, and possibly recourse to expert judgment. Second, if we assume that macro political risk is not regime-neutral (as suggested in Chapter 3), then we implicitly admit that by fine tuning our understanding of the features of a country's political arrangements it will be possible to also shed light on that country's risk environment. In sum, the conceptual toolkit of comparative politics can be used to the purposes of PRA. Models created to measure the multifaceted concept of the rule of law, for instance, can be adapted to compare countries across the dimension of likelihood of contract breach (to which the rule of law is negatively correlated from the theoretical and empirical point of view). In the next sections, an attempt will be made to apply lessons drawn from the branch of comparative politics dealing with the conceptualization and measurement of the quality of democracy to PR measurement. The first step in this direction will be to address conceptual and definitional conundrums.

7. Sources of conceptual confusion

If we take stock of the analysis conducted so far, we see that PR as a field of inquiry appears to be plagued by conceptual confusion stemming from at least three different sources: (1) the existence of *homonymies*; (2) the existence of *synonymies*; (3) *vagueness* in the relationship between the word and the referent. Homonymies occur when the same word is used with different meanings. Five alternative definitions were identified above, but at least one more can be mentioned, which constitutes a radical departure from PR as treated here: political risk is sometimes referred to as the risk of non-reelection of political leaders. For instance, Althaus (2008) defines PR as the calculation that political actors (of Western liberal-democracies) make before promoting a certain policy – that is, the calculation of the political cost of decisions in terms of lost votes in future elections. Synonymies in the literature also abound, the most widespread being those which equate political risk with political instability. This is indeed a conceptual loophole because although they are certainly interrelated, the two terms describe different things. Political instability appears to be a controversial concept in itself, especially if one looks at how its contrary – expressly, political stability – is defined. Surveying the relevant literature, Hurwitz for instance (1973) identifies five different approaches to political stability: "(a) the absence of violence; (b) governmental longevity/duration; (c) the existence of a legitimate constitutional regime; (d) the absence of structural change; and (e) a multifaceted societal attribute" (p. 449). This confusion has continued to linger for a long time, despite the attempts made by several authors to clearly separate PR from political instability (see for instance Robock, 1971). Another form of synonymy is the one that roughly equates political risk to country risk and sovereign risk (as made by Kobrak et al., 2004, p. 3). A third source of confusion has been individuated in the vagueness of the relationship between word and referent. Many authors, more or less unconsciously, end up equating political risk to the negative events that can affect the operations of MNEs. This is the approach, for instance, of the World Economic Forum (WEF) 2012 Report on Global Risk. Global risks are defined as "[h]aving global geographic scope, cross-industry relevance, uncertainty as to *how and when they will occur*, and high levels of economic and/or social impact requiring a multi-stakeholder response" (emphasis added). The semantic confusion is evident. Risk is a condition of a given subject: either one (individual, group, MNE, etc.) *is at risk*, or not. In definitions such as the one quoted above, PR is confused with particular *events* that should instead be classified as potential *causes* of risk.

A question arises at this point: should PR be considered an 'attribute' of the environment, independent of any actor that operates within the environment itself, or is it rather, as some authors seem to suggest, an 'attribute' of the international investor dependent on "the characteristics of the foreign investment: who owns it, what technology it uses, and to what economic sector it belongs" (Schmidt, 1986)? The question is not banal, as it bears important epistemic consequences (on the epistemological aspects of PRA, see Chapter 2). As in most instances, the truth perhaps lies somewhere in between, as political risk eventually arises from the interaction between economic operator and political environment. The problem with PR is that, as often happens in social sciences, an actual referent (that is, the 'real world' counterpart of a concept) is lacking. The concept is not matched by an object suitable for description but is rather a device built and used to capture a particular dimension of the interaction of MNEs with the environment wherein they operate, which is an intrinsically problematic task. A further remark could be added, relating to the so-called "language-in-use fallacy"(Sartori, 1984, p. 57) – that is, the difficulty in drawing a precise distinction between 'scientific' (or at least 'technical') use of the term and its use in common language. In fact, this formula seems to accurately describe the current situation of PR analysis, especially if one takes into account what Jarvis (2008) defines from the 1980s on as the abandonment of "theory for method" (p. 43), when scholars apparently stopped trying to develop general theories to explain, analyze and predict PR and focused on less ambitious, pragmatically oriented 'micro-studies'.

8. Rules for PR concept-building

The ambiguity surrounding the concept of political risk is due to several reasons: for one thing, as already stressed, the methodologies adopted by the numerous indexes providing country ratings and rankings in terms of potential PR for investors are heterogeneous and not always made explicit by the provider. As a result, in most cases a clear indication of how the concept has been converted into an index is lacking. Apparently, Sartori's aforementioned warning that "concept formation stands prior to quantification" has been largely overlooked in the elaboration of PR indexes. This section aims to propose a number of explicit rules for concept building in political risk.

The study of concepts is of paramount importance to the social scientist. It is not by chance that J.S. Mill (1843) devotes the first book of "A System of Logic" to "Names and Propositions". In the last few decades, starting with the seminal article by Giovanni Sartori on concept misformation in comparative politics (1970), a rich stream of literature has flourished on how multilevel concepts are formed in social sciences and how they *should* be formed in order to avoid aberrations such as *concept stretching*, which means increasing the *extension* (or *denotation*) of a concept as well as increasing, at the same time, its *intension* (or *connotation*). While the extension of a concept regards its empirical coverage – in other words, the cases to which it applies – intension regards the concept itself: its attributes and qualities. The rule for climbing and descending along a ladder of abstraction looks quite plain: there is a continuous trade-off between denotation and connotation, which means that, by going up the ladder in order to obtain a more abstract concept without losing focus, it is not possible to enlarge the extension/denotation of a concept (or rather, broadening the empirical coverage of that concept) without narrowing down its intension/connotation (that is, reducing its attributes). Thus, for instance, taking 'democracy' as our root concept, 'regime' would constitute a step upward along the ladder of abstraction ('regime' includes democracy, but also embraces authoritarian/totalitarian regimes and so on), while 'presidential democracy' would configure a descent along the ladder of abstraction. How does all this apply to political risk? As Jarvis (2008) rightly pointed out, "Defining political risk proves an elusive task if approached as a deductive-typological exercise, most obviously because its genealogy is discursive, its epistemology situated between disciplines rather than within a singular discipline, and because the generative agents of political risk are heterogeneous" (p. 1).

Although it is certainly impossible to deal with PR as with other less contested concepts, on the basis of what has been said so far some rules can be enunciated and applied to facilitate the task. First of all, it can be said that many authors more or less unconsciously apply the ladder of abstraction scheme when mentioning, alternatively, 'political risk' in general (pointing to the overall situation of a country) and 'political risks' (meaning by this the possibility that some specifically individuated events take place – an act of expropriation or the nationalization of an entire sector, for example). At this point another useful distinction can be mentioned – specifically, between "kind hierarchies" and "part-whole hierarchies" (Collier & Levitsky, 1997). Kind hierarchies are based on the idea that subordinate concepts are a 'kind of' in relation to superordinate concepts. Therefore, moving down along the ladder of abstraction, a subordinate concept is a kind of the superordinate. In part-whole hierarchies on the other hand, the superordinate concept is thought of as a whole, and the subordinate concept as a component or a part of it. In this sense, for example, if we consider a procedural, empirical concept of democracy as presenting the following four basic features – (1) universal suffrage, both male and female; (2) free, competitive, recurrent, and fair elections; (3) more than one party; (4) different and alternative media sources (see Morlino, 2011, ch. 3) – it is possible to notice how each feature constitutes a different concept (in the context of the multilevel concept of 'democracy'). Yet, all of the concepts can be virtually located at a lower level of abstraction *vis-à-vis* the overarching category of 'democracy'.

The relevance of the part-whole hierarchy scheme to PR is evident. As previously stated, the origins of political risk as a social science concept lie in the development of systems to assess country risk as an overarching concept. However, a distinction should be added here too: in spite of the recognition of the relevance of the political aspects of country risk, which have started to be assessed independently of purely economic indicators, for the sake of clarity the origins of the concept and its usage need to be recalled: PR in this sense should be thought of as a component of country risk. Bearing in mind the concept of PR and taking stock of its peculiarities, another point is worth stressing. The term (*signifier* in semantics) is the word we use to refer to something (signified); the meaning is essentially the connotation, or intension, pertaining to the term; the referent is the 'object', or real-world counterpart of the term. The problem when dealing with a concept such as PR is evident: how to treat a concept whose referent, assuming that it exists, is so fuzzy? How to circumvent, in our conceptual strategy, what can be defined as "reification, essentialism, and instrumentalist view of language" (Bevir & Kedar, 2008, p. 507)? The task is not easy at all, because the concept of risk itself entails a strong and inescapable subjective component; namely, the meaning of the term 'risk' is underpinned by its real-life referent (an ultimately unknowable future outcome) having been 'perceived' and 'weighted' by someone; or put simply, the term implies a subjective judgment or evaluation – a fact too easily overlooked in its use. The goal of transforming risk into an objectively, absolutely measurable substance is therefore impossible to attain. It is precisely for this reason that justifying and clarifying the choices made is indispensable when attempting to lay sound theoretical foundations for the conceptualization, operationalization and consistent measurement of political risk. Outlining the conceptual approach that will be adopted is of paramount importance to PRA in general, and even more so when its specific objective is to build PR indexes. In fact, while most PR indexes claim to adopt a 'pragmatic' rather than a 'theoretical' approach, as every social scientist knows, any index is nothing but a theory-laden model in which causal assumptions are always embedded. Indexes of PR are supposed to contain snapshot information on countries, but their essential purpose is predictive, not merely diagnostic, as they entail causal assumptions, for instance, about what makes a political regime more or less stable or more or less likely to enforce property rights for foreign investors. In his seminal work on social science concepts, Goertz (2006) distinguishes between the so-called factor-analytic approach and what he calls an 'ontological, realist and causal' approach. The first approach aims to measure an abstract concept (such as 'intelligence') by making inferences about its external manifestation (such as the ability to carry out a certain task in a certain time). The causal relationship then is akin to a top-down one in nature: the abstract concept manifests itself in a number of ways which can be translated into variables to be measured as 'symptoms' of the concept itself. The concept of 'legitimacy' can be taken as an example of the possible recourse to 'effect-driven', substitutable variables: legitimacy could be measured, for instance, by recurring to the size of a state's secret police aiming to crush dissenters (Gilley, 2006, p. 504). The second approach, adopted by Goertz, is *ontological* in that the sub-dimensions of the concept are substantial (for instance, free, fair and competitive elections are constitutive of democracy, not a 'symptom' thereof), *realist* in that it is not purely semantic but involves an empirical analysis of the concept referred to by the word, and *causal* in that it looks at the causal relationship between ontological attributes and causal hypotheses, explanations, and mechanisms. According to this approach, causality could be described as following a bidirectional pattern, because attributes influence and are in turn influenced by the overarching concept. Neither of these two approaches seems to be fit for PR analysis and assessment. The causal direction in this case is reversed, as illustrated in Figure 1.1. As already stressed, PR is a latent variable: it cannot be measured directly; therefore, other variables need to be chosen in order to measure it. In this respect, particular attention should be paid to the nature of the relationship between those variables, or dimensions, and the concept itself. Bollen and Lennox (1991, p. 305) distinguish between "indicators that influence, and those influenced by, latent variables". Concepts and measures of political risk cannot but adopt the first, 'causal' approach: PR as a construct necessarily incorporates a number of causal propositions with predictive purposes.

If we draw on the analysis conducted, some rules for PR concept-building can be enunciated: (1) when dealing with PR, a part-whole hierarchy approach is to be preferred to a classic, Aristotelian kind-hierarchy; (2) PR can be thought of as a 'three level concept', with a basic level, a secondary level (dimensions) and an indicator/data level; (3) in order to build consistent and reliable measurement techniques for PR, special attention should be paid to the relationship between the basic and the secondary level of the concept; (4) such relationship should be conceptualized as being causal and its direction as being bottom-up, configuring a model in which the dimensions are the explicative variables, and political risk the explained variable. These rules will prove useful both in assessing the performance of existing PRA methods and in formulating empirical definitions with unambiguous boundaries. Eventually, PRA will require clear-cut conceptual tools because conceptual confusion always has implications with respect to the choice of dimensions and sub-dimensions used to operationalize the concept itself. Error can easily occur if the dimensions and sub-dimensions used to measure the concept are not fit for the task – that is, if they are not causally linked to the concept itself. A good example of this is the above mentioned EIU's Political Instability Index 2009–10, which claims to measure instability as the "likelihood of future socio-political unrest" but actually operationalizes the concept in terms of a country's past record, thus in a sense overlooking the possibility of abrupt political change in more or less consolidated authoritarian regimes. This point is true both for firm-specific and generalist approaches to PRA. As already pointed out, the trend nowadays is towards a pragmatic approach to political risk analysis and assessment, focusing on the standpoint of the individual investor. While, as hinted at above, circumstances which represent risk for one investor may represent an

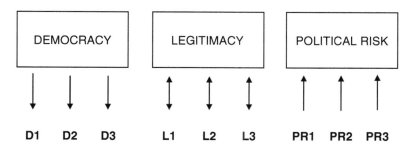

Figure 1.1 Direction of concept-dimensions causal relationship

opportunity for another, generalist political and country risk ratings still do provide important guidance for economic operators – especially small and medium-sized enterprises, most of which do not have an in-house political risk analysis division – in investment decisions, at least at an initial stage.

9. Some provisional conclusions

While in the past, political risk was often conceptualized in terms of hostile action by host countries' governments, its nature and sources have considerably changed due to the rapid pace of globalization of trade and investment, raising the level of scholarly interest across different fields, from international economics to international relations, from empirical political science to psychology and decision theory. In an era in which global equilibria have changed and once clear-cut distinctions such as 'developing' versus 'developed' countries are becoming more and more blurred, intelligence and risk management have become a major source of concern. The issue of how to analyze the relationship between politics and the activity of international investors has become even more pressing in light of the ongoing economic and financial crisis, a crisis whose causes are – at least partially – ascribable to questionable policy choices. Overviewing the prevalent political risk literature, some issues clearly emerge: first of all, given the multitude of meanings attached to this term, there is still confusion about what political risk exactly is, and how best to assess it. This holds true at every level of analysis, whether the approach be based on 'micro' or 'macro' political risk. A major challenge in this respect regards the question of how to design and conduct meta-studies of political risk assessment methodologies. For the reasons outlined above, in most cases opacity persists around the choices underlying the construction of models, as well as around the production and processing of the information that models factor in. In other words, how is it possible to better organize knowledge for predictive purposes in a field that has often been regarded as more of an 'art' than a 'science'? Are there ways to reach a higher level of transparency and accountability? It is worth noting that in comparing different PRA approaches it would also be important to avoid the problem of circularity in studies investigating various aspects of political risk itself: suffice it to mention that numerous works make use of the same political risk data, and their findings ultimately rely on the validity of such data (see for instance Diamonte et al., 1996; Erb et al., 1996: Oetzel et al., 2001; Simpson, 2007; Click & Weiner, 2010, who all use the same PR index in their studies). Finally, another question regards the possible contribution to political risk analysis and assessment of various disciplines, including, but not limited to, political science. In spite of claims of multidisciplinarity in PRA, efforts at developing a theory of political risk, including a reflection on its epistemological bases, have been limited and, in general, confined within the boundaries of positivist-oriented pragmatism. Somewhat surprisingly, virtually no author has so far proposed a critical reappraisal of PRA as a 'scientific' endeavor based on a study of the future. In an attempt to fill this gap, the next chapter delves into the explicit as well as the implicit epistemological claims made by scholars and practitioners in the field.

Notes

1　Sections 1–2 are based on Sottilotta, C.E. (2015). Political risk assessment and the Arab spring: What can we learn? *Thunderbird International Business Review*, 57(5), 379–390. © 2015 Wiley Periodicals, Inc. DOI: 10.1002/tie.21689.

2　For a historical account of country risk in the late nineteenth and early twentieth century, see Ferguson and Schularick (2004).

3　See for instance Mayer (1985, p. 10). The author surveys the (more or less) structured systems used by banks and other entities to assess country risk, considering political risk as a part of it.

4　See for instance Picht and Stüven (1991).

5　Thunell endorses Robock's definition of political risk, but in his study he conceptualizes political risk in terms of political instability, operationalized in various ways.

6　See for instance Ekpeyong and Umoren (2010, p. 28), who define political risk as "any politically induced event that has destabilizing effects on the polity, and distorts the functionality of an enterprise".

7　For an extremely clear account of the subject from the statistical point of view, see Scott Long (1997).

8　As in the case of the EIU Political Instability Index 2009–10 (EIU, 2009).

9　This is not to say that MNEs are passive actors in the relationship with foreign governments. To the contrary, as generally recognized by IR scholars (such as Nye, 1974), there are instances in which MNEs are capable of influencing national politics, at least to some extent, as their increasing importance "does limit state control over the domestic economy" (Kobrin, 2001, p.190). However, it should also be noted that normally the time horizon for change in domestic political structures is much longer than that of corporate actors. Hence, it is reasonable to adopt an analytical standpoint according to which the primary focus is on politics and policies influencing the actions of MNEs rather than the other way round.

10　On this point, see for instance Campisi and Caprioni (2016), who analyze political risks in the mining sector in China.

11　In this sense, see the famous 1970 decision of the International Court of Justice (ICJ) regarding the case of 'Barcelona Traction Light & Power Ltd.' (ICJ, 1970). For a more in depth account of legal issues related to the nationality of the firm, see for instance Fatouros (1983) and Winkler (2008).

12　Jones (2005) for instance argues that at the beginning of the twenty-first century "ownership, location and geography still mattered enormously in international business. [. . .] In some respects [. . .] more than in the past" (p. 29), while Pauly and Reich (1997) show that national institutions and tradition have a substantial impact on MNEs in terms of diverging patterns of internal governance, long-term financing structures, approaches to R&D as well as overseas investment and intra-firm trading strategies.

13　See for instance the Aon Political Risk Map (Aon, 2015). In 2012, Italian ECA SACE developed a similar map classifying risks also on the basis of the sector. In 2012 SACE proposed an industry-specific approach to risk assessment, whereby four different categories of investors (Bank, Construction Company, Exporter, Investor) were individuated and combined with three different categories of risk – two of which, 'political violence' and 'political-normative risk', were deemed relevant for any typology of investor.

14　There was consensus among oil industry experts on the fact that regime change in Libya would provide new opportunities for exploration and exploitation of resources (Park, 2012). If we set aside ethical concerns, it is undeniable that while situations of conflict are generally detrimental to economic activity, they also generate demand for military goods and thus profits for suppliers thereof (Wilkins, 2014).

15　For a comprehensive list of country risk indicators, see Kosmidou et al. (2008, p. 3).

16　See Bouchet et al. (2003, ch. 6).

17 The PRS Group, for instance, in the past has used a "modified Delphi technique" (Howell & Chaddick, 1994, p. 84) to obtain its country ratings. For an overview of Delphi and other forecasting techniques, see Chapter 4 below.
18 See MIGA (2009, p. 28).
19 Episodes of plain expropriation still occur today, as in the recent case of the Spanish Repsol Argentine subsidiary YPF, nationalized in April 2012 (see Peregil, 2012).
20 In this sense, suffice it to recall that OECD European countries imports of crude oil, natural gas liquids and refinery feedstocks from Libya dropped from 57.151 thousand metric tons in 2010 to 15.290 in 2011, reaching a low peak of 223 in the third quarter of the year, according to the International Energy Agency (2012) reflecting a dramatic drop in oil production which lasted for several months, due to the turmoil which culminated in the end of the thirty-year rule of Muammar Gaddafi.
21 See for instance English (2009).
22 See for instance King et al. (1994) and Brady and Collier (2004).
23 Forecasting methods based on the elicitation of expert judgment are discussed among the others in Chapter 4. For an overview of the techniques cited here, see Graefe and Armstrong (2011).
24 Howell and Chaddick (1994), Howell (2007) and Jensen (2008) being notable exceptions.
25 For a discussion and comparison of five different PRA models and their shortcomings, see Chapter 3.

References

Aliber, R.A. (1975). Exchange risk, political risk and investor demands for external currency deposits in the journal of money. *Credit and Banking*, 7, 161–179.

Alon, I. (1996). The nature and scope of political risk. In Stuart, E.W., Ortinau, K.J. & Moore, E.M. (Eds.), *Marketing: Moving toward the 21st century* (pp. 359–364). Rockhill: Southern Marketing Association.

Alon, I., Gurumoorthy, R., Mitchell, M.C. & Steen, T. (2006). Managing micropolitical risk: A cross-sector examination. *Thunderbird International Business Review*, 48(5), 623–642.

Alon, I. & Martin, M.A. (1998). A normative model of macro political risk assessment. *Multinational Business Review*, 6(2), 10–20.Althaus, C. (2008). *Calculating political risk*. London: Earthscan.

Aon (2015). *Political risk map*. Available at http://www.aon.com/2015politicalriskmap/2015-Political-Risk-Map.pdf [Accessed on 10 April 2016].

Berry, C. (2010). The convergence of the terrorism insurance and political risk insurance markets for emerging market risk: Why it is necessary and how it will come about. In Moran, T.H., West, G.T. & Martin, K. (Eds.), *International political risk management: Needs of the present, challenges for the future* (pp. 13–25). Washington, DC: The World Bank.

Bevir, M. & Kedar, A. (2008). Concept formation in political science: An anti-naturalist critique of qualitative methodology. *Perspectives on Politics*, 6(3), 503–517.

Bollen, K. & Lennox, R. (1991). Conventional wisdom on measurement: A structural equation perspective. *Psychological Bulletin*, 110(2), 305–314.

Bouchet, M.H., Clark, E. & Groslambert, B. (2003). *Country risk assessment: A guide to global investment strategy*. Chichester: John Wiley & Sons, Ltd.

Brady, H. & Collier, D. (Eds.) (2004). *Rethinking social inquiry: Diverse tools, shared standards*. Lanham: Rowman and Littlefield.

Brewers, T.L. (1981). Political risk assessment for foreign direct investment decisions: Better methods for better results. *Columbia Journal of World Business* (Spring), 16(1), 5–12.

Brink, C. (2004). *Measuring political risk: Risks to foreign investment*. Aldershot: Ashgate Publishing, Ltd.

Campisi, J. & Caprioni, E. (2016). Social & political risks: Factors affecting FDI in China's mining sector. *Thunderbird International Business Review* (Forthcoming).

Carter, J. (1977, December 31). Tehran, Iran toasts of the president and the shah at a state dinner. Online by Peters, G. & Woolley, J.T., *The American presidency project*. Available at http://www.presidency.ucsb.edu/ws/?pid=7080 [Accessed on 10 April 2016].

Chermack, J.M. (1992). Political risk analysis: Past and present. *Resources Policy* (September), 18(3), 167–178.

Ciarrapico, A.M. (1992). *Country risk: A theoretical framework of analysis*. Brookfield: Dartmouth.

Clark, E. (1997). Valuing political risk. *Journal of International Money and Finance*, 16(3), 477–490.

Click, R.W. & Weiner, R.J. (2010). Resource nationalism meets the market: Political risk and the value of petroleum reserves. *Journal of International Business Studies, Suppl. Part Special Issue: Conflict, Security, and Political Risk*, 41(5), 783–803.

Collier, D. & Levitsky, S. (1997). Democracy with adjectives: Conceptual innovation in comparative research. *World Politics*, 49(3), 430–451.

Diamonte, R.L., Liew, J.M. & Stevens, R.J. (1996). Political risk in emerging and developed markets. *Financial Analysts Journal*, 52(3), 71–76.

Dunning, J.H. (1988). The eclectic paradigm of international production: A restatement and some possible extensions. *Journal of International Business Studies*, 19(1), 1–31.

Eiteman, D.K. & Stonehill, A.I. (1973). *Multinational business finance*. Reading, Mass.: Addison-Wesley Educational Publishers Inc.

EIU (2009, March 25). Political instability index: Aux barricades! *The Economist*. Available at http://www.economist.com/node/13349331 [Accessed on 10 April 2016].

Ekpeyong, D.B. & Umoren, N.J. (2010). Political risk and the business environment: An examination of core challenges. *Journal of Financial Management and Analysis*, 23(1), 27–32.

English, K. (2009). Add political risk to bankers' management duties. *Bank News*, 109(12), 28–29.

Erb, C.B., Harvey, C.R. & Viskanta, T.E. (1996). Political risk, economic risk and financial risk. *Financial Analysts Journal*, November/December, 29–46.

Fatouros, A.A. (1983). Transnational enterprise in the law of state responsibility. In Lillich, R.B. (Ed.), *International law of state responsibility for injuries to aliens* (pp. 361–403). Charlottesville: University Press of Virginia.

Ferguson, N. & Schularick, M. (2004). The empire effect: The determinants of country risk in the first age of globalization, 1880–1913. *Working papers 04-03*, New York University, Leonard N. Stern School of Business, Department of Economics.

Fitzpatrick, M. (1983). The definition and assessment of political risk in international business: A review of the literature. *Academy of Management Review*, 8(2), 249–254.

Friedman, R. & Kim, J. (1988). Political risk and international marketing. *Columbia Journal of World Business*, 23(4), 63–74.

Gilley, B. (2006). The meaning and measure of state legitimacy: Results for 72 countries. *European Journal of Political Research*, 45, 499–525.

Giumelli, F. (2015). Sanctioning Russia: The right questions. *European Union Institute for Security Studies Issue Alerts*, 10, 1–2.

Goertz, G. (2006). *Social science concepts: A user's guide*. Princeton: Princeton University Press.

Graefe, A. & Armstrong, J.S. (2011). Comparing face-to-face meetings, nominal groups, Delphi and prediction markets on an estimation task. *International Journal of Forecasting*, 2, 183–195.

Green, R.T. (1972). Political instability as a determinant of US foreign investments. *Studies in Marketing*, 17, Bureau of Business Research, Graduate School of Business, University of Texas at Austin.

Green, R.T. (1974). Political structures as a predictor of radical political change. *Columbia Journal of World Business*, 9(1), 28–36.

Green, R.T. & Korth, C.M. (1974). Political instability and the foreign investor. *California Management Review*, 18(1), 23–31.

Haner, F.T. (1979). Rating investment risks abroad. *Business Horizons*, 22, 18–23.

Henisz, W. (2000). The institutional environment for multinational investment. *Journal of Law, Economics and Organization*, 16(2), 334–364.

Henisz, W. & Zelner, B.A. (2010). The hidden risks in emerging markets. *Harvard Business Review*, 88(4), 88–95.

Hoffmann, T.A. (2014). *Photography as meditation*. Santa Barbara: Rocky Nook Inc.

Hoti, S. & McAleer, M. (2004). An empirical assessment of country risk ratings and associated models. *Journal of Economic Surveys*, 18(4), 539–588.

Howell, L.D. (2007). Country and political risk assessment for managers. In Howell, L.D. (Ed.), *The handbook of country and political risk analysis* (pp.3–20). East Syracuse: PRS Group Inc.

Hurwitz, L. (1973). Contemporary approaches to political stability. *Comparative Politics, Special Issue on Revolution and Social Change*, 5(3), 449–463.

ICJ (1970). *Barcelona Traction, Light and Power Company, Limited (Belgium v. Spain)*. Available at http://www.icj-cij.org/docket/index.php?p1=3&p2=3&case=50&p3=4 [Accessed on 10 April 2016].

International Energy Agency (2012, July). *Monthly oil survey*. Available at http://www.iea.org/statistics/monthlystatistics/monthlyoilstatistics/ [Accessed on 10 April 2016].

Interview (2015l, December 28). Semi-structured written interview with managing director of international risk and due diligence consulting firm.

Jackman, S. (2008). Measurement. In Box-Steffensmeier, J.M., Brady, H.E. & Collier, D. (Eds.), *The Oxford handbook of political methodology* (pp. 119–151). Oxford: Oxford University Press.

Jarvis, D.S.L. (2008). Conceptualizing, analyzing and measuring political risk: The evolution of theory and method. *Lee Kuan School of Public Policy Research Paper No. LKYSPP08-004*. Available at http://ssrn.com/abstract=1162541 [Accessed on 10 April 2016].

Jarvis, D.S.L. & Griffiths, M. (2007). Learning to fly: The evolution of political risk analysis. *Global Society*, 21(1), 5–21.

Jensen, N.M. (2003). Democratic governance and multinational corporations: Political regimes and inflows of foreign direct investment. *International Organization*, 57(3), 587–616.

Jensen, N.M. (2008). Political regimes and political risk: Democratic institutions and expropriation risk for multinational investors. *The Journal of Politics*, 70(4), 1040–1052.

Jodice, D.A. (1984). Trends in political risk assessment: Prospects for the future. In Ghadar, F. & Moran, T.H. (Eds.), *International political risk management: New dimensions* (pp. 8–26). Washington, DC: Ghadar and Associates.

Jodice, D.A. (1985). *Political risk assessment: An annotated bibliography.* Westport: Greenwood Press.

Jones, G.G. (2005). Nationality and multinationals in historical perspective. Harvard Business School Working Paper 06-052. Available at http://www.hbs.edu/faculty/Publication%20Files/06-052.pdf [Accessed on 10 April 2016].

King, G., Keohane, R.O. & Verba, S. (1994). *Designing social inquiry: Scientific inference in qualitative research.* Princeton: Princeton University Press.

Kobrak, C., Kopper, C. & Hansen, H. (2004). Business, political risk and historians in the twentieth century. In Kobrak, C. & Hansen, H. (Eds.), *European business, dictatorship, and political risk, 1920–1945* (pp. 3–21). New York: Berghahn Books.

Kobrin, S.J. (1978). When does political instability result in increasing investment risk? *Columbia Journal of World Business*, 13(3), 113–122.

Kobrin, S.J. (1979). Political risk: A review and reconsideration. *Journal of International Business Studies*, 10(1), 67–80.

Kobrin, S. J. (2001). Sovereignty@Bay: Globalization, multinational enterprise and the international political system. In Brewer, T. and Rugman, A. (Eds.), *Oxford Handbook of International Business* (181–205). Oxford: Oxford University Press.

Kosmidou, K., Doumpos, M. & Zopounidis, K. (Eds.) (2008). *Country risk evaluation: Methods and applications.* New York: Springer.

Kynge, J. & Wildau, G. (2015, March 17). China: With friends like these. *The Financial Times.* Available at http://www.ft.com/intl/cms/s/2/2bb4028a-cbf0-11e4-aeb5-00144feab7de.html [Accessed on 10 April 2016].

Mayer, E. (1985). *International lending: Country risk analysis.* Reston: Reston Financial Services.

Micallef, J.V. (1982). Assessing political risk. *The McKinsey Quarterly*, Winter, 67–77.

MIGA (2009). *World investment and political risk report.* Available at http://www.miga.org/documents/flagship09ebook.pdf [Accessed on 10 April 2016].

MIGA (2010). *World investment and political risk report.* Available at http://www.miga.org/documents/WIPR10ebook.pdf [Accessed on 10 April 2016].

Mill, J.S. (1843). *A system of logic, ratiocinative and inductive, being a connected view of the principles of evidence and the methods of scientific investigation: Vol. I.* London: John W. Parker, West Strand.

Morlino, L. (2011). *Changes for democracy: Actors, structures, processes.* Oxford: Oxford University Press.

Noorderhaven, N.G. & Harzing, A. (2003). The "country-of-origin effect" in multinational corporations: Sources, mechanisms and moderating conditions. *Management International Review*, 43(2), 47–66.

Nye, J.S. (1974). Multinationals: The game and the rules: Multinational corporations in world politics. *Foreign Affairs* (October). Available at https://www.foreignaffairs.com/articles/1974-10-01/multinationals-game-and-rules-multinational-corporations-world-politics [Accessed on 10 April 2016].

Oetzel, J.M., Bettis, R.A. & Zenner, M. (2001). Country risk measures: How risky are they? *Journal of World Business*, 36(2), 128–145.

Ohmae, K. (1990). *The borderless world: Power and strategy in the interlinked economy.* New York: Harper Business.

Park, J. (2012). Petroleum development opportunities in Libya after the Arab spring. *OpenOil Site.* Available at http://openoil.net/2012/11/21/petroleum-development-opportunities-in-libya-after-the-arab-spring/ [Accessed on 10 April 2016].

Pauly, L.W. & Reich, S. (1997). National structures and multinational corporate behavior: Enduring differences in the age of globalization. *International Organization*, 51(1), 1–30.

Peregil, F. (2012, April 17). Argentina announces expropriation of Repsol oil subsidiary YPF. *El Pais*. Available at http://elpais.com/elpais/2012/04/16/inenglish/1334595212_305415.html [Accessed on 10 April 2016].

Picht, H. & Stüven, V. (1991). Expropriation of foreign direct investments: Empirical evidence and implications for the debt crisis. *Public Choice*, 69, 19–38.

PRS Group (2016). *Our two methodologies*. Available at https://www.prsgroup.com/about-us/our-two-methodologies/prs [Accessed on 10 April 2016].

Reich, R. (1990). Who is us? *Harvard Business Review*. January-February. Available at https://hbr.org/1990/01/who-is-us [Accessed on 10 April 2016].

Robock, S.H. (1971). Political risk: Identification and assessment. *Columbia Journal of World Business*, 6(4), 6–20.

Root, F.R. (1972). Analyzing political risks in international business. In Kapoor, A. & Grub, P. (Eds.), *Multinational enterprise in transition: Selected readings and essays* (pp. 354–365). Detroit: Darwin Press.

Rummel, R.J. & Heenan, D.A. (1978). How multinationals analyze political risk. *Harvard Business Review*, 56(1), 67–76.

Sartori, G. (1970). Concept misformation in comparative politics. *American Political Science Review*, 64(4), 1033–1053.

Sartori, G. (1984). Guidelines for concept analysis. In Sartori, G. (Ed.), *Social science concepts: A systematic analysis* (pp. 15–48). Beverly Hills: SAGE Publications Inc.

Satyanand, P.N. (2011). How BRIC MNEs deal with international political risk. In Sauvant, K., Sachs, L., Davies, K. & Zandvliet, R. (Eds.), *FDI perspectives: Issues in international investment* (pp. 36–38). New York: The Vale Columbia Center on Sustainable International Investment.

Schedler, A. (2012). Measurement and judgment in political science. *Perspectives on Politics*, 10(1), 21–36.

Schmidt, D.A. (1986). Analyzing political risk. *Business Horizons*, 29, 43–50.

Scott Long, J. (1997). *Regression models for categorical and limited dependent variables*. Thousand Oaks: SAGE Publications, Inc.

Sethi, P.S. & Luther, K.A.N. (1986). Political risk analysis and direct foreign investment: Some problems of definition and measurement. *California Management Review*, 28(2), 57–68.

Simon, J.D. (1982). Political risk assessment: Past trends and future prospects. *The Columbia Journal of World Business*, 17(3), 62–71.

Simon, J.D. (1984). A theoretical perspective on political risk. *Journal of International Business Studies*, 15(3), 123–143.

Simpson, J. (2007). Expert political risk opinions and banking system returns: A revised banking market model. *American Review of Political Economy*, 5(1), 14–33.

Tetlock, P. (2006). *Expert political judgment: How good is it? How can we know?* Princeton: Princeton University Press.

Thunell, L.H. (1977). *Political risks in international business: Investment behavior of multinational corporations*. New York & London: Praeger.

Vernon, R. (1971). *Sovereignty at bay: The multinational spread of U.S. enterprises*. London: Longman.

Weiss, M.A. (2015). Arab league boycott of Israel. *Congressional Research Service Report*. Available at https://www.fas.org/sgp/crs/mideast/RL33961.pdf [Accessed on 10 April 2016].

Wilkins, G. (2014, September 14). Growing global conflict a bonanza for arms makers. *The Sydney Morning Herald.* Available at http://www.smh.com.au/business/world-business/growing-global-conflict-a-bonanza-for-arms-makers-20140915-10h19u.html [Accessed on 10 April 2016].

Winkler, M. (2008). *Imprese multinazionali e ordinamento internazionale nell'era della globalizzazione.* Milano: Giuffré.

Zink, D.W. (1973). *The political risks for multinational enterprise in developing countries with a case study of Peru.* New York: Praeger.

2 Thinking about a theoretical framework

> Theory is your best friend.
> (G. Jasso, 2013)

1. Introduction

As already explained in the previous chapter, political risk is a multifaceted, under-theorized concept lying at the crossroads of different disciplines. From the standpoint of corporate actors, it can be defined as the probability that political decisions, events or conditions will significantly affect the profitability of a given economic action undertaken in a foreign country. Scholarly contributions on the subject have always oscillated between skepticism – events such as revolutions would be referred to as 'black swans' – that is, intrinsically unpredictable – and the belief that forecasting, if not *predicting*,[1] the occurrence of disruptive events of a social and political nature is possible and indeed useful. This chapter presents a reflection on a perennial problem within political risk literature: the quest for sound theoretical bases for political risk analysis and assessment. This section introduces the topic. The second section of the chapter discusses the epistemological aspects of PRA. The third section proposes a heuristic approach to PRA based on the concept of 'levels of analysis'. The fourth section wraps up the contents of the chapter by introducing a discussion on some recent geopolitical developments in the MENA region which will be further explored in Chapter 3.

As Jarvis (2008, p. 3) rightly pointed out, political risk as a field of inquiry "can [. . .] be claimed by political science, development studies, international relations, international business, economics, and economic geography, a feature which has undoubtedly been the principal reason hindering its theoretical consolidation and advancement". Similar claims about the theoretical underdevelopment of this field are extremely common in the literature on the subject (see for instance Fitzpatrick, 1983, p. 249; Simon, 1984, p. 124; Sethi & Luther, 1986, p. 58; Jarvis & Griffith, 2007, p. 10). The very entry of the International Encyclopedia of Political Science dedicated to PRA reads:

> Social science research and nonacademic interpretations of current affairs influence all three phases – namely, the analysis, assessment, and management

of political risk. In principle, political risk could also be useful in analyzing the general judgment and policy design of politicians under conditions of uncertainty. However, political risk analysis is undertheorized in this regard and currently remains rooted in the intersection between politics and business.

(Matthee, 2011, p. 2011)

Indeed, the ambiguity of political risk can also be traced to the fact that it was traditionally developed as a component of country risk, the measurement of which, as the name itself suggests, means focusing on the country as a whole as a unit of analysis. Country risk ratings always contain elements of judgment of a government's actions, its policies and eventually its creditworthiness.[2] Nonetheless, as further explained below, the conceptual and physical boundaries of political risk escape the static nature of national borders, especially if one equates a country with its government and its creditworthiness, as was the case when the first models for assessing country risk were developed.

A clear indication on how to organize the diverse literature streams and epistemologies which are actually or potentially relevant to PRA is missing in the current debate. Several issues which are clearly theoretical in nature remain unexplored, as the aforementioned case of the relationship between political regimes proper and political risk. The same can be said about the international dimension of PR – that is, the 'external variables', such as wars, but also more generally the processes and mechanisms triggered by globalization. While in the past some commentators have already called for a more central role for academic scholars in PRA (see for example LaPalombara, 1982), a reappraisal of political risk from the social scientist's standpoint today is more urgently needed than ever: at a time when the development of complex statistical techniques has generated an abandonment of 'theory' for 'method' (Jarvis & Griffiths, 2007, p. 18), the recent occurrence of political and economic large-scale 'black swan' events such as the international financial crisis[3] or the Arab uprisings proves that methods are worthless if used in an a-theoretical manner. On the other hand, skeptics have often labeled efforts at predicting social events as crystal ball exercises (Adler, 2001), thus discouraging practitioners from engaging with theoretical issues. On this count, it should be added that most works on the subject focus on the *management* of political risk and normally only provide cursory coverage of what comes conceptually and logically 'before' the use of PR data by managers and practitioners in general. Such issues as how PR data is produced, the explicit or implicit assumptions made with regard to its nature, and how the concept of PR relates to the disciplines of political science and international relations as a whole are sometimes mentioned *en passant*, but they are seldom addressed satisfactorily.

It should also be recalled that, to add complexity to the matter, risk assessment and risk perception are closely intertwined. After all, assessment deriving from analysis is heavily influenced by the way in which risks are weighed by decision-makers (be they politicians or 'experts'). In addition, risk perception works both ways: by this term, one might refer to the perception of risks by the investor, but also to the perception of risk (to the foreign investor) by the host country's policy makers, who might be interested in changing such perception for the better to attract FDI. Any attempt at 'objectivizing' risk by focusing on its sources while forgetting to analyze the features of the subject in relation to which risk arises would be misleading. The approach adopted is a multidisciplinary one, as "disciplinary segregation" (Crouch, 2005, p. 9) is not viable when studying the complex interplays between states, societies, enterprises and markets. In a way, PRA epitomizes the need for business scholars to recognize that a reentry of political science – as well as of other disciplines normally labeled as 'soft' sciences – into the analysis of the markets and the economy is inevitable (Crouch, 2005, p. 10).

2. Epistemological issues

Lying as it does at the crossroads of different disciplines, even a superficial exploration of the epistemological ramifications of PRA is a daunting task. To shed some light on this subject, we should once again recall what political risk is about. At its core, political risk analysis and assessment is about estimating the likelihood of future events. Thus, the political risk analyst is expected not only to know thoroughly the present conditions of a given country, region or industry but also to be able to inform the decision-maker – that is, his or her client – about the possible futures that lie ahead, considering both the most and the least likely. In a nutshell, to use Donald Rumsfeld's famous catchphrase about "known knowns, known unknowns and unknown unknowns" (Graham, 2014), the political risk analyst is normally expected to:

1   Master the 'known knowns' – or rather, the available information; in this sense, a 'country expert' is supposed to have a profound understanding of a "country's politics, history, culture, law, economics and international relations and a knowledge of the investing firm's likely place in that economy" (Howell, 1986, p. 51);
2   Be able to provide a credible representation of the "known unknown", which means being aware of the limits of his or her knowledge and providing as accurate an estimate as possible of the uncertainty surrounding possible alternative outcomes. This is exactly what the US intelligence community did not manage to do when providing public as well as classified assessments about Saddam Hussein's alleged possession of weapons of mass destruction: as Jervis (2010) argued, its judgments "were stated with excessive certainty" (p. 126).
3   Be aware of the fact that there are always "unknown unknowns", sometimes referred to as black swans which, in the words of Taleb (2007), are events which (a) are outliers in the sense that they lie outside of regular expectations because of a lack of experience or imagination, (b) have an extreme impact, and (c) are *ex post* predictable as, when looking at them in retrospect, the human intellect easily elaborates explanations for them (pp. xvii–xviii). A recent example of a black swan is the tragic crash of a Germanwings plane in the French Alps on March 24, 2015, after the copilot took over the flight controls and deliberately steered the plane into the ground.[4]

These three sets of activities give rise to a number of questions about the nature of sociopolitical knowledge – namely, what (we think) we know, how (we think) we know it and the use that we make of it (how do we select information to transform it into intelligence?), in particular as far as the ability or inability to foresee future events and to assess their likelihood is concerned.[5] In fact, with respect to this last point, because of its future-oriented nature, PRA has much in common with the eclectic field of inquiry known as futures studies. According to the World Futures Studies Federation (WFSF),[6] futures studies provide a conceptual umbrella for a plurality of approaches towards the study of alternative futures: the possible, the probable as well as the desirable ones.

The origins of futures studies can be traced back to the 1960s, when a group of intellectuals – including Bertrand de Jouvenel, Gaston Berger, Jerome Monod, Fred Polak, John McHale and Eleonora Barbieri Masini (Stevenson, 2006, p. 1147) – embarked on a collective enterprise aimed at developing "the habit of forward-looking" (Jouvenel, 1965, p. 2). Such an enterprise, claims Jouvenel, cannot be scientific in the sense that there are no facts in the future, as by definition the future is not the realm of "true or false" but the realm of "possibles" (Jouvenel, 1965, p. 2). And yet, argues Jouvenel, while there cannot be a science of the future, we cannot avoid thinking about the future (or rather, the possible futures lying ahead). And since that is inevitable, it is preferable to do it explicitly rather than implicitly. It is interesting to notice that the same line of reasoning was fully embraced by the first futurists working towards the development of new tools for strategic and political forecasting at the RAND Corporation:

> The fact remains [. . .] that for better or for worse, trend predictions – implicit or explicit, "scientific" or intuitive – about periods as far as twenty or even fifty years in the future do affect current planning decisions (or lack of same) in such areas as national defense, urban renewal, resource development, etc. Thus, almost anything further we can learn about the basis, the accuracy, and the means for improving such long-term forecasts will be of value.
>
> (Gordon & Helmer, 1964, p. v)

Although its scope is evidently more limited, as it deals with a particular category of possible future events from the standpoint of a precise type of actor, both its multidisciplinarity and its emphasis on exploring future alternatives with intellectual rigor suggest that PRA has much in common with futures studies. Greenfield FDI decisions are typically based on long-term assessments and planning mirroring those described above. In sum, if we concede that PRA is mostly – although not exclusively[7] – about studying and managing possible futures, then there are at least two basic questions that need addressing: (1) the possible ontological commitments for PRA – that is, on which philosophical grounds it is possible to conceive of a theory for political risk – and (2) the nature of the future forecasting/predicting activity which is central to PRA. In his reflection on the epistemological foundations for futures studies, Bell (1997, pp.191–238) identifies two broad categories of theories of knowledge, a 'positivist' and a 'postpositivist' one, and then goes on to propose a third view, critical realism, as a more suitable approach to the study of futures. In light of the previously proposed definition of PRA as a forward-looking, future-oriented activity, this subsection follows the same analytical path traced by Bell to sketch out an epistemology for PRA.

2.1 Positivism, post-positivism and critical realism

First of all, it must be acknowledged that political risk analysis both as a practice and as a field of inquiry is influenced by the outright positivism (Moss,1984; Hovenkamp, 1990; Alvey, 2005) still prevailing in economic disciplines. In very general terms, positivism can be described as the 'received view' (Hacking, 1981) – that is, a transcultural, cumulative theory of knowledge according to which the reality is a 'given' which indeed can be known through empirical experience allowing for scientific generalizations. As already recognized by Milton Friedman (1966) in his famous essay on "The methodology of positive economics", typical dichotomies in the economic literature are for instance 'normative' versus 'positive', 'objective' versus 'subjective', 'descriptive' versus 'prescriptive', 'ought' versus 'is' analyses. The dominant pattern of positive economic analysis is epitomized by the standard template applied to contributions in leading economic journals: an introductory section; a section describing the model applied, which inevitably presumes specific criteria of 'truthlikeness' (namely, statistical testing conventions); a subsequent segment commenting on the empirical results; and a final one summarizing the conclusions (Boland, 1991, p. 97). The assumption that systematic knowledge can be reached by observing the reality of things – an idea dating back to Francis Bacon's logic of induction – has proved remarkably resilient in contexts in which a pragmatic mindset is the norm and decisions have to be made quickly. This is in spite of the fact that clear-cut distinctions between normative and positive analyses – as well as the allegedly 'objective' or value-free nature of economic disciplines – have been questioned over time (Sen, 1967; Boland, 1991; Putnam & Walsh, 2011). Although, as further explained in Chapter 3, modeling sociopolitical variables is an intrinsically problematic task, there is a constant temptation for the analyst coupled with strong demand from the management of the investing firm (Interview, 2015a) to 'objectivize' or 'positivize' those variables so as to incorporate them more easily in the firm's decision-making processes. Such tendency can be easily illustrated by making reference to the countless indexes built by political risk consultancies with the aim of comparing the level of political risk to direct investment across countries, as for instance the Political Risk Services (PRS) Group's Global Risk Index (PRS, 2014), Aon's Political Risk Map (Aon, 2016), Euromoney's country risk score containing a political risk indicator (Euromoney Country Risk, 2016), the Political Monitor's Political Risk Index for Asia (Political Monitor, 2016) and Verisk Maplecroft's Political Risk Analytics (Verisk Maplecroft, 2016) to mention but a few of them. As claimed by a major consulting firm proposing "a detailed three-stage methodology for integrating political risk into an organization's existing risk management programs", the overarching idea is that "political risk can indeed be measured and managed" (Beardshaw et al.,

2015). Such statements, common as they are in the 'real' business world, would hardly be accepted a-critically by a hypothetical 'post-positivist' social scientist. In fact, if on the one hand PRA is heavily influenced by the pragmatic empiricism of the economic disciplines, on the other it also inevitably draws from the theoretically and methodologically multifarious world of social sciences which have fully embraced post-positivism in all its declinations – intending by post-positivism that, broadly speaking,

> the purpose of scientific activity no longer stands out as a statistical putting together of surface phenomena in an observed reality . . . [but rather] . . . to conceive this reality as an expression for, or a sign of, deeper-lying processes.
>
> (Alvesson & Sköldberg, 2009, p. 18)

Central features of post-positivism are also the rejection of the unity of science and the dismissal of the idea that scientific knowledge has nothing to do with the identity or the beliefs of the investigator – a well-known critical view embodied by Kuhn's classic essay on the structure of scientific revolutions. In sum, according to Kuhn (1996),

> Observation and experience can and must drastically restrict the range of admissible scientific belief, else there would be no science. But they cannot alone determine a particular body of such belief. An apparently arbitrary element, compounded of personal and historical accident, is always a formative ingredient of the beliefs espoused by a given scientific community at a given time.
>
> (p. 4)

It is curious to notice that practitioners and business scholars started talking about political risk as a measurable entity precisely at a time when positivism was undeniably under attack, although such occurrence is easily explained if we remember once again that for a long time political risk has been confined outside of the scope of methodological debates in the social sciences. In fact, from a post-positivist standpoint, objections might well be raised along the lines that it does not make any sense to talk of PR as a given or a measurable entity, because the different meanings of the words 'political risk' would vary so much from one subject to the other as to make them 'incommensurable' in the sense outlined by Feyerabend (1993). On the other hand, it is difficult to deny that pushing post-positivist views to their extreme consequences, as done on a large scale by the postmodernist movement debuting in the 1960s, inevitably leads to "the point where knowledge becomes a closed system, a language game" (Morçöl, 2001, p. 105). As Rosenau (1991) puts it, such a refusal to offer criteria for evaluating knowledge means that there is "no basis for definitively assessing the superiority of one theory over another" and that therefore a "denial of universal truth, or any approximation to it, follows logically" (p. 135). Where does this leave us in our quest for an epistemological approach suitable to the study of PRA? An uncompromising denial of the possibility to know about social reality would obviously wipe out any chance of a theory that may serve as a compass in the practice of PRA. On the other hand, pretending to reduce political risk to a quantity that we can measure just as we measure the GDP or the demographics of a country, all the while ignoring the complexities and ambiguities that underpin the concept, would be equally counterproductive. As already anticipated, a possible way out of this *cul-de-sac* is to resort to a critical realist approach along the lines of Bell's reflection on the epistemological foundations of futures studies.

Critical realism as an approach to the philosophy of science is usually associated with the early work of Roy Bhaskar (1975, 1989). According to Bell, critical realism can be defined as a post-positivist, post-Kuhnian theory of knowledge according to which science relies on the assumption that the world really 'is', in the sense that it exists independent of the subject; truth can be known within the limits of the human senses and discernment; although cultural, personal and social biases can threaten the validity of science, they can be self-consciously 'guarded against' at least to some extent via inter-subjective evaluation; different research traditions overlap sufficiently for possible contradictions among them to be exposed and critically tested (Bell, 1997, pp. 207–208). In sum, critical realism embraces a fallibilist worldview in the Popperian sense of the term. As is well known, according to Popper, "the method of science is criticism, i.e. attempted falsifications" (Popper, 1962, p. 52). While denying the possibility to *verify* inductively the statements of empirical sciences, Popper proposes falsifiability as a criterion of demarcation to admit a statement within the realm of empirical science: thus, the logical form of a scientific system "shall be such that it can be singled out, by means of empirical tests, in a negative sense: it must be possible for an empirical scientific system to be refuted by experience" (Popper, 2005, p. 18). A conception according to which the nature of knowledge is conjectural and "the claim that plausibility, not absolute certainty is the most that can be claimed from scientific labors" (Bell, 1997, p. 236) is well suited to PRA if we look at it through the analytical lens of futures studies. As Jones (2012) puts it, "if-then" statements are the order of the day for the political risk analyst. If Scotland secedes from the UK, then it "may have to pursue some kind of currency board arrangement" (Booth, 2013); "if the Taliban takes Helmand, then Afghanistan could go the way of Syria" (Rashid, 2015); "if the naysayers manage to blow up the newly minted agreement [on the Iranian nuclear, a.n.], it will be a disaster for the United States – and will only push Iran closer to the bomb" (Nossel, 2015): in a nutshell, political analysis is replete with arguments following a similar logical structure which, relying on the available information, essentially purport to predict a given outcome, provided that some conditions are met. Since what is at stake in PRA is the evaluation of different scenarios that may or may not come true in the future, the key task is to build arguments that can be compared and defended in front of an audience – most of the time made up of individuals with very diverse backgrounds – which is likely to challenge them (Jones, 2012). At this point, a crucial question arises with regard to the very nature of these acts of foresight. Is the political risk analyst a fortune-teller or a scientist? In a nutshell, is the purpose of PRA to *predict*, or rather to *forecast*, the occurrence of future events?

2.2 Predicting versus forecasting

Political scientists have been traditionally reluctant to embark in systematic and explicit futures thinking. As Crick (2015) wrote, "it is curious that an exercise of mind so common to economists and so talked about by sociologists has been so neglected by students of politics" (p. 347). Similarly, Schneider (2014) notes that political scientists overall are still disinclined to engage in the 'dirty business' of prediction, also in light of the disappointing track record of forecasting techniques such as opinion polls applied to anticipating the outcome of political elections. In the same vein, according to Schrodt, one of the 'seven deadly sins' in contemporary quantitative political analysis is precisely the "disparaging of prediction as the criteria for validating a model, instead preferring 'explanation'", while "papers and articles that attempt to forecast are simply dismissed by the discussant/referee with a brusque 'That's only a forecast'" (Schrodt, 2014, p. 289). Quoting Hempel and Oppenheim (1948), Schrodt argues that what distinguishes 'pre-scientific' from scientific explanation is precisely the predicting power of the latter, of which the former is lacking. This contention is in line with Popper's view that

> the use of a theory for predicting some specific event is just another aspect of its use for explaining such an event. And since we test a theory by comparing the events predicted with those actually observed, our analysis also shows how theories can be tested.
>
> (Popper, 1957, p. 124)

Schrodt (2010, 2014) provocatively attributes this attitude to the fact that most models developed by political scientists are worthless for prediction – although with some notable exceptions such as the Political Instability Task Force (PITF).[8] Thus, rejecting prediction as a legitimate endeavor derives from the human impulse to 'move the goal posts' if one cannot score the goal. Nonetheless, it can be argued that there are deeper reasons for such a reluctance, one of which lies precisely in the semantic ambiguity surrounding the idea of 'predicting' as opposed to 'forecasting'. While these two terms are often used interchangeably, they actually refer to two different concepts. According to Jantsch (1967, p. 15), "a forecast is a probabilistic statement, on a relatively high confidence level, about the future. A prediction is an apodictic (non-probabilistic) statement, on an absolute confidence level, about the future." Banal as it may seem at first sight, this distinction bears remarkable methodological consequences, as it reflects two very different ways of conceiving of the future and preparing for it. As effectively stated by Bauer (2014),

> A prediction shows where things are headed, with an appearance of precision, but experience suggests you have no reason to believe it. Why bother responding when the future will almost certainly turn out to be something

else? [. . .] A forecast, in contrast, is energizing and empowering. Its essential plurality, the probabilities of possibilities, implies choices to be made. A forecast tells us not only that different outcomes are possible and, to varying degrees, likely, but that several different possibilities can occur simultaneously within the area and time it covers.

(pp. 112–113)

Such demarcation allows us to appreciate an important point: in its singularity, a *prediction* is much easier to discard than a forecast. At a time when even the apparent linearity, uniformity and predictability of the Newtonian natural sciences has started to be questioned – for instance, by the predicaments of 'chaos theory' (Kiel & Elliot, 2013, p. 1) – it is indeed little wonder that scholars prudently shun prediction of future sociopolitical events as an attainable goal while falling back on the seemingly more reassuring, less pretentious concept of 'explanation'. It is in this sense that Popper rebuffs the possibility of *prediction* based on the alleged existence of general laws governing the motion of society. Since social dynamics are in no way analogous to those of physical bodies, "there can be no such laws" (Popper, 1957, p. 115). Does this mean that we are to abandon any pretense of using theory to predict sociopolitical events? Certainly not. However, in light of what has been said so far, it must be acknowledged that political risk analysis is – or should be – about *forecasting* rather than *predicting*. As they embody a probabilistic view of the future, forecasts are by definition provisional and fallible, but they also constitute an inestimable conceptual tool to prepare for different possible futures. Thus, a probabilistic conception of causality is central to effective PRA. Gerring (2005) proposes a minimal definition of causation in probabilistic terms, holding that "minimally, causes may be said to refer to events or conditions that raise the probability of some outcome occurring (under ceteris paribus conditions). X may be considered a cause of Y if (and only if) it raises the probability of Y" (p. 169). This view of causation in the interaction between MNEs and a host country's political environment can also be framed in terms of the agency-structure debate in the social sciences. The very nature of political risk as discussed so far implies that it arises from the (future) interaction between the international investor, or the MNEs, and a given 'environment' assumed to have certain structural features that may favor/hinder the actor's initiatives. A 'strong' state may actually act as an enabling 'structure' for the international investor by providing, for example, public goods such as security and order, but it may also have a detrimental effect, such as in the case of widespread corruption or creeping expropriation – that is, the enforcement of discriminatory legislation which penalizes the international investor. How much agency do MNEs have? To what extent do 'state structures' constitute constraints or enabling conditions to an MNEs' action? If we take a look at the existing approaches to PRA in light of the agency-structure framework, at least two different orientations can be individuated. The first could be defined as 'structuralist', and it is based on the general assumption that a careful examination of the features of a country's power structure can help predict the occurrence of political events. This is the case of the CIA-sponsored

State Failure Task Force and in general of all PR indexes mentioned above. The second approach focuses instead on actors – a prominent example being behavioral approaches to political science. For instance, Bueno de Mesquita (2010) applies game theory to successfully predict policy outcomes. While its potential for reaping accurate and reliable forecasts applied to individual cases is high, a major drawback of this approach is that it is difficult – if not impossible – to use it for large-scale cross-country analyses aimed at producing country ratings.

This view of causation brings us back to critical realism as suggested 'ontological commitments' (Bevir, 2008) for political risk. Speaking of the sources of political risk to foreign investment, are we trying to attribute causal powers to something that is not an actor but rather a structure? In this respect, is there a way to avoid reification, meant as "the illegitimate attribution of agency to entities that are not actors" (Sibeon, 1999)? The approach defended here is in line with the distinction drawn by Lewis (2002, pp. 20–21).[9] Within an Aristotelian framework, it is possible to distinguish the *efficient* cause (the sculptor who realizes a work) from the *material* cause (the material used by the sculptor cannot be said to have 'causal powers', yet it constrains the outcome). In other words, just as the features of the craftsperson's product depend on the available tools and raw materials, so the outcomes of social actors' initiatives depend on preexisting social structure, which cannot initiate activity but still constrains the actors' choices. Similarly, studying political risk from a 'structural' point of view does not mean ignoring the fact that risk mainly depends on the features, perspectives and choices of the relevant actor – in our case, the international investor. Rather, it means focusing the attention on the environmental constraints with which any actor has to cope when making investment decisions. In Rees' words,

> the focus of critical realism is [. . .] on the interplay between micro-practices and macro-structures. [. . .] The generalization of insights from qualitative research in general and from case studies in particular is possible, but it will depend on the postulation of plausible causal mechanisms, the collection of evidence for or against their existence, and the elimination of possible alternatives. This is the painstaking critical realist-informed approach that could be usefully applied to comparative case studies of MNEs.
>
> (Rees, 2012, p. 12)

3. Heuristic issues

As already stressed, references to the multidisciplinarity of political risk abound in the extant literature, as well as allusions to its 'theoretical underdevelopment' (see for instance Robock, 1971; Brewer, 1981; Jarvis, 2008; Petersen, 2012). Nevertheless, in most cases precise mention of *which* theories should be applied, or *how* to apply them, is lacking. Brink (2004, p. 30) suggests 'problem solving theory' as a theoretical grounding for PR. Císař (2007) sketches the boundaries of a 'general' theory for (macro) political risk in terms of political stability, modernization and political development, discussing the implications of Przeworski's concept of a political regime for PRA also in light of Haber's definition of authoritarianism (Haber, 2006) and Bueno De Mesquita's 'selectorate theory' (Bueno De Mesquita et al., 2003). However, he warns that they are limited to a specific notion of political risk based on the assumption that "the central reason of political risk is regime change and persistence" (Císař, 2007, p. 93). Petersen (2012) locates political risk at the intersection between security studies as a field within IR and multidisciplinary 'risk studies' cutting across sociology, economics and natural sciences. Jensen et al. (2012) shed light on various theoretically relevant and under-explored aspects of PRA (such as democracy and the risk of expropriation, partisan governments and their effects on FDI, the role of multinational lobbying on political decision-makers), without proposing a unique overarching paradigm for political risk. In sum, the quest for the 'holy grail of political risk theorizing' (Jarvis, 2008, p. 59) is not likely to find an end in the short term. As a matter of fact, the scope of PRA is so wide that, once we set aside its epistemological and methodological aspects, it seems that pretending to unify it under a single theoretical framework is bound to be a Sisyphean toil. Nonetheless, this does not mean that the PR analyst should refrain from recurring to theory. The copious literature on political and social change seems to have many lessons to teach its practitioners, although with the inevitable warning that its language and concepts need to be adapted to business 'jargon' in order to generate useful conceptual tools for corporate actors (Císař, 2007, p. 7).

As already hinted at, thinking of a theory for PRA raises at least two different sets of problems. The first is a heuristic one, as it relates to the issue of *how* to make sense of content belonging to very different disciplines – in sum, how to organize the extant theories and approaches that may offer relevant contributions to PRA? Once the first problem is solved, more concrete issues can be tackled; or rather, once the various streams of literature which bear potential or actual influence on the methods and practice of PRA have been organized according to reasonable criteria, it will be possible to delve more deeply into *what* each and every relevant discipline and theory has to say about PRA in terms of its content. In PRA, the unit of analysis, the types of risks analyzed and even the very claims about which variables are relevant, as well as the intensity and direction of causal relationships between them, may vary notably. The unit of analysis can be a whole country, a given industry,[10] the individual MNE or even the different branches of a single MNE operating in foreign countries. In this sense, as already explained in Chapter 1, Robock (1971) introduced a distinction between 'micro' and 'macro' political risk which has since become very popular in the literature (see for instance Lax, 1983; Alon & Martin, 1998; Rugman & Collinson, 2008, p. 391; Alon & Herbert, 2009; Rachman, 2014; Kansal, 2015). The first regards the aspects of political change that are selectively directed toward specific fields of business activity. When authors dealing with PR write about it in general terms, they mostly refer to the second or 'macro' political risk related to the possible occurrence of large-scale political phenomena, which may affect all foreign enterprises. In this second sense, PR perception derived from PRA is bound to bear important consequences on the decision-making processes for both governments and private actors. Furthermore, the typologies of risk developed over time by analysts and scholars are very diverse. The model proposed by Brink (2004) with its 103 contextualized, measurable risk factors and their 411 risk factor indicators epitomizes the prevalent approach in macro political risk assessment: one based on risk-events checklists. As the objective is to compare countries across a number of dimensions which are associated with different risks for investors, generally those dimensions (such as stability of government, corruption and rule of law) are listed along with indicators whose scores are assigned to the different countries to sketch out their political risk profile. Even when there is agreement on the dimensions which are relevant to PRA, the intensity and sometimes even the polarity (positive or negative) of the effect of a given variable on the political risks for the investor remain controversial issues. For instance, as shown in Chapter 3, one of the hypotheses embedded in the model proposed by the EIU to forecast political instability in 2009–10 was that a consolidated democratic regime and a consolidated authoritarian regime were equally stable, or, more precisely, equally likely to survive.[11] Other empirical works, however, suggest that there is in fact a difference between democratic and authoritarian regimes in that political risk is higher in the latter than in the former (Jensen 2008, 2012; Sottilotta, 2015). Thus, in this case, although it can be safely claimed that there is agreement on the impact of different political regime types on political risk in a given country, whether or not the impact of democracy on PR is positive may to some extent remain a contested notion, also influenced by the definition and operationalization of the concept of democracy.

At this point, the problem should be clear: against the backdrop of the intrinsic complexity characterizing PRA, how is it possible to make sense of literatures and narratives which come from different disciplines; how to organize them so that they can be compared and properly 'exploited' for a better understanding of political risk? With an eye to suggesting a much-needed solution to this heuristic problem, it is possible to borrow from the 'level of analysis' approach as famously proposed by Waltz (2001). Although dealing with a different set of questions – namely, the causes of war – Waltz introduces the concept of 'levels of analysis' or 'images' to organize a very diverse and copious literature on that subject. No matter what each and every political theorist holds true about the causes of war, Waltz's argument goes, whether they be optimist or pessimist, realist or liberal, they cannot escape the necessity of placing their analysis at one of three possible levels or images: the first refers to *human behavior*, as it aggregates all those approaches whose take on the causes of conflict hinges on human nature or behavior; the second refers to the *states*, as in order to explain conflict, it focuses on the internal structures and institutions of states; the third is the international system, described as *international anarchy*, as it looks at the international, systemic causes of war. In its clarity, the appeal of Waltz's intuition to PR scholars is considerable. Although some adjustments are obviously needed in order to transfer such construct to PRA, the relevance of Waltz's heuristic approach to this field of inquiry is conspicuous. Indeed, whether one thinks about international business studies focusing on the individual MNE, or rather studies in international political economy (IPE) focusing on the interaction between MNEs and governments, whatever the discipline or the approach chosen to study political risk, consciously or unconsciously the observer must settle on a level of analysis. While, as already stressed, Robock's original distinction between micro and macro PR was useful insomuch as it introduced a more nuanced understanding of political risk, in the words of a senior analyst (Interview, 2015a) today there is "a huge gap to be filled" between the 'micro' and the 'macro' – that is, between the firm and the 'big picture' level of analysis. In fact, as also noted by Fägersten (2015), it is possible to detect a logical discrepancy in this micro-macro distinction. While at the 'micro' level the focus is on the *point of view* from which risk assessment is made (the individual firm as opposed to virtually all firms), at the 'macro' level the focus is on the *sources* of risk – that is, the magnitude of the phenomenon. This means that phenomena which according to the prevalent orientation in the literature would be defined as 'macro' risks, such as revolutions, may actually have very diverse impacts on different sectors and even on different firms operating within the same industry. 'Micro' in this sense is not the contrary of 'macro', as they do not represent two extremes of the same category – rather, this apparent distinction is in fact only a juxtaposition. The micro-macro dichotomy makes sense if we recognize that not only can the sources of risk be both 'micro' (or 'local') and 'macro' (that is governmental, regional, international) but also the impact of risk can be 'micro' and 'macro': a 'macro' risk such as the risk of revolution can have different 'micro' effects on different firms or industries, disrupting activities in some cases while creating opportunities in others. A level of analysis approach can be applied both to the standpoint of the impact (a specific project; a specific firm; a specific industry; all industries) and to the sources of political risk. Once again, the Aristotelian concept of a 'ladder of abstraction' as already recalled in Chapter 1 is useful to understand the terms of the problem. Concepts, in the sense of "central elements of propositions" (Sartori, 1970, p. 1040) can be thought of as distributed along a vertical structure. The more one ascends such structure, the higher the level of abstraction or generality of the concepts. As Sartori points out, there are two ways of climbing up a ladder of abstraction: broadening the extension of a concept by diminishing its attributes (which means reducing its connotation), or the procedure entailed by conceptual stretching – that is, broadening the extension without diminishing the intension, which inevitably produces an obfuscation of the connotation. This means that the higher we place ourselves on the ladder of abstraction, the more general an outlook we attain: applying this logic to PRA, as far as sources of risk are concerned, the global level of analysis accounts for the more general, while traveling down the ladder we encounter the regional, state and local levels. Equally, from the standpoint of the category of investors, the impact of risk-events can be general or, going down the ladder of abstraction, affect a whole sector or industry, a firm in its entirety, or a single project. Table 2.1 summarizes the approach described resorting to a matrix intersecting different levels of analysis for both political risk sources and impacts, and providing examples of possible risks. As for the application of this approach to the sources of political risk, at least four levels of analysis

Table 2.1 PR-source and PR-impact levels of analysis

Particular ⬆ / General ⬇ (General)

Impact / Source	Project	Firm	Industry	General
Local	local protest (e.g., attack on a single plant)	civil war (e.g., attack on multiple plants or headquarters)	civil war (different sectors = different effects, e.g., oil extraction; tourism)	civil war (e.g., disruption of trade routes and strategic infrastructure)
State	contract repudiation by host government	expropriation (firm)	nationalization (sector)	nationalization (general)
Regional	conclusion of PTA: project becomes unprofitable due to increased competition	conclusion of PTA: firm threatened by increased competition	conclusion of PTA: whole sector affected (e.g., agriculture)	proliferation of PTAs (e.g., general rise in protectionism worldwide)
Global	project halted in compliance with international sanctions	boycott of a firm (e.g., for its nationality)	global terrorism (different sectors = different effects, e.g., aviation)	global terrorism (general disruptive effects)

can be identified: (a) the local level, as for example in the case of oil firms facing threats to specific oilfields in Iraq due to the turmoil caused by the Islamic State of Iraq and Syria (ISIS) and the resulting deterioration in the country's security situation (Raval, 2014); (b) the state level, as for instance in the case of several Latin American countries (namely, Venezuela, Bolivia and Ecuador) which have passed laws forcing companies exploiting natural resources to renegotiate the terms of their concession contracts in ways that limit their rights, *de facto* eliminating the right to bring disputes to the International Center for the Settlement of Investment Disputes (ICSID) (Pastrana, 2011); (c) the regional level, considering that any business venture today must pay attention to the politics of 'regions', due to trends such as the proliferation of preferential trade agreements (PTAs) or the 'regionalization of security' (Hurrell, 1995; Stein & Lobell, 1997; Fawcett, 2013), as well as to purely geopolitical reasons (sometimes framed as 'bad neighborhoods' as better explained in Chapter 3); and (d) the 'global' level, as some threats to businesses may arise from the international arena: for instance, in the case of the ongoing Syrian conflict involving both governmental and nongovernmental actors, or the introduction of international sanctions altering the business environment of a country as in the case of those imposed against Russia in the wake of the annexation of Crimea (Bayley, 2014; Birnbaum, 2014). 'Global' risks may also emerge as byproducts of globalization (Marchetti & Vitale, 2014; WEF, 2015). Cyber political risks, for instance, as discussed in Chapter 6 below, are intrinsically a-territorial yet virtually ubiquitous.

This matrix also provides a heuristic device that can be used to systematize the miscellaneous disciplines and theories relevant to PRA. Thus, the study of IR and subfields such as global politics or IPE come to the fore when the focus is on the regional and/or global source level of analysis – for instance, when it comes to studying nongovernmental actors such as transnational terrorist groups; the conceptual categories of comparative politics as a subfield of political science, on the other hand, can be used when the task of the analyst is to build cross-country comparisons and to study the state level in general. Similarly, management and business economics as fields of research will typically focus on the behavior of the individual firm but also have to consider the PR source level of analysis, identifying local, national, regional, global political threats and so on with virtually any scientific field that may have a contribution to make to the purposes of political risk analysis. The central point is that any inquiry about the international or domestic sources of political risk will also need to select an *impact* level of analysis, be it a single project, a firm, a whole industry or virtually all potential investors. Equally, any analysis starting from a specific point of view will inevitably take into account the *sources* of risk that can be organized as proposed along a particular general continuum.

An important observation must be made entering into the merits of PRA: in practice, most political risk analysis on a comparative basis is still state-centric, especially when performed by Export Credit Agencies (ECAs) and insurers, but also by consulting firms. A state-centric perspective is also adopted by PR analysts trying to account for the 'global' dimensions of political risk. For instance, although it recognizes the relevance of 'global' factors – explicitly, those variables which are not endogenous to the domestic political system – Eurasia's Global Political Risk Index (GPRI) still uses *countries* as units of analysis. The same applies to PR consulting firms such as PRS, Euromoney and the EIU, as well as to scholars such as Marchetti and Vitale (2014) in putting forward proposals on how to add 'external variables' to political risk forecasting models, as opposed to 'internal' or 'domestic' ones. This means that at the highest level of generality, the crux of the various issues surrounding PRA hinges precisely on the changing nature of the state and 'statehood' and its interaction with the market. Although it is undeniable that over the last few decades state sovereignty has been eroded by a fast-paced process of economic and financial globalization, the state – although of course to varying degrees – still retains substantial influence in shaping the business environment in a given country. In Boyer's words, "The domain for state intervention is [. . .] large indeed, and comprises education and training, the access and financing of healthcare and last, but not least, the production of knowledge" (Boyer, 1996, p. 64). And, although the role of non-state actors should not be underestimated, "[n]ational governments still make the primary decisions regarding economic matters; they continue to set the rules within which other actors function, and they use their considerable power to influence economic outcomes" (Gilpin, 2001, p. 18). Of course, in today's asymmetric international system there is much variation in terms of state capability. The very notion of 'Westfalian state' is contested today. If we look at the state in functional terms, we can define it with Ghani and Lockhart (2009, p. 124) as "a set of institutes fulfilling a set of exclusive functions". Those functions, though, may be fulfilled more or less effectively, 'failed states' being one of the extremes of a continuum in this sense.[12] It should also be noted that making the analytical choice of focusing on the state level does not mean ignoring the role of non-state actors – in some cases when the civil society in a given country is particularly vital, at times of crisis it may indeed take over some of the state's function to avoid state failure.[13] Put simply, such interpretation of the interaction between state and market seems particularly fit as an overarching approach to PRA because its conceptual underpinnings and its parsimony make it suitable for discussion even outside academic circles – an extremely important asset for a theory that aims to be 'practically' relevant.

4. Bridging the theory–practice gap

Discussing the theoretical implications of PRA requires an exercise in mental agility, which after all is a fundamental asset for "strategic leaders in a globalizing world" (Pisapia, 2009, p. 46). Going back and forth from theory to practice, or rather from *theories* to *practices* in the quest for insights about the sociopolitical future, is indeed an exercise in 'consilience', in the understanding highlighted by Wayman (2014) of the

> [c]ross-fertilization of ideas from a variety of perspectives, including not only varieties of political science and economics, but also mathematics,

demography, public health, evolutionary biology, and, where possible, even the physical sciences and certain humanities . . . [postulating that] . . . at a higher level these apparently diverse perspectives can be merged into an underlying or some underlying modes of inquiry.

(p. 4)

In this sense, 'cross-disciplinary communication' (Jones, 2012) – which means combining insights, jargons, methods normally confined within the boundaries of specific disciplines and more or less segregated epistemic communities – is also a major challenge for the political risk analyst. In the background, there is always the ultimate goal of PRA – that is, making sense of a chaotic reality by turning information into intelligence and recognizing that while it is not possible to predict the future through 'general laws', embracing a probabilistic view of causality in the sociopolitical world does indeed enable the observer to assess different scenarios and detect trends. Although, going back to Popper (1957, p. 115), "trends which have existed for hundreds or even thousands of years [. . .] may change within a decade or even more rapidly than that", recognizing the existence and direction of a trend can help the corporate actor to turn immeasurable uncertainty into measurable risk for better decision-making.

Summing up the main arguments put forward in this chapter, it is possible to conclude that although PRA is by definition a practice-oriented activity, a reflection on its theoretical aspects is in order to expose potential conceptual loopholes which are likely to result in flawed assessments. As far as the epistemological aspects are concerned, it has been argued that critical realism constitutes a suitable ontological framework for the study of political risk, while a falsificationist logic provides for a pragmatic rule of thumb to avoid oversimplifications; PRA has been presented as an exercise in futures studies; a clear distinction has been drawn between the concepts of prediction and forecast, suggesting that the second be preferred to the first as it better reflects the intrinsic plurality of possible futures. In relation to what has been defined as the *heuristic* problem in political risk studies, it has been argued that the traditional micro-macro political risk divide is partly misleading and could be replaced with a slightly more complex framework based on the concept of 'level of analysis' whereby it is possible to combine *impacts* and *sources* of political risk; besides allowing for a more accurate classification of risks, such framework also purveys an overarching conceptual tool to organize the miscellaneous disciplines and theories that may come to relevance on each occasion in the analysis and assessment of PR. In more general terms, the analysis conducted leads to the conclusion that a sound theoretical grounding of political risk as a social science concept is key to the work of the analyst. What it is, where it arises from, and what are the assumptions underpinning such concept, in particular as regards the nature of the state and its interaction with the markets, are crucial questions that must be addressed if PRA is to benefit from rigorous futures thinking. Moving once again the focus from theory to practice, the next chapter will show how 'theory' as discussed in this chapter shapes the way in which practitioners think of and measure political risk.

Notes

1 On the distinction between forecasting and predicting, see Section 2.
2 As in the case of the downgrading of Japan's credit rating to 'A' by rating agency Fitch in April 2015 due to a negative assessment over premier Shinzo Abe's fiscal policy (Harding, 2015), or in the case of downgrading of Brazil's credit rating to 'junk' status in September 2015 over the situation of political gridlock caused by president Dilma Roussef's government (Primo Braga, 2015).
3 "If these things were so large, how come everyone missed them?" Queen Elizabeth II famously asked during a 2008 briefing at the London School of Economics, referring to the credit crunch which had recently occurred (Beattie, 2008).
4 This was possible thanks to a post-9/11 security regulation which enables plane cockpits to be locked from the inside in the case of a hijacking. Such occurrence is tragically ironic considering that the 9/11 attacks have been described by many as a 'black swan' themselves (Gobry, 2015).
5 On the distinction between forecasting and expert judgment, see Chapter 5.
6 The WFSF was founded in 1973 to bring together under the aegis of UNESCO "scholars, teachers, researchers, foresight practitioners, policy analysts, activists, students and others with a long-range view" (WFSF, 2016).
7 On this point, see Chapter 5.
8 For a description of the PITF, see Chapter 4.
9 Both Lewis' and Sibeon's arguments are based on a critical realist approach, as developed by Bhaskar (1975, 1989) and Archer (1995).
10 See for instance Lax (1983) and Moody (2005).
11 By this token, in 2010, Tunisia was deemed to be more stable than both Italy and France.
12 An example of an attempt at to build country rankings in terms of likelihood of 'vitality and stability' is Fragile State Index of the Fund for Peace (2014).
13 On this point see for instance Minakov (2015), who focuses on the resilience of the Ukrainian civil society after the political crisis affecting Ukraine after the Russian annexation of Crimea.

References

Adler, R. (2001, November 29). The crystal ball of chaos. *Nature*, 414, 480–481.

Alon, I. & Herbert, T.T. (2009). A stranger in a strange land: Micro political risk and the multinational firm. *Business Horizons*, 52(2), 127–137.

Alon, I. & Martin, M.A. (1998). A normative model of macro political risk assessment. *Multinational Business Review*, 6(2), 10–19.

Alvey, J.E. (2005). Overcoming positivism in economics: Amartya Sen's project of infusing ethics into economics. *Journal of Interdisciplinary Economics*, 16(3), 227–245.

Aon (2016). *Political risk map 2016*. Available at http://www.aon.com/2016politicalrisk map/index.html [Accessed on 10 April 2016].

Archer, M.S. (1995). *Realist social theory: The morphogenetic approach*. Cambridge: Cambridge University Press.

Alvesson, M. & Sköldberg, K. (2009). *New vistas for qualitative research*. Thousand Oaks: SAGE Publications, Inc.

Bauer, J.C. (2014). *Upgrading leadership's crystal ball. Five reasons why forecasting must replace predicting and how to make the strategic change in business and public policy*. Boca Raton, London, New York: CRC Press.

Bayley, C. (2014, November 24). How sanctions against Russia are hitting UK businesses. *BBC News (Online)*. Available at http://www.bbc.com/news/business-30209319 [Accessed on 10 April 2016].

Beardshaw, P., Cattaneo, B. & Gomes, R. (2015). Managing political risk: Controlling loss, finding opportunity. *Accenture Paper*. Available at https://www.accenture.com/ t20150715T045906__w__/us-en/_acnmedia/Accenture/Conversion-Assets/DotCom/ Documents/Global/PDF/Industries_13/Accenture-Managing-Political-Risk-Control ling-Loss-Finding-Opportunity.pdf [Accessed on 10 April 2016].

Beattie, A. (2008, November 14). Good question, ma'am. *The Financial Times*. Available at http://www.ft.com/intl/cms/s/0/5b306600-b26d-11dd-bbc9-0000779fd18c.html# axzz43oIFGQXt [Accessed on 10 April 2016].

Bell, W. (1997). *Foundations of future studies: Human science for a new era*. Volume 1 "History, Purposes, and Knowledge". New Brunswick, NJ: Transaction Publishers.

Bevir, M. (2008). Meta-methodology: Clearing the underbrush. In Box-Steffensmeier, J.M., Brady, H.E. & Collier, D. (Eds.), *The Oxford handbook of political methodology* (pp. 49–70). Oxford: Oxford University Press.

Bhaskar, R. (1975). *A realist theory of science*. Leeds: Leeds Books.

Bhaskar, R. (1989). *Reclaiming reality: A critical introduction to contemporary philosophy*. London: Verso.

Birnbaum, M. (2014). Investors abandon Russia as Putin risks economy for Crimea. *The Independent*. Available at http://www.independent.co.uk/news/world/europe/investors-abandon-russia-as-putin-risks-economy-for-crimea-9792222.html [Accessed on 10 April 2016].

Boland, L.A. (1991). Current views on economic positivism. In Greenaway, D., Bleaney, M. & Stewart, I. (Eds.), *Companion to contemporary economic thought* (pp. 88–104). New York: Routledge.

Booth, P. (2013). Can the euro survive? *European Financial Review*. Available at http:// www.europeanfinancialreview.com/?p=791 [Accessed on 10 April 2016].

Boyer, R. (1996). State and market: A new engagement for the twenty-first century? In Boyer, R. & Drache, D. (Eds.), *States against markets: The limits of globalization* (pp. 62–85). London: Routledge.

Brewer, T. L. (1981). Political risk assessment for foreign direct investment decisions: Better methods for better results. *Columbia Journal of World Business* (Spring), 5–12.

Brink, C. (2004). *Measuring political risk: Risks to foreign investment*. Aldershot: Ashgate Publishing, Ltd.

Bueno de Mesquita, B. (2010). *The predictioneer's game: Using the logic of brazen self-interest to see and shape the future*. New York: Random House.

Bueno de Mesquita, B., Smith, A., Siverson, R.M. & Morrow, J. (2003). *The logic of political survival*. Cambridge, MA: MIT Press.

Císař, O. (2007). *Political risk assessment*. Master's Thesis, Masarykova Univerzita Fakulta Sociálních Studií Katedra Politologie. Available at http://is.muni.cz/th/42699/ fss_m/political_risk_assessment.pdf [Accessed on 10 April 2016].

Crick, B. (2015). Futuribles: Studies in conjecture, edited by Bertrand de Jouvenel; The pure theory of politics, by Bertrand de Jouvenel (1964). In Bell, S. (Ed.), *Defending politics: Bernard Crick at the political quarterly* (pp. 347–348). Chichester: Wiley-Blackwell, in association with The Political Quarterly.

Crouch, C. (2005). *Capitalist diversity and change: Recombinant governance and institutional entrepreneurs*. London: Oxford University Press.

Euromoney Country Risk (2016). *Methodology*. Available at http://www.euromoneycountryrisk.com/Methodology.aspx [Accessed on 10 April 2016].

Fägersten, B. (2015). Political risk and the commercial sector – Aligning theory and practice. *Risk Management*, 17, 23–39.

Fawcett, L. (2013). The regionalization of security: A comparative analysis. In Prantl, J. (Ed.), *Effective multilateralism through the looking glass of East Asia* (pp. 43–69). Basingstoke: Palgrave MacMillan.

Feyerabend, P. (1993). *Against method: Outline of an anarchist theory of knowledge*. London: Verso.

Fitzpatrick, M. (1983). The definition and assessment of political risk in international business: A review of the literature. *Academy of Management Review*, 8(2), 249–254.

Friedman, M. (1966). The methodology of positive economics. In Friedman, M. (Ed.) *Essays in Positive Economics* (pp. 3–43). Chicago: University of Chicago Press.

Fund for Peace (2014). Fragile states index. *Foreign Policy*. Available at http://foreignpolicy.com/fragile-states-2014/ [Accessed on 10 April 2016].

Gerring, G. (2005). Causation: A unified framework for the social sciences. *Journal of Theoretical Politics*, 17(2), 163–198.

Ghani, A. & Lockhart, C. (2009). *Fixing failed states: A framework for rebuilding a fractured world*. Oxford: Oxford University Press.

Gilpin, R. (2001). *Global political economy: Understanding the international economic order*. Princeton: Princeton University Press.

Gobry, P.E. (2015, March 26). The germanwings crash, and the folly of risk analysis. *The Week*. Available at http://theweek.com/articles/546460/germanwings-crash-folly-risk-analysis [Accessed on 10 April 2016].

Gordon, T.J. & Helmer, O. (1964). Report on a long-range forecasting study. *RAND Paper*. Available at http://www.rand.org/content/dam/rand/pubs/papers/2005/P2982.pdf [Accessed on 10 April 2016].

Graham, D.A. (2014). Rumsfeld's knowns and unknowns: The intellectual history of a quip. *The Atlantic*. Available at http://www.theatlantic.com/politics/archive/2014/03/rumsfelds-knowns-and-unknowns-the-intellectual-history-of-a-quip/359719/ [Accessed on 10 April 2016].

Haber, S. (2006). Authoritarian government. In Wittman, D. & Weingast, B. (Eds.), *The Oxford handbook of political economy*. Oxford: Oxford University Press, online version. Available at http://www.stanford.edu/~haber/papers/Haber-Logic-of-Authoritarian-Government.pdf [Accessed on 10 April 2016].

Hacking, I. (1981). Introduction. In Hacking, I. (Ed.), *Scientific revolutions* (pp. 1–5). Oxford: Oxford University Press.

Harding, R. (2015, April 27). Fitch downgrades Japan's credit rating on fiscal policy concerns. *The Financial Times*. Available at http://www.ft.com/intl/cms/s/2/d83bbbee-ecc3-11e4-b82f-00144feab7de.html#axzz3lXzIPYPq [Accessed on 10 April 2016].

Hovenkamp, H. (1990). Positivism in law & economics. *California Law Review*, 78, 815–851.

Howell, L.D. (1986). Area specialists and expert data: The human factor in political risk analysis. In Rogers, J. (Ed.), *Global risk assessments: Issues concepts and applications, Book 2* (pp. 47–84). Riverside: Global Risk Assessment Inc.

Hurrell, A. (1995). Explaining the resurgence of regionalism in the world order. *Review of International Studies*, 21(4), 331–358.

Interview (2015a, July 22). Semi-structured face-to-face interview with CEO of political risk and due diligence consulting firm.

Jantsch, E. (1967). *Technological forecasting in perspective*. Paris: OECD.

Jarvis, D.S.L. (2008). Conceptualizing, analyzing and measuring political risk: The evolution of theory and method. *Lee Kuan Yew School of Public Policy Research Paper No. LKYSPP08-004*. Available at http://dx.doi.org/10.2139/ssrn.1162541 [Accessed on 10 April 2016].

Jarvis, D.S.L. & Griffiths, M. (2007). Learning to fly: The evolution of political risk analysis. *Global Society*, 21(1), 5–21.

Jasso, G. (2013, July 20). *Keynote speech.* Conference on Linking Theory and Empirical Research in the Social Sciences – Major Challenges and Current Debates, WZB, Berlin.

Jensen, N.M. (2008). Political risk, democratic institutions, and foreign direct investment. *The Journal of Politics*, 70(4), 1040–1052.

Jensen, N. M. (2012). Democracy and the political risk of expropriation for international business. In Jensen, N.M., Biglaiser, G., Li, Q., Malesky, E., Pinto, P.M., Pinto, S.M. & Staats, J.L. (2012). *Politics and foreign direct investment* (pp. 27–52).Ann Arbor: The University of Michigan Press.

Jensen, N.M., Biglaiser, G., Li, Q., Malesky, E., Pinto, P.M., Pinto, S.M. & Staats, J.L. (2012). *Politics and foreign direct investment.* Ann Arbor: The University of Michigan Press.

Jervis, R. L. (2010). *Why intelligence fails: Lessons from the Iranian revolution and the Iraq war.* Ithaca and London: Cornell University Press.

Jones, E. (2012, December 14). *Political risk: Setting the stage.* Paper presented at the LUISS School of Government Annual Conference on Investing in the Age of Political Risk, Rome. Available at https://erikjones.net/2015/11/28/political-risk/#more-400 [Accessed on 10 April 2016].

Jouvenel, B. (1965). Futuribles. Available at https://rand.org/content/dam/rand/pubs/papers/2008/P3045.pdf [Accessed on 10 April 2016].

Kansal, V. (2015). Political risk: A conceptualization. *The Journal of Political Risk*, 3(4). Available at http://www.jpolrisk.com/political-risk-conceptualization [Accessed on 10 April 2016].

Kiel, L.D. & Elliot, E. (2013). *Chaos theory in the social sciences: Foundations and applications.* Ann Arbor: The university of Michigan Press.

Kuhn, T. (1996). *The structure of scientific revolutions.* Chicago & London: University of Chicago Press.

LaPalombara, J. (1982). Assessing the political environment for business: A new role for political scientists? *PS: Political Science & Politics*, DOI: 10.1017/S1049096500059886.

Lax, H.L. (1983). *Political risk in the international oil and gas industry.* Boston: IHRDC.

Lewis, P.A. (2002). Agency, structure and causality in political science: A comment on Sibeon. *Politics*, 22(1), 17–23.

Marchetti, R. & Vitale, M. (2014). Towards a global political risk analysis. *Working Paper, LUISS Dept. of Political Science*, 5, 1–73.

Matthee, H. (2011). Political risk analysis. In Badie, B., Berg-Schlosser, D. & Morlino, L. (Eds.), *International encyclopedia of political science* (pp. 2011–2014). Thousand Oaks: SAGE Publications, Inc.

Minakov, M. (2015, May 9). *The third sector entering the first: Cooperation and competition of civil society, state and oligarchs after Euromaidan.* Paper presented at the Conference on Risks and Opportunities in the State-Civil Society Relations, LUISS Guido Carli, Rome.

Moody, R. (2005). *The risks we run: Mining, communities and political risk insurance.* The Netherlands: International Books.

Morçöl, G. (2001). What is complexity science: Postmodernist or postpositivist? *Emergence: A Journal of Complexity Issues in Organizations and Management*, 3(1), 104–119.

Moss, S. (1984). The history of the theory of the firm from Marshall to Robinson and Chamberlin: The source of positivism in economics. *Economica*, 51, 307–318.

Nossel, S. (2015, July 30). This is what will happen if congress blows up the Iran nuclear deal. *Foreign Policy*. Available at http://foreignpolicy.com/2015/07/30/congress-iran-nuclear-deal-obama-veto-kerry-mccain/ [Accessed on 10 April 2016].

Pastrana, J. (2011, September 1). Concerns of nationalization through expropriation in Latin America. *Association of Corporate Counsel*. Available at http://www.acc.com/legal resources/quickcounsel/cnela.cfm?makepdf=1 [Accessed on 10 April 2016].

Petersen, K.L. (2012). Risk analysis: A field within security studies? *European Journal of International Relations*, 18(4), 693–717.

Pisapia, J. (2009). *The strategic leader: New tactics for a globalizing world*. Charlotte: Information Age Publishing, Inc.

Political Monitor (2016). *Asia political risk index – Risk in the world's most dynamic region*. Available at https://politicalmonitor.com.au/content/asia-political-risk-index#political_risk_index [Accessed on 10 April 2016].

Popper, K. (1957). *The poverty of historicism*. Boston: The Beacon Press.

Popper, K. (1962). *Conjectures and refutation: The growth of scientific knowledge*. New York: Routledge Classics.

Popper, K. (2005). *The logic of scientific discovery*. London: Routledge.

Primo Braga, C.A. (2015). Brazil's credit rate downgrading: Another bump on the road to recovery. *IMD Blog*. Available at http://www.imd.org/news/Brazil-credit-rate-down-grading.cfm [Accessed on 10 April 2016].

PRS (2014). *Global PRS risk index as of April 2014*. Available at https://www.prsgroup.com/risk-index/global-prs-risk-index-as-april-2014 [Accessed on 10 April 2016].

Putnam, H. & Walsh, V. (Eds.) (2011). *The end of value-free economics*. London: Routledge.

Rachman, G. (2014, March 17). Unrest in Europe raises global concerns. *The Financial Times*. Available at http://www.ft.com/cms/s/0/5df7c230-9fb0-11e3-b6c7-00144feab7de.html#axzz3wZuUGrBQ [Accessed on 10 April 2016].

Rashid, A. (2015, December 21). If the Taleban takes Helmand, then Afghanistan could go the way of Syria. *The Spectator*. Available at http://blogs.spectator.co.uk/2015/12/if-the-taleban-takes-helmand-then-afghanistan-could-go-the-way-of-syria/ [Accessed on 10 April 2016].

Raval, A. (2014, July 8). Fears grow over long-term hit to Iraq oil output. *The Financial Times*. Available at http://www.ft.com/intl/cms/s/0/9757170a-0672-11e4-ba32-00144feab7de.html#axzz3wZuUGrBQ [Accessed on 10 April 2016].

Rees, C. (2012, July 5–7). *Agency and institutions in MNE research: The contribution of critical realism?* Paper presented at the 28th EGOS Colloquium, Helsinki.

Robock, S.H. (1971). Political risk: Identification and assessment. *Columbia Journal of World Business*, 6(4), 6–20.

Rosenau, P.M. (1991). *Post-modernism and the social sciences: Insights, inroads, and intrusions*. Princeton: Princeton University Press.

Rugman, A.M. & Collinson, S. (2008). *International business*. Harlow: Pearson Education.

Sartori, G. (1970). Concept misformation in comparative politics. *American Political Science Review*, 64(4), 1033–1053.

Schneider, G. (2014). Forecasting political events with the help of financial markets. In Wayman, F.W., Williamson, P.R., Bueno de Mesquita, B. & Polachek, S. (Eds.), *Predicting the future in science, economics, and politics* (pp. 213–234). Cheltenham and Northampton: Edward Elgar Publishing.

Schrodt, P.A. (2010, September 2–5). Seven deadly sins in contemporary quantitative political analysis. Paper prepared for the theme panel A Sea Change in Political Methodology? at the Annual Meeting of the American Political Science Association, Washington.

Schrodt, P.A. (2014). Seven deadly sins of contemporary quantitative political analysis. *Journal of Peace Research*, 51(2), 287–300.

Sen, A.K. (1967). The nature and classes of prescriptive judgements. *The Philosophical Quarterly*, 17(66), 46–62.

Sethi, P.S. & Luther, K.A.N. (1986). Political risk analysis and direct foreign investment: Some problems of definition and measurement. *California Management Review*, 28(2), 57–68.

Sibeon, R. (1999). Agency, structure, and social chance as cross-disciplinary concepts. *Politics*, 19(3), 139–144.

Simon, J.D. (1984). A theoretical perspective on political risk. *Journal of International Business Studies*, 15(3), 123–143.

Sottilotta, C.E. (2015). Political risk assessment and the Arab spring: What can we learn? *Thunderbird International Business Review*, 57(5), 379–390.

Stein, A.A. & Lobell, S.E. (1997). Geostructuralism and world politics: The end of the cold war and the regionalization of international security. In Lake, D.A. & Morgan, P.M. (Eds.), *Regional orders: Building security in a new world* (pp. 101–124). University Park: Penn State University Press.

Stevenson, T. (2006). Eleonora Masini: Nurturing visions of the future. *Futures*, 38, 1146–1157.

Taleb, N.N. (2007). *The Black Swan: The impact of the highly improbable*. New York: Random House.

Verisk Maplecroft (2016). *Political risk analytics*. Available at https://maplecroft.com/themes/pr/ [Accessed on 10 April 2016].

Waltz, K. (2001). *Man, the state and war: A theoretical analysis*. New York: Columbia University Press.

Wayman, F.W. (2014). Scientific Prediction and the human condition. In Wayman, F.W., Williamson, P.R., Bueno de Mesquita, B. & Polachek, S. (Eds.), *Predicting the future in science, economics, and politics* (pp. 3–20). Cheltenham and Northampton: Edward Elgar Publishing.

WEF (2015). *Global risk report*. Available at http://www3.weforum.org/docs/WEF_Global_Risks_2015_Report15.pdf [Accessed on 10 April 2016].

WFSF (2016). *About future studies*. Available at http://www.wfsf.org/about-us [Accessed on 24 March 2016].

3 From theory to practice

A case study of the Arab Spring

There is nothing more practical than a good theory.

(Lewin, 1952, p. 169)

1. Introduction

The purpose of this chapter is to show how theoretical problems that practitioners may sometimes consider too abstract to be relevant to everyday PR assessment in fact have too large a practical impact to be ignored or easily circumvented. Thus, in light of the premises laid out in Chapters 1 and 2, the next sections elaborate on some key methodological issues affecting PRA. The remainder of the chapter is organized as follows.[1] Section 2 discusses the quantitative-qualitative divide in PRA, arguing that the differences between quantitative and qualitative methods are more blurred than appears at first sight. Section 3 deals with the crucial problem of how to assess the effectiveness of PR formal models. Section 4 reviews and compares five different PR assessment models, while Section 5 explains why the massive and unexpected wave of social and political turmoil which began sweeping across the Middle East and North Africa region from the winter of 2010–11 provides an interesting PR case study which can be used to discuss theoretical and methodological issues. Keeping the 'Arab Spring' case study in mind, Section 6 highlights the shortcomings of the PR models considered, while Section 7 sets out to debunk them by describing their built-in limitations and providing some suggestions on possible improvements. The overall purpose of the chapter is to show the intrinsic difficulty of measuring the likelihood of political phenomena, introducing two crucial aspects which influence the effectiveness of PR models: the role of 'quantification' operations in the creation of political forecasts, and the role of expertise in the production of political risk analysis and assessments. Both aspects will be explored more deeply in Chapters 4 and 5 below, which are dedicated to forecasting and expert judgment in PRA respectively.

2. On the quantitative-qualitative divide: The 'power of numbers' versus human judgment

As stressed throughout the book, the primary aim of PRA is to identify and assess the likelihood of sociopolitical developments that may harm a given business venture. These operations are based on forward-looking causal thinking, which implies the use or manipulation of existing data, but frequently also the *production* of new data. A traditional distinction, already recalled in Chapter 1, sets apart qualitative versus quantitative approaches to PRA. The former are often described as 'subjective' techniques based on the analyst's or manager's 'judgment', while the latter may include statistical procedures using "external economic indicators, internal economic indicators, and political indicators" (Kim, 2011, p. 377). Pahud de Mortanges and Allers (1996), for instance, propose the following classification: (1) *Qualitative unstructured* methods, such as the so-called 'grand tours' and 'old hands' as described in Chapter 1; (2) *Qualitative structured* methods, including the Delphi technique, standardized 'checklists' and scenarios; and (3) *Quantitative methods* which are supposed to "reduce the bias of the subjectivity of qualitative methods [. . .] through use of certain measurable factors that act as lead indicators" (p. 307). However, after sketching out this classification, the authors warn that to serve the purpose, "reliable data have to be collected adequately, sophisticated computer programs are required, and *experts* are needed to carefully interpret the results" (p. 308, emphasis added). In sum, even when political risks are carefully operationalized,[2] their success for use in forecasting models "is highly dependent on the quality of the data, mainly on effective classification of the events" (Burnley et al., 2008, p. 3): as further highlighted in Chapter 5, in spite of claims of the higher level of 'objectivity' of quantitative methods, it is virtually impossible to exclude elements of human judgment from PR assessment. To look at a typical instance, in surveying 'quantitative' country risk analysis methods and their political risk component, along with some genuinely quantitative indicators such as the number of strikes, riots or coups, Nath (2008) lists variables which would hardly qualify as 'quantitative', such as 'high and low' political violence or the ICRG political risk rating. This is not to deny that the use of purely quantitative indicators is possible and sometimes even indispensable in PRA, provided that the nature of the measured phenomena allows for the construction of such indicators. Rather, the point that is worth underscoring here is that at its very core, political risk assessment entails an element of human judgment, which may take very diverse forms. 'Subjective' judgment is key when it comes to choosing a given approach, selecting an indicator or even constructing an index. It should be stressed that this is a feature which PRA shares with the social sciences in general. On the one hand, diverging opinions still exist about whether or not quantitative and qualitative social research are fundamentally different in terms of logic of inference (Brady, 2004), while on the other hand there is a widespread convergence on the idea that in both cases causal language should be used with caution in social sciences and that the quantitative template leaves some important problems unsolved, for instance in the case of omitted variables and endogeneity (Collier et al., 2004). In any case, it can be said that 'quantitative' and 'qualitative' as methodological categories are far less discrete than might initially appear (Creswell, 2014, p. 87), especially as far as PRA is concerned. In fact, any exercise in political risk measurement is influenced by two sets of problems which are not only relevant to PRA but have larger implications for global economic governance as well as for public and private policy-making: the 'power of numbers' and the role of 'expertise'. With regard to the first issue, it should be stressed that today the production, publication and commercialization of indicators or composite indexes is crucial to generate website traffic and/or to boost the demand for the provider's consultancy services (Davis et al., 2012, p. 14). Although quantitative indexes or rankings are admittedly no substitute for in-depth tailor-made reports, it can certainly be said that there is a demand for them from consumers of PR intelligence services also owing to their success as 'marketing devices' (Interview, 2015a; Interview, 2015f), epitomized by the fact that all major PR consultancies offer similar products, as for instance the PRS Group's Global Risk Index, Aon's Political Risk Map, Euromoney's country risk score containing a political risk indicator, the Political Monitor's Political Risk Index for Asia, or the Verisk Maplecroft's Political Risk Atlas mentioned in Chapter 2. Obviously, PR indexes are just one of many categories of tools for PRA, and certainly not the sharpest one in terms of accuracy, as will be shown throughout the chapter. Yet, to the extent that they represent a response, however partial, to the long-standing quest for measurability in a world which is perceived as magmatic and unpredictable, they can be connected to the pervasive trend towards practices of 'quantifying, classifying, and formalizing' as defining aspects of modern life (Lampland & Star, 2008). Upon closer examination, the appeal of the idea of quantification applied to political risk can be explained by making reference to at least four – however controversial – features of numerical indicators vis-à-vis qualitative assessments – that is, their putative (1) objectivity; (2) persuasiveness; (3) brevity; and (4) comparability. As already highlighted in Chapter 2, objectivity is the ever-elusive chimera of positivists. Approaching numbers as strategies of communication, Porter (1996) points out that the resonance of the concept of 'objectivity' is overwhelmingly positive, having to do with the "exclusion of judgment, the struggle against subjectivity . . . [which] . . . has long been taken to be one of the hallmarks of science " (p. ix). Translating a message into numbers is to "summarize complexity, not by accident but by design, and speak with a quantitative and apparently objective authority that commands respect" (Morse, 2004, p. xiv). The aura of apparent impartiality assumed by the 'quantified' entity leads to the second point mentioned above – that is, the persuasiveness of numbers: indexes in this sense can be thought of as numbers whose 'vested authority' augments as they circulate:

> 'Raw' information typically is collected and compiled by workers near the bottom of organizational hierarchies; but as it is manipulated, parsed and moved upward, it is transformed so as to make it accessible and amenable for those near the top, who make the big decisions. This "editing" removes assumptions, discretion and sociology of quantification ambiguity, a process that results in "uncertainty absorption": information appears more robust than it actually is.
>
> (Espeland & Stevens, 2008, p. 421)

Brevity and comparability are also perceived as major advantages of the 'indexation' of political risk: while the simplification of complex phenomena is per se key to the appeal and impact of indicators (Davis et al., 2012, p. 8), it is also indispensable to conduct large-N comparisons and to facilitate decision making.

For the reasons sketched out above, it can be said that indexes are indeed 'powerful': as Krause Hansen (2012, p. 509) put it, they "are [. . .] capable of creating connections and effects of power", and they are systematically 'mobilized' in favor of development or investment strategies by governmental and nongovernmental actors, as stressed by Mühlen-Schulte (2012). Discussing the normative agendas behind indexes as tools for 'global benchmarking', Broome and Quirk (2015, p. 814) admit:

> It is hard to think of any area of International Relations, from international security to global political economy, grand strategy, climate change, human rights, international development, and global public policy, which has not been pulled into this politics of numbers.

Providing a more concrete example closer to the subject of our inquiry, it may be useful to recall that, for one thing, the classification of countries as more or less risky by export credit agencies or insurers has an immediate impact on the protocols defining the lines of credit or pricing of insurance products offered to companies willing to branch out in foreign markets.

Critiques of an excessive reliance on indicators have been put forward by several authors. Eberstadt (1995) openly condemns the 'tyranny of numbers', asserting, on the basis of various case studies, that "the policies of liberal and affluent states have been miscast or deleteriously directed through an ill-advised use of, or reliance on, statistical data" (Eberstadt, 1995, p. 15). In discussing appeals to numbers as powerful tools to legitimate decisions in virtually every field of the human experience, from policy-making processes to investment decisions, Fioramonti (2014, p. 12) warns against their power of persuasion – due to the fact that they appear to be so much less 'debatable' and more 'transparent' than verbal analyses. The 'overselling' of quantitative indicators of political stability and the rule of law is criticized by Bradley (2015) and discussed with reference to the Freedom House's encouragement of direct policy interventions and investment decisions on the basis of questionable causal relationships posited via measurement indicators.

Examples of how metrics and measurements "hit the target but miss the point" (Wachter, 2016) while still retaining their influence and epistemic status as key technologies for knowledge and decision-making abound. Bhuta (2012) for instance exposes the limitations of the USAID state frailty index, stressing that although the index was used only once to actually select target countries for aid programming, the generation of the index "was never discontinued, [. . .] it is said that 'anyone with a dot gov email address can receive it' and requests to be added to the distribution list have been steadily growing [since its inception in 2006]" (p. 156). Another famous example of the 'trust in numbers' – and of the major pitfalls it entails – is the Reinhart and Rogoff (2010) study on "Growth in a time of debt".[3] The main argument of the study, which relies on a data set incorporating "over 3,700 annual observations covering a wide range of political systems, institutions, exchange rate arrangements, and historic circumstances" (Reinhart & Rogoff, 2010, p. 2), is that while

> the link between growth and debt seems relatively weak at 'normal' debt levels, median growth rates for countries with public debt over 90 percent of GDP are roughly one percent lower than otherwise; average (mean) growth rates are several percent lower.

(Reinhart & Rogoff, 2010, p. 3)

Since its publication, this study had been widely used as an authoritative source in support of the implementation of austerity measures – for instance, by EU commissioner Olli Rehn, former US central banker and Secretary of Treasury Timothy Geithner as well as many other US budget 'hawks'.[4] Thus, astonishment became general when a student from the University of Massachusetts Amherst was able to show – as part of his homework – that the data in the Reihnart and Rogoff paper was fundamentally flawed to the point that the conclusions it drew were untenable (Herndon et al., 2013): a striking example of how, just like in the 'Emperor's new clothes' fairytale, claims supported by numbers acquire an aura of truth and prestige which makes them less likely to be questioned. In this respect, it should be stressed that notwithstanding the difficulty to replicate (and thus to 'falsify') quantitative economic studies (Chang & Li, 2015), the extent and the persistence of economists', policy-makers' and investors' faith in numbers are impressive (Green & Gabor, 2012).

If quantitative methods and indexes have their limits, on the other hand 'qualitative' methods – that is, those hinging on expert judgment – are encumbered by their own problematic aspects. Just like the 'power of numbers', the 'power of expertise' (Rose & Miller, 1992) also plays a role in generating a sense of overconfidence in the expert's opinion. Although at first glance they are diametrically opposite (if complementary) categories of techniques, a dimension along which forecasting based on expert judgment and PR quantitative models overlap is that of how to make them 'accountable'. Numbers may give the illusion of objectivity, but, in the end, as will be shown in the next sections, attempts at translating sociopolitical variables into measurable entities entail precise, if not always specified, philosophical, epistemological and methodological assumptions, some of which may lead to incongruous results in the measurement of political risk.

3. Testing the effectiveness of PR models: A difficult task

As anticipated, a major problem associated with political risk models regards their accountability: relevant as PR assessment may be as part of a company's strategic planning, the lack of information about the extent to which PR ratings are accurate casts doubts over their credibility and usefulness to the decision-maker. The challenge of testing these models' relevance is made particularly daunting by the lack of transparency and of data in general, in particular with respect to the problem of measuring the actual versus the estimated losses brought about by political events. More specifically, collecting data on politically motivated losses for research purposes is difficult both because it requires time and resources and because companies are inherently reluctant to share information about their losses in general. In addition, as already hinted at in Chapter 1, finding adequate proxies of this particular category of losses is also a challenging task. A few studies took up the issue of political risk modeling assessment. In a groundbreaking study in this field, Howell and Chaddick conducted a comparison across three different approaches to political risk assessment (the Economist, BERI and PRS Group), building a loss indicator for thirty-six countries (ranging from 0 to 10), based on the Overseas Private Investment Corporation's (OPIC) record of payments for claims related to expropriation, inconvertibility, war damage and civil strife damage, and on information drawn from Foreign Economic Trends, news reports and corporate reports or interviews (Howell & Chaddick, 1994, p. 73). The accuracy of political risk indexes for the period 1987–92 was then tested against the loss index resorting to multiple correlation and stepwise regression. The authors found that, among the three indexes examined, the one presenting the highest level of correlation with the losses was the PRS Group's, followed by BERI, with the Economist's PR index scoring worse than the other two.

Apart from providing much-needed insights into the performance of PR indexes, studies like the one mentioned here allow an assessment of the effect of individual components concurring to the construction of total indexes (and also to rule out some of those components in cases of high multicolinearity, for instance). Nonetheless, the operation of building a loss index poses a number of methodological challenges in itself, especially regarding – although not limited to – the above-mentioned time and resource-heavy quest for reliable information on losses incurred by enterprises. In light of those challenges, the limitations of a loss indicator built to the purposes of studies such as the one brought up here are manifold: for one thing, it covered only thirty-six countries and contained information limited to losses by US enterprises. In addition, the extent to which results can be generalized is often limited. An attempt at replicating the study for the period 1994–2004 was made by Nel (2009) but with diverging results compared to the original. Differences in the outcome of the study might be explained by the partially different research design and country sample, and epitomize the difficulties that observers inevitably encounter when trying to test the predictive power of PR models. The problem, however, is the general lack of available data, not only as far as losses are concerned, but also as regards country ratings proper. In a comparative analysis of country risk ratings, Oetzel, Bettis and Zenner solve the first problem by using currency fluctuations as a surrogate for overall country risk. However, although their original intention was to compare eleven country risk measures across seventeen countries during a period of nineteen years, the researchers were compelled to limit their study to four out of eleven measures, citing among other reasons that "either because it was cost prohibitive to purchase them [. . .] or because access was limited by the publisher" (Oetzel et al., 2001, p. 134). Other, but inevitably less accurate, proxies for direct losses ascribable to political events are inflows of FDI, widely used in panel regressions, and volatility in stock exchange indexes – the debatable assumption underpinning both approaches being that political risk can be isolated as a relevant determinant of FDI flows and stock exchange indexes volatility.

4. Five models for PR rating: OECD, ONDD, EIU, PRS, SACE

As anticipated, the performance of the existing methods for obtaining political risk country ratings is rarely satisfactory, and when it comes to assessing their effectiveness as forecasting tools some shortcomings inevitably emerge. To better illustrate this point, it is timely to (1) present some of those models and (2) provide concrete examples of the effects of those shortcomings. The second task will be carried out in the next section, which addresses the problem of meta-assessment of political risk. We turn now to the first task.

In an attempt to keep up with the fast pace of economic and financial globalization, a number of agencies, public and private, have developed systems to respond to the transnational investor's increasing need for reliable ways of categorizing countries on the basis of potential risk for business operations. PR country ratings basically aim at providing a comparative snapshot of the political risk situation of the countries considered. As already shown, political risk can be conceptualized in many different ways, and such diversity in the approaches to operative definitions is widely reflected in the numerous, diverse methodologies adopted for assessment. Table 3.1 summarizes the definitions and methodologies adopted by five different agencies: the Organization for Economic Cooperation and Development (OECD), the Office Nationale du Ducroire (ONDD),[5] the Economist Intelligence Unit (EIU), Political Risk Services (PRS) and the Servizi Assicurativi per il Commercio Estero (SACE). These models were selected for inclusion in this study for a number of reasons: first, because analyzing them allows for a comparison across different categories of actors providing political risk ratings: an international organization (OECD), ECAs (ONDD and SACE), private consulting firms (EIU and PRS); second, although they are all 'Western', these actors vary notably in terms of geographic bases and approaches, allowing for some diversity in the sample; finally, because the data on political risk used here was freely available on their websites (OECD, PRS, EIU, SACE) or because they accepted to provide it (ONDD). The first step toward an assessment of the performance of such indexes is to give them a closer look.

The OECD proposes a notion of country risk as a function of two categories of variables: transfer and convertibility risk (that is, "the risk a government imposes capital or exchange controls that prevent an entity from converting local currency into foreign currency and/or transferring funds to creditors located outside the country") and cases of *force majeure* (that is, "war, expropriation, revolution, civil disturbance, floods, earthquakes"). The first set of variables is embedded in the Country Risk Assessment Model (CRAM); the second, since it is related to phenomena that are difficult to quantify, is incorporated in the model through a country-by-country qualitative assessment integrating political risk and/or other factors not accounted for by the CRAM.

Table 3.1 PR definitions and models compared

Agency	PR definition	Model Type	Model Essential Features	Critical aspect(s)
OECD	"Country risk is composed of transfer and convertibility risk, and cases of force majeure (e.g. war, expropriation, revolution, civil disturbance, floods, earthquakes)."	Country risk rating	2 components: 1. The Country Risk Assessment Model (CRAM) produces a quantitative assessment of country credit risk based on 3 groups of risk indicators (payment experience of Participants, financial situation and economic situation). 2. A qualitative assessment of the CRAM results by country risk experts from OECD members, considered country-by-country to integrate political risk and/or other risk factors not taken (fully) into account by the CRAM.	Expert judgment Not an actual forecast
ONDD	"Any event occurring abroad which assumes the nature of *force majeure* for the insured or for the debtor, such as in particular, wars, revolutions, natural disasters, currency shortages, government action."	Risks for Export Credit: Short term PR Medium-long term PR Risks for FDI: War risk Expropriation / government action Transfer risk	The classification largely relies on the ECA's obligations under the OECD Arrangement. Scheme testing a set of quantitative indicators against additional qualitative elements (full methodology not disclosed). Countries classified in categories ranging from 0 to 7 (7 = highest risk).	Expert judgment Not an actual forecast
EIU	"The level of threat posed to governments by social protest."	Political Instability Index	2 component indexes – an index of underlying vulnerability and an economic distress index. The overall index is a simple average of the two component indexes. 15 indicators in total – 12 for the underlying and 3 for the economic distress index (see Annex 1).	Causal assumptions Not an actual forecast Weights
PRS	"The political risk rating is to provide a means of assessing the political stability of the countries covered by *ICRG* on a comparable basis."	Political risk rating	12 dimensions: Government stability, socioeconomic conditions, investment profile, internal conflict, external conflict, corruption, military in politics, religious tensions, law and order, ethnic tensions, democratic accountability, bureaucracy quality (see Annex 2).	Expert judgment Causal assumptions Weights
SACE	"The whole of decisions, conditions or events of political nature able to trigger directly or indirectly a financial loss or a physical damage for an	Political risk index[6]	3 dimensions: Expropriation risk, (sub-dimensions: rule of law, property rights, government intervention, control of corruption); Transfer risk (sub-dimensions: regulatory quality, monetary policy, investment freedom, financial freedom); and Political Violence risk (sub-dimensions:	Causal assumptions Not an actual forecast Weights

The ONDD, a Belgian ECA, relies on a similar methodology. However, to the purposes of its activity, the ONDD differentiates between political risk for short-term (less than one year) and medium-term/long-term export credits (more than one year) on the one hand, and three categories of risk (war risk, expropriation/ government action and transfer risk) for FDI on the other.

The EIU (2009) builds a model which aims at measuring the level of threat posed to governments by social protest. The overall index on a scale of 0 (lowest vulnerability) to 10 (highest vulnerability) consists of two components: an index of underlying vulnerability and an economic distress index. The overall index is a simple average of the two component indexes. There are fifteen indicators in all, twelve for the 'underlying' vulnerability and three for the economic distress index. The former include inequality, state history, corruption, ethnic fragmenta-tion, trust in institutions, status of minorities, history of political instability, pro-clivity to labor unrest, level of social provision, a country's neighborhood, regime type, regime type and factionalism. The latter are economic distress, unemploy-ment and level of income per head.

The PRS political risk model, measuring risk within an eighteen-month time horizon, consists of twelve variables to which different weights are assigned. The variables are government stability (12 pt.), socioeconomic conditions (12 pt.), investment profile (12 pt.), internal conflict (12 pt.), external conflict (12 pt.), cor-ruption (6 pt.), military in politics (6 pt.), religious tensions (6 pt.), law and order (6 pt.), ethnic tensions (6 pt.), democratic accountability (6 pt.) and bureaucracy quality (6 pt.).

As far as the SACE model is concerned, PR is broken down into three compo-nents: expropriation risk (whose sub-dimensions are rule of law, property rights, government intervention, control of corruption); transfer risk (sub-dimensions: regulatory quality, monetary policy, investment freedom, financial freedom); and political violence risk (sub-dimensions: voice and accountability, political stabil-ity, rule of law). Before we proceed to a comparison of the existing indexes, some preliminary concerns should be addressed regarding the rationale for comparing models which at first glance appear to be quite different. As regards the OECD model, it is important to point out that although countries are ostensibly classified on the basis of country risk, comparing it to political risk models seems reason-able for at least two reasons: (1) because it incorporates a political component, but, since the details of the models are not disclosed, it is impossible to assess it separately, and (2) because the OECD classification is used as a benchmark for PR ratings both by private agencies and by ECAs (ONDD and SACE are bound by the OECD Arrangement on Officially Supported Export Credits, and they both use the OECD rating as a basis for assessing the transfer risk component of politi-cal risk). Similarly, although the EIU model is conceptually and technically meant to measure political instability, its focus on structural vulnerability and economic distress makes it comparable to the other models in the context of a case study focusing on the Arab Spring. Since, as will be better illustrated in the next section, the objective is to test the performance of various models against the occurrence of widespread social turmoil, the five models considered seem equally fit for comparison – in this sense, looking at how they fare may provide useful insights into their performance in a comparative perspective.

A few preliminary comments can be made about the five rating systems described. As far as the OECD and the ONDD are concerned, the most critical aspects regard the methods and criteria according to which expert judgment contributes to the ratings. When it comes to the EIU, the most problematic aspect apparently relates to the causal assumptions embedded in the model – for instance, as regards the relationship between regime and political stability. The PRS model relies on a web of country experts, and, in this sense, to the purposes of an assessment of its accuracy, at least three main concerns arise: (1) issues related to expert judgment; (2) like in the case of the EIU, the problem of causal assumptions; and (3) the theoretical foundations for attributing different weights to individual determinants of risk. Since it relies on secondary data, SACE's model does not raise issues of expert judgment, but, apart from that, the same concerns mentioned with regard to the PRS model apply to it.

A relevant, cross-cutting issue regards the very nature of the PR indexes under examination. In fact, although risk analysis and assessment are intrinsically forward-looking tasks, many PR indexes today still do not actually convey information about the estimated likelihood of future events. To the contrary, they mostly constitute mere snapshots of a country's present situation. After reviewing fourteen PR rating systems, Howell (2014, p. 314) for instance finds that only a few of them provided actual forecasts, and he explicitly recommends that PR indexes become actual forecasts rather than mere assessments of current conditions. In this sense, it is important to notice that among the models presented here, only that of PRS explicitly aims to provide actual loss forecasts.

5. MENA countries and the Arab Spring as a PR case study

If we think of the Arab Spring from the point of view of the PR data user, simple yet intriguing questions arise: how well did political risk models do in forecasting the occurrence of widespread turmoil in the MENA region? Is it possible to gain some insights from a comparative analysis of the performance of PR indexes in this respect? Before turning to these questions, it is important to pinpoint the rationale for considering the Arab Spring a political risk case study suitable to providing insights into PR assessment tout-court.

The overall economic ramifications of the Arab Spring have been relevant and far-reaching. Domestic political unrest combined with external shocks produced by the economic and financial crisis in Europe concocted a 'perfect storm' (Kahn, 2014, p. 1) in the MENA countries. Table 3.2 and Figure 3.1 show the impact of the 2010–11 events on the GDP growth rate of six economies in the region. The slump is particularly impressive in the case of Libya, where cuts in oil and gas output due to the rebellion against Muhammar Gaddafi's regime and international sanctions had an immediate and visible impact on GDP. It is not surprising, then, that the share price of the Italian energy firm ENI, the leading energy company in Libya, fell 5.1 percent on February 2011, the biggest drop since July 2009. As

Table 3.2 The Arab Spring and GDP growth rate in six economies in the MENA region

Country	2007	2008	2009	2010	2011	2012	2013
Bahrain	8.29	6.25	2.54	4.33	2.10	3.59	5.41
Egypt, Arab Rep.	7.09	7.15	4.69	5.14	1.82	2.19	2.11
Libya	6.35	2.67	−0.79	5.02	−62.08	104.49	−13.55
Syrian Arab Rep.	5.70	4.50	6.00	3.20	−2.30	N/A	N/A
Tunisia	6.71	4.24	3.04	3.51	−1.92	4.09	2.89
Yemen, Rep.	3.34	4.01	4.13	3.32	−15.09	2.47	4.16

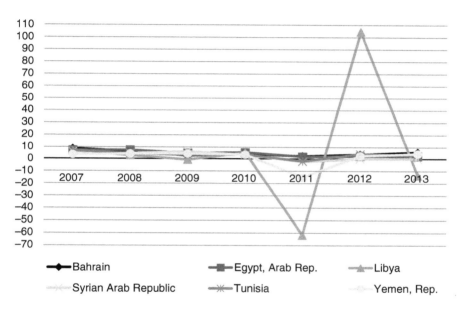

Figure 3.1 The Arab Spring and GDP growth rate in six MENA countries

of October 2011, the overall cost of the Arab uprisings were reported to exceed $55 billion, with countries affected by civil wars (Libya and Syria) bearing the economic brunt, although high losses in terms of GDP were also borne by Egypt, Tunisia, Bahrain and Yemen. Two years later, a study report released by the bank HSBC estimated that the Arab uprisings would cost the MENA economies about $800 billion in lost output by the end of 2014.

Lost output also means losses for foreign companies, in a region where they have traditionally invested in strategic sectors such as energy, construction, infrastructure, telecommunications and tourism. Just like political turmoil, those losses came largely unexpected. In addition, the recovery of normal economic activity was hindered both by ongoing unrest and by the widespread perception of increased risk deriving from social and political sources.

According to World Bank economists Burger et al. (2015), the Arab Spring and its aftermath in the MENA region provides a relevant frame of reference to explore the relationship between political instability and FDI in particular as regards sector-specific effects. Based on an analysis of quarterly FDI inflows to MENA countries in the 2003–12 period, the authors found that political instability conceptualized as political risk is strongly correlated with decreases in incoming greenfield FDI flows, especially in the non-resource manufacturing sector. On a side note, it is interesting to notice that the World Bank study in question develops a sophisticated econometric model but admittedly incorporates within it data produced by the International Country Risk Guide based on "experts' subjective assessments of a country's socio-economic conditions, investment profile, internal and external conflict, corruption, the influence of the military in politics, religious tensions, law and order, ethnic tensions, democratic accountability, and bureaucratic quality in a country" (Burger et al., 2015, p. 8).

According to arbitration firm Norton Rose, typical sources of loss to foreign investors were physical damage to property during riots, cancellation of concessions by incoming governments, or major policy changes contradicting the investors' legitimate expectations. Nonetheless, losses also originated from soaring oil prices in the immediate aftermath of the Arab uprisings, as well as from the disruption of supply routes. According to consulting firm Grant Thornton (2011), six months into the uprisings, more than a fifth (22 percent) of privately owned companies reported a negative impact on their business. This figure was highest in North America where 26 percent of businesses reported a negative impact. The MIGA-EIU Political Risk Survey 2013 confirms that the recent evolution in the political landscape of the MENA region took a heavy toll on economic growth, with most investors concerned about political violence, terrorism and breach of contract. Widespread political instability in the aftermath of the Arab Spring has also made it more difficult for companies to claim compensation under the existing bilateral investment treaties (BITs) protecting foreign investors.

The increase in the real and perceived probability of losses inflicted on foreign investors from the end of 2010 onwards is reflected by the slump in incoming foreign direct investment reported by the World Bank: net FDI in the MENA region in 2012 was 26 percent lower than in 2011 – 38 percent lower if only developing MENA countries are taken into account (World Bank, 2014). According to the *Financial Times*, the number of FDI projects in Libya and Yemen had declined by 80 percent, in Egypt by 29 percent, in Syria by 29 percent and in Tunisia by 14 percent in 2012 vis-à-vis the previous year. The impact of political uncertainty on the countries directly undergoing political change was significant also in terms of tourist arrivals in the aftermath of the uprisings (Masetti et al., 2013). From the picture sketched out above, it clearly emerges that the level of political risk in the MENA region increased dramatically vis-à-vis the years prior to 2010: thus, taking a closer look at the predictive performance of PR indexes against the backdrop of the drastic political change which occurred appears to be a reasonable strategy to shed some light on their shortcomings as well as on possible improvements.

6. PR models and the Arab Spring

Let us go back to the first question posed at the beginning of the previous section. How well did political risk models do in predicting the occurrence of widespread turmoil in the MENA region? Table 3.3 shows the political risk 'top fifteen' of EIU, PRS and SACE before the outbreak of the Arab upheavals. Because the rankings by OECD and ONDD are based not on continuous but on categorical values, the countries belonging to the top risk categories (6 and 7) are shown separately in Table 3.4.

What is evident at first glance is that none of the countries which were on the verge of dramatic political change were included in the 'top fifteen' in terms

Table 3.3 Top risk countries according to PRS, SACE, EIU

#	PRS	#	SACE	#	EIU
1	Somalia	1	Somalia	1	Zimbabwe
2	Congo, D.R.	2	Iraq	2	Chad
3	Iraq	3	Afghanistan	3	Congo, D.R.
4	Sudan	4	Congo, D.R.	4	Cambodia
5	Cote d'Ivoire	5	Zimbabwe	4	Sudan
6	Haiti	6	North Korea	6	Iraq
7	Guinea	7	Sudan	7	Cote d'Ivoire
8	Zimbabwe	8	Myanmar	7	Haiti
9	Nigeria	9	Uzbekistan	7	Pakistan
10	Myanmar	10	Liberia	7	Zambia
10	Pakistan	11	Eritrea	7	Afghanistan
12	Venezuela	12	Turkmenistan	7	Central African Republic
13	North Korea	13	West Bank Gaza	13	North Korea
13	Niger	14	Haiti	14	Bolivia
15	Ethiopia	15	Iran	14	Ecuador

Note: Data for PRS refers to October 2010, for SACE to 2008, for the EIU to 2009–10.

Table 3.4 Top risk countries according to OECD and ONDD

OECD		ONDD	
"category 7" countries	Afghanistan, Belarus, Bosnia and H., Ethiopia, Iraq, Lebanon, Liberia, Malawi, Maldives, Mauritania, Moldova, Myanmar, Nepal, Nicaragua, Niger, Pakistan, Rwanda, Sierra Leone, Somalia, Sudan, Tajikistan, Togo, Ukraine, Venezuela, Yemen	"category 7" countries	Afghanistan, Iraq, Palestine, Somalia
		"category 6" countries	Burundi, Chad, Congo, Eritrea, Ethiopia, Guinea, Haiti, Iran, Korea (North), Kyrgyzstan, Myanmar, Pakistan, Sudan, Western Sahara, Zimbabwe

Note: Data contained in the table refers to year 2010.

of political risk in the ranking provided by PRS, SACE and EIU. Tunisia and Egypt, the countries which experienced a drastic change of regime, ranked 93rd and 32nd respectively out of 140 countries according to the PRS's approach, 134th and 106th out of 165 according to the EIU's, and 109th and 62nd out of 209 according to SACE. According to the EIU political instability index, in 2009–10 Tunisia scored better for political stability and economic distress than Italy, France and the UK (which occupied respectively the 110th, 121st and 132nd position in the ranking). Such a depiction of the MENA countries as extremely stable is in line with a forecast on the future of Egypt made by the EIU together with the Columbia Program on International Investment in their jointly written "World investment prospects to 2011" report, stating that "[w]ith political liberalisation not matching that in the economy, discontent could lead to unrest, although it is unlikely that this would seriously destabilise the country's longstanding political regime" (EIU & the Colombia Program on International Investment, 2007, p. 182).

The absence of any of the autocracies of the MENA region (apart from Yemen) in the list of top risk countries is equally striking in the case of the OECD classification. The same can be said for the ONDD: a closer look at ONDD's war risk rating for 2010 reveals that, in a scale going from 1 to 7 where 1 is the lowest and 7 is the highest risk category, Tunisia was awarded a 2 (just like countries such as Greece, Hong Kong and Japan), Egypt a 3, and Syria a 4.

If we add the time dimension to this cross-sectional analysis, another observation can be made: if we compare the PRS political risk rating dating back to October 2010 with that relating to January 2011, while Tunisia's score plunged (according to the PRS's coding system, the higher the risk, the lower the score a country receives), Egypt's score remained virtually unchanged. This epitomizes what can be considered yet another shortcoming of PR indexes: the fact that they generally do not seem to systematically take into account possible regional contagion effects. Neglecting geopolitical aspects can be misleading. Algeria, for instance, was largely 'immune' from the Arab Spring (Bouandel, 2015, p. 455), yet its proximity to Libya caused its level of political risk to soar, as suggested by the occurrence of episodes such as the attack against the In Amenas oil plant jointly run by BP, Norway's Statoil and the Algerian state oil company, which resulted in the massacre of thirty-nine foreign workers in January 2013.

The comments made by the British coroner in charge of investigating the death of seven British citizens killed during the In Amenas attack deserve special attention as they go straight to the core of the risk assessment method adopted by BP and provide a strikingly clear example of the problem of weighting variables in PR indexes mentioned in Section 4:

The JV risk assessment system clearly identified terrorism as a key risk. However, the practice adopted within both the BP and JV risk matrices in 2012 was that different types of risk were amalgamated within the risk matrix calculations. [. . .] In the approach adopted by the JV, the assessed risk of terrorist attack was amalgamated with another related but separate risk – the risk to pipeline security. A threat to the gas pipeline was considered to be a less probable event than a terrorist attack on personnel, and was rated with a lower score. The effect of amalgamating these two risks within the matrix was a reduction in the overall residual risk rating for a terrorist attack. [. . .] It seems to me that it does defeat the purpose of such a detailed risk assessment exercise if high residual risks are obscured by considering them in combination with lesser risks.

(In Amenas Inquest Team, 2015, pp. 46–47)

As different risk ratings are associated to different security protocols, this example clearly shows how a flawed rating may immediately translate into serious damage, including the loss of human lives. If we come back to the more general point about the contagion effect, another argument in support of its relevance for inclusion in PR indexes is the fact, well known to scholars of political change, that democratization waves have often unfolded in the past according to regional trends (Huntington, 1991). None of the models analyzed seems to incorporate this hypothesis. To be sure, if modeling social reality is quite a difficult task, modeling the impact of international variables on political risks is even harder. However, in light of democratization theory applied in this case to the Arab Spring, it might be time to start making efforts in this direction.

7. Risk dimensions and built-in causal hypotheses: PR and regime type

A datum that any conscious user of PR ratings should take into account is clear at this point: any sub-dimension which is operationalized to numerically represent a component of risk is a statement about a causal relationship linking one or more 'independent' or 'explanatory' variables with a 'dependent' or 'outcome' variable. A good example to illustrate the relevance of this assertion and its impact on PR assessment is the relationship between a country's political regime and its risk profile. Although a rich stream of literature exists about the determinants of FDI, little has been said about the mechanisms that link political institutions to risk for foreign investors – although the question has emerged over time. In their PR meta-assessment study of 1994, for instance, Howell and Chaddick criticize the Economist's model because it incorporates an inverse causal relationship between authoritarianism and political stability, given that it considers authoritarianism as a factor that jeopardizes instead of enhancing the stability of a given polity. Historically, Howell and Chaddick (1994) hold, "authoritarian rule has been both characterized and justified as necessary or contributing to stability" (p. 76). If we follow this line of reasoning, at least in the short term authoritarianism could be positively linked to stability, and the theoretical foundations of the Economist's approach would be flawed. Interestingly and somewhat surprisingly, the more recent EIU Political Instability Index seems to have embraced such criticism, as when it comes to assess political stability, it assigns the same 'stability score' to democracies and to autocracies, while attributing a lower score to hybrid regimes, although, as further illustrated below, this approach is anything but unproblematic.

Coming back to the main problem at issue, we see there are a number of ways in which a country's institutional arrangements may influence the activity of foreign investors. Notably, a major source of concern is the possibility of expropriations of foreign investments. Research by the World Bank (Eden et al., 2012), besides providing empirical support for the distinction between sovereign risk (risk of government default) and political risk (of which expropriation risk can be considered to be a subtype), also confirms the existence of a correlation between poor policy performance and both types of risk. Although expropriation proper remains perhaps the most catastrophic event for the international enterprise, politically induced losses can also derive from far less spectacular moves by the host government, such as the aforementioned creeping expropriation – that is, the introduction of adverse fiscal regulation, which normally falls outside the scope of expropriation risk insurance.

Another obvious source of risk is the occurrence of political violence or regime change, as in the case of the MENA countries examined above. In this case, losses may derive from damages to plants and/or to the personnel, not to mention the possible repercussions in terms of share price due to the ensuing climate of uncertainty that inevitably affects business operations. Although all political in nature, these risks are quite different and should therefore be measured recurring to different tools. For instance, while expropriation risk presupposes the existence of a government with the capacity to enforce regulation and materially execute expropriation, violence risk may instead be higher in cases in which institutions are weak. Building on the work of Jensen (2008) and Jensen and Young (2008), two sets of simple models are presented here to test the effect of different institutional arrangements on two categories of political risk: expropriation risk and war risk. The baseline model is a replication of the ordered probit model estimated by Jensen (2008, p. 1046) to assess the impact of democracy on political risk-pricing categories:

$$Risk = \alpha + \beta 1 \; Democracy + \beta 2 \; GDP \; Growth + \beta 3 \; GDP + \beta 4 \; Europe + \beta 5 \; Latin \; America + \beta 6 \; SS \; Africa + \beta 7 \; North \; Africa + \beta 8 \; Eastern \; Europe + \beta 9 \; Asia + \beta 10 \; Oceania + \varepsilon_i$$

In the first set of models (see Table 3.5) the dependent variable is expropriation risk measured in terms of insurance pricing for the year 2012. The rating chosen is the ONDD one. Data on the explanatory variables is from the years 2009–10, meaning that in all calculations the output is lagged two years behind the explanatory variables. Thus, although the models are formally cross-sectional, in practice they contain information on the interaction between institutional environment and risk over time. The source of data on GDP and GDP growth (expressed in US dollars) is the World Bank World Development Indicators database. Data on democracy is from the well-known Polity IV "Political Regime Characteristics and Transitions, 1800–2011" data set (Jaggers & Gurr, 2013).

Table 3.5 Political regime and expropriation risk

	democracy1 b/t	hybrid1 b/t	exprop_res b/t
exprop2012			
democ	-0.023***		
	(-3.55)		
gdpg_log	0.305**	0.184	
	(3.04)	(1.85)	
gdp_log	-0.842***	-0.769***	-0.729***
	(-5.11)	(-4.51)	(-4.42)
europe	-0.559	-0.415	-0.519
	(-1.19)	(-0.93)	(-1.18)
latamcarib	1.292**	1.650***	1.755***
	(2.58)	(3.39)	(3.75)
subsaharanafrica	0.912	1.009*	0.952*
	(1.95)	(2.20)	(2.19)
northafricamiddlee~t	1.881***	1.624***	1.656***
	(4.42)	(3.88)	(3.69)
eefsu	1.081*	1.152**	1.106**
	(2.43)	(2.94)	(2.80)
asia	0.843	1.014*	1.176**
	(1.77)	(2.20)	(2.58)
oceania	0.224	0.749	0.350
	(0.49)	(1.29)	(0.56)
o.northamerica	0.000	0.000	0.000
	(.)	(.)	(.)
Aut_dum		0.928***	0.833**
		(3.35)	(2.86)
Hyb_dum		0.505	0.518
		(1.82)	(1.85)
rent from natural ~o			0.019*
			(2.42)
cut1			
Constant	-7.661***	-6.569***	-6.261***
	(-4.48)	(-3.58)	(-3.58)
cut2			
Constant	-6.839***	-5.707**	-5.456**
	(-4.18)	(-3.24)	(-3.24)
cut3			
Constant	-6.134***	-4.974**	-4.699**
	(-3.81)	(-2.86)	(-2.83)
cut4			
Constant	-5.077***	-3.899*	-3.654*
	(-3.30)	(-2.32)	(-2.29)
cut5			
Constant	-4.133**	-2.961	-2.717
	(-2.74)	(-1.79)	(-1.75)
cut6			
Constant	-3.767*	-2.605	-2.356
	(-2.49)	(-1.57)	(-1.51)
N	127.000	127.000	139.000
Pseudo R2			
chi2	171.216	163.070	169.248

* p<0.05, ** p<0.01, *** p<0.001

The democracy indicator is an additive 0–10 scale derived from codings of four main components: the competitiveness of political participation, the openness and competitiveness of executive recruitment, and constraints on the chief executive. Another important feature of the models presented, which distinguishes them from the one originally estimated by Jensen (2008), is that a further 'political regime' dummy variable is used to introduce a more refined distinction, to gain insights about the risk environment in the so-called hybrid regimes.

In fact, in recent years, growing attention has been paid to institutional arrangements that cannot be satisfactorily classified as democratic but at the same time cannot be labeled as traditional authoritarian regimes either. A vast array of definitions was developed to designate such arrangements, such as 'competitive authoritarianisms' (Levitsky & Way, 2002), 'partial democracies' (Epstein et al., 2006), 'electoral authoritarianisms' (Schedler, 2009), to quote only a few of them. Conceptual endeavors by Diamond (2002) and more recently Morlino (2009, 2011) led to the following definition of a hybrid regime:

> A set of institutions that have been persistent, be they stable or unstable, for at least a decade, have been preceded by authoritarianism, a traditional regime (possibly with colonial characteristics), or even a minimal democracy, and are characterized by the break-up of limited pluralism and forms of independent, autonomous participation, but the absence of at least one of the four aspects of a minimal democracy.
>
> (Morlino, 2011, p. 56)

To the purposes of this study, the empirical notion of a hybrid regime hinges on the aspect of duration over time: following Morlino (2011), in order to single out empirical instances of hybrid regimes, data provided by Freedom House (2016) was used to create a dummy variable called 'Hyb_dum' for those countries whose regimes were classified as 'partially free' for at least ten consecutive years between 1989 and 2010. Countries which do not meet this requirement are classified as authoritarian or democracies, on the basis of the Freedom House and Polity IV data.

As far as the first set of models is concerned (Table 3.5), the existence of a statistically significant and inverse relationship between the level of democracy and expropriation risk is confirmed. Controls include the level of GDP and regional dummies (model 1: 'Democracy1'). Democracy is a good predictor for lower risk of expropriation also when including in the baseline model a measure of rents from natural resources, which is associated with lower levels of democracy (in line with the extant literature on the so-called 'resources curse' as reviewed for instance by Frankel, 2010), but the hybrid regime dummy apparently bears no statistically significant effect on the explained variable.

When it comes to the second set of models (Table 3.6), however, results are different. The dependent variable here is ONDD's category for 'war risks', which include "risks of external conflict and the risks of domestic political violence. Apart from the extreme case of civil war, domestic political violence also covers risks of terrorism, civil unrest, socio-economic conflicts and racial and ethnic tension" (ONDD, 2013).

Table 3.6 Political regime and war risk

	democracyw1 b/t	hybridw1 b/t	war_res b/t
war2012			
democ	-0.026***		
	(-3.61)		
gdpg_log	0.108	-0.071	
	(0.98)	(-0.61)	
gdp_log	-0.770***	-0.656***	-0.709***
	(-5.84)	(-5.02)	(-5.67)
europe	-0.469	-0.111	-0.715
	(-0.89)	(-0.25)	(-1.17)
latamcarib	0.659	1.386***	0.570
	(1.41)	(3.50)	(0.95)
subsaharanafrica	0.487	0.745	-0.235
	(0.90)	(1.67)	(-0.37)
northafricamiddlee~t	1.916***	1.737***	0.962
	(4.02)	(3.67)	(1.40)
eefsu	0.896	1.104**	0.234
	(1.92)	(3.07)	(0.39)
asia	0.652	1.011**	0.116
	(1.37)	(2.68)	(0.19)
oceania	0.275	1.305*	0.039
	(0.49)	(2.14)	(0.05)
o.northamerica	0.000	0.000	0.000
	(.)	(.)	(.)
Aut_dum		1.418***	1.229***
		(4.13)	(3.68)
Hyb_dum		1.075***	0.971***
		(3.54)	(3.36)
rent from natural ~o			0.018**
			(2.75)
cut1			
Constant	-7.201***	-5.422***	-6.649***
	(-5.26)	(-3.98)	(-4.86)
cut2			
Constant	-6.377***	-4.459***	-5.648***
	(-4.68)	(-3.30)	(-4.13)
cut3			
Constant	-5.475***	-3.442*	-4.718***
	(-4.05)	(-2.55)	(-3.45)
cut4			
Constant	-4.741***	-2.682*	-3.989**
	(-3.51)	(-1.97)	(-2.90)
cut5			
Constant	-4.041**	-2.016	-3.242*
	(-3.02)	(-1.48)	(-2.38)
cut6			
Constant	-3.191*	-1.189	-2.253
	(-2.45)	(-0.91)	(-1.71)
N	132.000	132.000	147.000
Pseudo R2			
chi2	145.186	147.902	151.173

* p<0.05, ** p<0.01, *** p<0.001

Even after controlling for GDP and resource rents, the model proposed supports the hypothesis that, although operating in both an authoritarian and a hybrid regime increases the likelihood of incurring political violence compared to operating in a democracy, there is a statistically significant difference between authoritarian and hybrid regimes. That is, there is further empirical evidence, adding to the extant literature, suggesting that political risks are not regime-neutral. At the same time, though, such evidence seems to be in contrast with models such as the EIU's political instability index, which, as already stressed, assumes that authoritarian and democratic regimes are equally stable, and more stable than hybrid regimes.

8. Drawing some lessons

In spite of the existence of extremely sophisticated statistical techniques, modeling political risk today remains a difficult task. When it comes to fitting the likelihood of political events into a quantitative model, it is virtually impossible to escape the necessity of recurring to qualitative assessments whose nature remains largely subjective even when expressed in numbers. All PR measurement approaches entail a procedure of operationalization whereby causal hypotheses are made to the purposes of translating elusive concepts into figures. This makes it especially difficult to test the effectiveness of PR models. Difficulties in this sense include, but are not limited to, the extremely cumbersome quest for data about actual versus forecasted losses. The Arab Spring, as an example of widespread turmoil on a regional scale, offered food for thought with respect to the unsatisfying performance of PR forecasting models. As the events in the MENA region began unfolding in December 2010, uncertainty in the business environments of the countries swept up in social and political change suddenly skyrocketed, together with the likelihood of heavy losses for the companies operating in the region. The models analyzed in this chapter epitomize some common criticalities that can be summarized as follows: (1) with the exception of the PRS model, they are not actual forecasts but rather assessments of current conditions; (2) causal assumptions are often embedded into them without being tested rigorously; (3) the rationale/theoretical justification for assigning different weights to the independent variables they feature is not made explicit; and (4) they all seem to have failed in adequately capturing the 'contagion effect' taking place as turmoil spread from one country to another.

The first two points appear to be particularly relevant as they are generalizable to every PR analysis endeavor. It is crucial for PR models to give formal recognition to the fact that PR analysis and assessment are forward-looking tasks and explicitly provide probability estimates of possible outcomes. It is equally crucial to ensure that the causal relationships postulated by the models are defendable in light of the relevant literature or, where possible, are supported by empirical evidence as in the case, presented here, of the relationship between institutional arrangements and PR. This also holds true with regard to the usage of weights to attach different values to the independent variables. The last point raised epitomizes the difficulties entailed in trying to model the international and regional dimensions of political risk. Although there have recently been some contributions to PRA from scholars in the fields of international relations and globalization studies, the literature on the subject is even scarcer than the one on PR and political regimes. Against the backdrop of shifting sociopolitical paradigms, famously defined by Beck (1992) as the emergence of a 'risk society', some have questioned whether globalization magnifies political risks such as transnational terrorism (Howell, 2006), whether there exists a negative relationship between globalization and the level of political risks in a given country (Li & Schaub, 2004; Marchetti & Vitale, 2014), or, rather, whether the impact of globalization could be mixed (Blomberg & Rosendorff, 2009). As a matter of fact, there currently is no agreement in this respect. A further gap within the literature can be identified in the lack of insights related to the regional aspects of political risks following the recent developments both in the Mediterranean and/or in the Eurasian regions, which provided 'food for thought' to reflect on the meaning of assessing political risk within unstable regions, such as the post-Soviet geopolitical space[7] or North Africa.[8]

Notes

1 Sections 3–7 are based on Sottilotta, C.E. (2015). Political risk assessment and the Arab spring: What can we learn? (pp. 380–390), Thunderbird International Business Review, 57(5) 379–390. © 2015 Wiley Periodicals, Inc. DOI: 10.1002/tie.21689.
2 See for instance the early warning tool for political conflict developed by Jenkins and Bond (2001).
3 Also cited in this sense by Fioramonti (2014).
4 Waldron (2013) for instance lists eleven US Republicans who publicly used the Reinhard and Rogoff study to make the case for drastic spending cuts.
5 Since November 2013, the ONDD changed its name into Credendo Group. However, hereinafter the name ONDD is maintained in view of the fact that the ECA's denomination was ONDD when the data used in this study was produced.
6 To the purpose of the present work, since the case studies adopted assume a time horizon prior to 2011, SACE's approach to political risk is the one described in Ferrari and Rolfini (2008).
7 On the connection between political risk and the energy sector in this region, see for instance Asche et al. (2000).
8 For a discussion of political stability in the MENA region, see Sottilotta (2013).

References

Asche, F., Osmundsen, P. & Tveterås, R. (2000). European market integration for gas? Volume flexibility and political risk. *CESifo working paper*, vol. 358.
Beck, U. (1992). *Risk society: Towards a new modernity*. London: SAGE Publications Ltd.
Blomberg, B.S. & Rosendorff, B.P. (2009). A gravity model of globalization, democracy, and transnational terrorism. *Non-published Research Reports: Paper 1*. Available at http://create.usc.edu/sites/default/files/publications/agravitymodelofglobalizationdemo cracyandtransnationalte_0.pdf [Accessed on 10 April 2016].
Bouandel, Y. (2015). Algeria the limits of revolution and democratization. In Sadiki, L. (Ed.), *The Routledge handbook of the Arab spring: Rethinking democratization* (pp. 451–462). Oxon: Routledge.

Bradley, C.G. (2015). International organizations and the production of indicators: The case of Freedom House. In Merry, S.E., Davis, K.E. & Kingsbury, B. (Eds.), *The quiet power of indicators: Measuring governance, corruption, and rule of law* (pp. 27–74). New York: Cambridge University Press.

Brady, H.R. (2004). Doing good and doing better: How far does the quantitative template get us? In Brady, H.R. & Collier, D. (Eds.), *Rethinking social inquiry: Diverse tools, shared standards* (pp. 53–83). Lanham, MD: Rowman and Littlefield.

Broome, A. & Quirk, J. (2015). The politics of numbers: The normative agendas of global benchmarking. *Review of International Studies*, 41(5), 813–818.

Burger, M., Ianchovichina, E. & Rijkers, B. (2015). Risky business: Political instability and greenfield foreign direct investment in the Arab world. *The World Bank Economic Review*, 1–26. (Forthcoming, First published online on June 10). Available at http://wber.oxfordjournals.org/content/early/2015/06/10/wber.lhv030.abstract [Accessed on 10 April 2016].

Burnley, C., Buda, D. & Kayitkire, F. (2008). Quantitative global model for armed conflict risk assessment. *OPOCE*. Available at http://publications.jrc.ec.europa.eu/repository/handle/JRC46309 [Accessed on 10 April 2016].

Bhuta, N. (2012). Governmentalizing sovereignty: Indexes of state fragility and the calculability of political order. In Davis, K., Fisher, A., Kingsbury, B. & Merry, S.E. (Eds.), *Governance by indicators: Global power through classification and rankings* (pp. 134–162). Oxford: Oxford University Press.

Chang, A.C. & Li, P. (2015). Is economics research replicable? Sixty published papers from thirteen journals say "usually not". *Finance and economics discussion series 2015-083*. Washington, D.C.: Board of Governors of the Federal Reserve System.

Collier, D., Seawright, J. & Munck, G.L. (2004). The quest for standards: King, Keohane, and Verba's Designing Social Inquiry. In Brady, H.R. & Collier, D. (Eds.), *Rethinking social inquiry: Diverse tools, shared standards* (pp. 21–50). Lanham, MD: Rowman and Littlefield.

Creswell, G.W. (2014). *Research design: Qualitative, quantitative, and mixed methods approaches*. Thousand Oaks: SAGE Publications, Inc.

Davis, K., Kingsbury, B. & Merry, S.E. (2012). Introduction: Global governance by indicators. In Davis, K., Fisher, A., Kingsbury, B. & Merry, S.E. (Eds.), *Governance by indicators: Global power through classification and rankings* (pp. 3–28). Oxford: Oxford University Press.

Diamond, L. (2002). Thinking about hybrid regimes. *Journal of Democracy*, 13(2), 21–35.

Eberstadt, N. (1995). *The tyranny of numbers: Mismeasurement and misrule*. Washington, DC: The AEI Press.

Eden, M., Kraay, A. & Rong, Q. (2012, October). Sovereign defaults and expropriations: Empirical regularities. *Policy Research Working Paper 6218, the World Bank*. Available at https://openknowledge.worldbank.org/handle/10986/12055 [Accessed on 10 April 2016].

EIU (2009). *Political instability index*. Available at http://viewswire.eiu.com/site_info.asp?info_name=social_unrest_table&page=noads&rf=0 [Accessed on 10 April 2016].

EIU & the Colombia Program on International investment (2007). *World investment prospects to 2011: Foreign direct investment and the challenge of political risk*. Available at http://graphics.eiu.com/upload/wip_2007_web.pdf [Accessed on 10 April 2016].

Epstein, D.L., Bates, R., Goldstone, J., Kristensen, I. & O'Halloran, S. (2006). Democratic transitions. *American Journal of Political Science*, 50(3), 551–569.

Espeland, W.N. & Stevens, M.L. (2008). A sociology of quantification. *European Journal of Sociology*, 49 (3), 401–436.

Ferrari, F. & Rolfini, R. (2008). Investing in a dangerous world: a new political risk index. SACE working paper n. 6. Available at http://sace.it/docs/default-source/documenti-importati-(pubblicazioni)/investing_in_a_dangerous_world_-_ferrari_rolfini_-_sace_wp_n-6a-pdf.pdf [Accessed on 10 April 2016].

Fioramonti, L. (2014). *How numbers rule the world: The use and abuse of statistics in global politics.* London and New York: Zed Books.

Frankel, J.A. (2010). The natural resource curse: A survey. *Working Paper 15836, National Bureau of Economic Research.* Available at http://www.nber.org/papers/w15836.pdf [Accessed on 10 April 2016].

Freedom House (2016). *Freedom in the world comparative and historical data, individual country ratings and status.* Available at https://freedomhouse.org/report-types/freedom-world [Accessed on 10 April 2016].

Grant Thornton (2011, June 21). *Business counts the cost of the Arab spring.* Available at http://www.gti.org/IBR2011/Arab-Spring.asp [Accessed on 10 April 2016].

Green, P. & Gabor, G. (2012). *MisLeading indicators: How to reliably measure your business.* New York: Praeger.

Herndon, T., Ash, M. & Pollin, R. (2013). Does high public debt consistently stifle economic growth? A critique of Reinhart and Rogoff: Political economy research institute. *University of Massachusetts Amherst Working Papers Series No. 322.* Available at http://www.peri.umass.edu/fileadmin/pdf/working_papers/working_papers_301-350/WP322.pdf [Accessed on 10 April 2016].

Howell, L.D. (2006, March 22). *Political risk assessment in a globalization context.* Paper presented at the Annual Meeting of the International Studies Association, Town & Country Resort and Convention Center, San Diego, California, USA.

Howell, L.D. (2014). Evaluating political risk forecasting models: What works? *Thunderbird International Business Review*, 56, 305–316.

Howell, L.D. & Chaddick, B. (1994). Models of political risk for foreign investment and trade: An assessment of three approaches. *Columbia Journal of World Business*, 29(3), 70–91.

Huntington, S. (1991). *The third wave: Democratization in the late twentieth century.* Norman: University of Oklahoma Press.

In Amenas Inquest Team (2015). *Inquest conclusion.* Available at http://www.inamenasinquest.org.uk/ [Accessed on 10 April 2016].

Interview (2015a, July 22). Semi-structured face-to-face interview with CEO of political risk and due diligence consulting firm.

Interview (2015f, November 11). Semi-structured face-to-face interview with senior regulatory risk and business intelligence consultant.

Jaggers, K. & Gurr, T.R. (2013). POLITY™ IV PROJECT political regime characteristics and transitions, 1800–2010 dataset users' manual. Monty G. Marshall Center for Systemic Peace and Societal-Systems Research Inc. Available at www.systemicpeace.org/polity/polity4.htm [Accessed on 10 April 2016].

Jenkins, J.C. & Bond, D. (2001). Conflict carrying capacity, political crisis and reconstruction. *Journal of Conflict Resolution*, 45(1), 3–31.

Jensen, N. (2008). Political regimes and political risk: Democratic institutions and expropriation risk for multinational investors. *Journal of Politics*, 70, 1040–1052.

Jensen, N. & Young, D.J. (2008). A violent future? Political risk insurance markets and violence forecasts. *Journal of Conflict Resolution*, 52, 527–547.

Kahn, M. (2014). *The economic consequences of the Arab spring.* Atlantic Council: Rafik Hariri center for the Middle East Issue Brief. Available at http://www.atlanticcouncil.

org/images/publications/The_Economic_Consequences_of_the_Arab_Spring.pdf [Accessed on 10 April 2016].

Kim, K.A. (2011). *Global corporate finance: A focused approach*. Singapore: World Scientific Publishing.

Krause Hansen, H. (2012). The power of performance indexes in the global politics of anticorruption. *Journal of International Relations and Development*, 15, 506–531.

Lampland, M. & Star, S.L. (Eds.) (2008). *Standards and their stories: How quantifying, classifying, and formalizing practices shape everyday life*. Ithaca: Cornell University Press.

Levitsky, S. & Way, L.A. (2002). Elections without democracy: The rise of competitive authoritarianism. *Journal of Democracy*, 13(2), 51–65.

Lewin, K. (1952). *Field theory in social science: Selected theoretical papers by Kurt Lewin*. London: Tavistock.

Li, Q. & Schaub, D. (2004). Economic globalization and transnational terrorism: A pooled time-series analysis. *The Journal of Conflict Resolution*, 48(2), 230–258.

Marchetti, R. & Vitale, M. (2014). Towards a global political risk analysis. *Working Paper, LUISS Dept. of Political Science*, 5, 1–73.

Masetti, O., Körner, K., Forster, M. & Friedman, J. (2013). *Two years of Arab spring: Where are we now? What's next?* Frankfurt: DB Research, Deutsche Bank.

Morlino, L. (2009). Are there hybrid regimes? Or are they just an optical illusion? *European Political Science Review*, 1(2), 273–296.

Morlino, L. (2011). *Changes for democracy: Actors, structures, processes*. Oxford: Oxford University Press.

Morse, S. (2004). *Indexes and indicators in development: An unhealthy obsession with numbers*. London: Earthscan.

Mühlen-Schulte, A. (2012). Full faith in credit? The power of numbers in rating frontier sovereigns and the global governance of development by the UNDP. *Journal of International Relations and Development*, 15, 466–485.

Nath, H.K. (2008). Country risk analysis: A survey of the quantitative methods. Available at http://dx.doi.org/10.2139/ssrn.1513494 [Accessed on 10 April 2016].

Nel, D. (2009). The predictive power of political risk forecast models: An empirical analysis. *Strategic Review for Southern Africa*, 31(1), 99–127.

Oetzel, J.M., Bettis, R.A. & Zenner, M. (2001). Country risk measures: How risky are they? *Journal of World Business*, 36, 128–145.

Office National Du Ducroire (ONDD) (2013). *Data set of historical classifications for country risk and political risk*.

Pahud de Mortanges, C. & Allers, V. (1996). Political risk assessment: Theory and the experience of Dutch firms. *International Business Review*, 5(3), 303–318.

Porter, T.M. (1996). *Trust in numbers: The pursuit of objectivity in science and public life*. Princeton: Princeton University Press.

Reinhart, C.M. & Rogoff, K.S. (2010). Growth in a time of debt. *Working Paper 15639, National Bureau of Economic Research*. Available at http://www.nber.org/papers/w15639 [Accessed on 10 April 2016].

Rose, N. & Miller, P. (1992). Political power beyond the state: Problematics of government. *The British Journal of Sociology*, 43(2), 173–205.

Schedler, A. (2009). Electoral authoritarianism. In Landman, T. & Robinson, N. (Eds.), *The SAGE handbook of comparative politics* (pp. 381–393). London: SAGE Publications, Inc.

Sottilotta, C.E. (2013). Political stability in authoritarian regimes: Lessons from the Arab uprisings. *Istituto Affari Internazionali Working Papers Series, 3, ISSN 2280-4331*.

Available at http://pubblicazioni.iai.it/content.php?langid=1&contentid=822 [Accessed on 10 April 2016].

Wachter, R.M. (2016, January 16) How measurement fails doctors and teachers. *The New York Times*. Available at http://www.nytimes.com/2016/01/17/opinion/sunday/how-measurement-fails-doctors-and-teachers.html [Accessed on 17 January 2016].

Waldron, T. (2013, April 16). 11 republicans who cited a faulty study to push for drastic spending cuts. *Think Progress*. Available at http://thinkprogress.org/economy/2013/04/16/1875541/11-republicans-who-cited-a-flawed-study-to-push-for-drastic-spending-cuts/ [Accessed on 10 April 2016].

World Bank (2014). *World Development Indicators*. Washington, DC: The World Bank.

4   Forecasting political events

Issues and techniques

Prediction is very difficult, especially about the future.

(N. Bohr, quoted by Ellis, 1970, p. 431)

1. Forecasting political events

As argued in Chapter 2, one way to look at political risk analysis is to consider it as the production of conjectural knowledge based on a study of the future. In this sense, it is safe to say that forecasting broadly defined as a set of activities aimed at estimating the likelihood of future events lies at the heart of PRA. This chapter provides a critical review of several techniques which are widely used to forecast political events. What is evident at first glance is that as already stressed above, none of the techniques explored here can be classified as purely quantitative or, conversely, purely qualitative: as further explained in Chapter 5, 'expert' judgment plays a cross-cutting role in this respect. This section introduces the topic of the chapter. Section 2 consists of six sub-sections dedicated to statistical extrapolation, game theory and simulations, expert political forecasting, the Delphi technique, opinion polls and prediction markets, and scenario analysis.

Many studies in psychology and behavioral economics have shown that human beings tend to be risk averse (see for instance Kahneman & Tversky, 1979; Rabin, 2003; Simonsohn, 2009). At the same time, a certain amount of risk is inevitable – even necessary – when making an investment. A constant quest for prediction and predictability emerges from this apparent oxymoron, from Stonehenge's druids using "rock alignments to predict coming changes in the seasons" (Bauer, 2014, p. 15) to ancient Rome's haruspices practicing divination through the inspection of the entrails of animals. The *I Ching* or the *Book of Change*, one of the most influential and ancient books in Chinese literature, was used as a decision-making tool for kings over "questions . . . [which] often concerned the Great Affairs of State" (Minford, 2014, p. 9), and its influence stretches to today's business world. As one prominent commentator wrote, the book can still be used as a tool for today's leaders: "like a wanderer, an international business executive is exposed to uncertainties and danger when he is on the road as the environment of the host country is different from that of his home country" (Mun, 2007, p. 366). Apollo's oracle at Delphi was for centuries a central institution in Greece with the Pythia, the god's priestess, functioning as a 'professional' consultant offering advice to supplicants who traveled long distances to obtain her insights into the future. It is interesting to notice that the Pythia provided specific political recommendations – for instance, advising Athens on where to establish new colonies and on the appointment of religious officials, not to mention the role played by the Oracle in the start of the Peloponnesian War (Scott, 2014). In sum, endeavors at developing techniques for forecasting the impact of future events before starting a new venture have a long and cross-cultural history. The universal aspiration of human beings to know in advance the future developments of history is also a recurrent theme in literature, from Oedipus' self-fulfilling prophecy to Hari Seldon, depicted by Isaac Asimov (2010) in his Foundation trilogy as the founder of 'psychohistory', a discipline combining social sciences and mathematics which enables scientists to make broad predictions about large-scale sociopolitical events.

Considering its long history and powerful allure, it is therefore not surprising that governmental as well as nongovernmental actors nowadays invest heavily in political forecasting. In fact, as Sherden (1997) censoriously points out, the prognostication business has turned into a lucrative industry employing hundreds of thousands of practitioners, which thrives in spite of the shockingly poor track record of 'fortune sellers'. Although Sherden is certainly right in pointing out the failures of professional prognosticators, there are at least two orders of reasons why dismissing all attempts at political forecasting as useless would be counterproductive: first, because as shown in the next sections, not all efforts at forecasting political events have been in vain; second, because from a pragmatic vantage point, it is extremely unlikely that unsatisfactory track records will be sufficient for consumers of PRA to renounce political forecasting tout-court. After all, the very fact that 'fortune sellers' keep selling their services testifies that there is constant demand for them and that they are considered to bring value to businesses undertaking FDI. What should be immediately clarified, however, is that it makes no sense to talk about the effectiveness of forecasting techniques in general terms: rather, the question is which forecasting technique is more suited to a specific type of risk-event. In other words, a technique which is well suited to a certain type of risk-event may be completely useless for another type of risk-event: as already stressed, political risks change across many dimensions, critically depending on factors such as geography, business culture, political regime and even local politics. This means that prior to any attempt at forecasting, we should clearly define the nature of the question we intend to submit to the forecaster's metaphorical 'crystal ball'. Rare events, for instance, such as terrorist attacks, respond to a different logic (and statistical distribution) than more common events that can still be considered political in nature, such as the request of a bribe by a government official in a country displaying a high level of corruption; wondering which candidate will win a presidential election is very different from trying to infer what kind of foreign policy a newly elected cabinet is going to pursue. What is more, both questions in turn change considerably if we move from the short to the medium and long term, as introducing the time dimension further complicates things for aspirant forecasters: as scenario-planning expert Cronje (2014) explains, modeling the long-term dynamics of political systems poses challenges similar to those faced by biologists in the first half of the twentieth century trying to create a model for the life of plants: in fact, they realized that it made no sense to break them down into parts to be observed in isolation and that studying a living organism means studying a complex system whose entirety is much more than the mere addition of parts. Analogously, it is perfectly useless to study the individual behavior of each and every motor vehicle circulating in a given urban environment, as it takes only one actor (a vehicle breaking down for instance) to set in motion a chain of events eventually culminating in a large-scale gridlock (Cronje, 2014). The point is that in a complex system characterized by the presence and interaction of a large number of actors, even an imperceptible change can trigger huge effects later in time. Wondering whether or not a revolution will take place at a given point in time is a daunting question, yet it is very different from aiming to grasp the long-term ramifications of a revolution. This is precisely the meaning of the so-called 'butterfly effect' in chaos theory. As first observed by mathematician and weather scientist Edward Lorenz, in systems with bounded solutions "slightly differing initial states can evolve into considerably different states" (Lorenz, 1963, p. 130); this means that "two particular weather situations differing by as little as the immediate influence of a single butterfly will generally after sufficient time evolve into two situations differing by as much as the presence of a tornado" (Lorenz, 1972, p. 1).

While an elaborated discussion of the promises and pitfalls of chaos theory for political forecasting is beyond the scope of this book, it should be noted that one key implication of such theory applicable to PRA is that the longer the time horizon considered, the more difficult it is to gauge the potentially far-reaching consequences of seemingly irrelevant events occurring at a given moment in the life of an investment. In light of this difficulty and of the numerous, diverse events which may give rise to political risks, the literature on political forecasting is as sparse as that on political risk proper. In a study aiming to map policy-orienting foresight exercises sponsored by governmental but also corporate actors in Europe and worldwide, Popper et al. (2007) found that the most used techniques were literature reviews, expert panels and scenarios, while other commonly used techniques included futures workshops, brainstorming, trend extrapolation, interviews, questionnaires/surveys, Delphi, key technologies, megatrend analysis and SWOT analysis. Such diversity fits well with the idea that there are no absolutely 'effective' or 'ineffective' methods, nor is it possible to argue for a superiority of quantitative over qualitative techniques, as argued by some (see for instance Lyons, 2012). Moreover, as already stressed and also shown by Popper et al. (2007), most methods for forecasting sociopolitical events can be classified as 'mixed'. Keeping this in mind, as anticipated, the next section reviews and discusses seven categories of widely used forecasting techniques, highlighting their potentialities as well as limitations for application in PRA.

2. A review of the existing techniques

2.1 Statistical extrapolation

A preliminary, fundamental distinction to be drawn when examining statistical extrapolation techniques[1] is the one between cross-sectional techniques, such as bivariate or multiple regression analysis, and time series, such as time series regression analysis, auto-regressive integrated moving average (ARIMA) models and exponential smoothing. In its simplest version, regression analysis is based on the idea that a 'dependent' or 'explained' variable (Y) can be forecast by looking at only one predictor (X), usually referred to as 'independent' or 'explanatory' variable, the basic model being:

$$Y = \beta_0 + \beta_1 X + \varepsilon$$

Where parameter β_0 refers to the intercept, β_1 refers to the slope of the line describing the behavior of the variables, and ε refers to the error term. Regression analysis can be used whenever it is reasonable to assume that there is a linear relationship between variables – for instance, in the case of the relationship between education and income level in a given population. Cho (1972) for instance used a multiple regression model to measure the level of crime in big cities. When the dependent variables are binary or ordinal, nonlinear regression models such as logit and ordered probit are preferred. An example of the latter are the models described in Chapter 3, where the dependent variables are expropriation risk and war risk according to ONDD ratings.

Broadly speaking, time series analysis focuses on data organized according to a specified temporal order. When such data is available, it is possible to use time series to extrapolate information about the past and forecasts about the future behavior of the variables considered. As observed by Makridakis et al. (1998, pp. 25–26), in order to select an appropriate forecasting technique it is necessary to look at the types of data patterns. Four such patterns can be identified: (1) horizontal (stationary), when data values oscillate around a constant mean; (2) seasonal, when a series is influenced by seasonal factors, as in the case of household energy consumption for heating or the production of ice cream; (3) cyclical, when the rise and fall in the values of the series does not exhibit a seasonal pattern (for instance, in the case of the macroeconomic business cycle or the housing market); and (4) trend, when a long term increase or decrease in the values of the data can be observed (for instance, in the case of today's negative demographic trends in many advanced and emerging economies). In many empirical instances, data can exhibit mixed patterns, which obviously further complicates the task of devising models suitable to achieving accurate forecasts. As stressed by Ostrom (1990, pp. 5–6), while time series regression analysis postulates a structural equation model – that is, the specification of a causal structure which is subsequently tested using time series data – ARIMA time series models follow an inverse logic, as the variables and lag structure of the model are based on what fits the data, using the most recent observation as the starting value and subsequently analyzing recent forecasting errors to allow for adjustments for future forecasting (Armstrong, 1985, p. 175). Exponential smoothing is another popular forecasting technique based on time series, widely used for forecasting data with no trend or seasonal pattern, such as the demand for fuel oil, the intuition behind exponential smoothing being that older observations are assigned exponentially decreasing weights, which means that more recent observations weigh more in relative terms than older ones. Applications of time series forecasting techniques are virtually endless, this method being applicable for instance to series regarding GDP growth, unemployment rate, military expenditure, the occurrence of civil or international conflicts, the electoral performance of a given party or coalition, electoral turnover, and many other variables, provided that they can be represented as a chronologically ordered series. Bhasin and Gandhi (2013), to provide a recent example, use a cross-national time series model to investigate the timing and targeting of suppression of dissent before elections in about sixty nondemocratic regimes between 1990 and 2008.

While in some cases political data can be relatively tractable, most of the time 'quantitative' political forecasters face daunting challenges connected to data collection as well as model building. Nonetheless, in the last few decades both public and private actors have devoted a remarkable number of resources to the development of quantitative techniques for political forecasting. This is the case, for instance, of three major event-coding data sets currently available today: the Global Database of Events, Language, and Tone (GDELT), the open source Phoenix data project and the Integrated Crisis Early Warning System (ICEWS) Program sponsored by the US Defense Advanced Research Projects Agency (DARPA). As highlighted by Ulfelder (2015), compared to past efforts at coding political events worldwide, they all are 'higher resolution' data sets relying on country-months, rather than country-years, as units of analysis, and they also rely on advances in information technologies[2] to tackle one of the most relevant problems in the development of large-scale event data sets – that is, the fact that they have traditionally resorted to time-consuming and resource-heavy manual coding. The quality of these data sets in terms of predictive power is high. ICEWS data for instance allowed for highly accurate short-term (three months into the future) predictions (Ward et al., 2012), while the PITF, a US-sponsored precursor of the ICEWS, developed a global model for forecasting political events capable of distinguishing countries that experienced instability from those that did not with a two-year lead time and over 80 percent accuracy – with reference to a data set covering cases of onset of political instability worldwide from 1955 to 2003 (Goldstone et al., 2010). Such accomplishments have generated a wave of optimism about the alleged omnipotence of statistical methods for political forecasting. Methods traditionally confined to 'hard' sciences, such as models based on the so-called 'power laws', are now increasingly applied with promising results to forecast sociopolitical events – for instance, terrorist attacks (see Marcovina & Pellero, 2015). Successful baseball and election forecaster Nate Silver became the iconic epitome of a 'new era' in which almost flawless prediction of political events would at last be possible, enabling qualified observers to finally get rid of the 'veil of Maya' of intrinsically flawed human judgment (Lyons, 2012; Ward & Metternich, 2012). This outburst of enthusiasm, however, has fueled a heated debate in the 'quants' epistemic community, with Ulfelder, himself a prominent quantitative scholar and forecasting practitioner, arguing that for a number of reasons "the world can't have a Nate Silver" (Ulfelder, 2012a). To better illustrate the main stumbling blocks faced by approaches aiming to extrapolate forecasts from past events, it is useful to recall a few remarks by Makridakis et al. (1998): "Quantitative forecasting can be applied when three conditions exist: 1. Information about the past is available. 2. This information can be quantified in the form of numerical data. 3. It can be assumed that some aspects of the past pattern will continue into the future" (p. 9). What happens if we apply this checklist to the state of the art in political forecasting? As far as the first point is concerned – that is, considering data availability – it should be noticed that the landscape is very heterogeneous. As stressed by Ulfelder (2012a), while for some categories of political events (such as elections in mature democracies) high-quality data abounds, when it comes to phenomena such as coups, revolutions and large-scale terroristic attacks, the data available is in fact too sparse or low quality for yielding accurate forecasts, no matter how sophisticated the available models are. Coming to the second point, that is the 'measurability' of both the explicative and the explained variables, one of the leitmotifs of this book is precisely the gargantuan challenge faced by political risk analysts in this respect. Even measures of variables that are relatively easy to define, such as GDP growth or the inflation rate, are not necessarily reliable for a number of reasons, from the intentional manipulation of statistics by governments – as recently happened in several cases including Greece (Franchet, 2010) and Argentina (The Economist, 2012) – to the limited resources available for the production of such statistics (Ulfelder, 2012a). Complexity grows exponentially when it comes to operationalizing multifaceted concepts such as 'conflict', 'inequality' or 'democracy' – providing indicators thereof being a preliminary operation indispensable to statistical extrapolations.[3] As far as the third point is concerned, statistical extrapolation techniques are clearly based on the epistemological assumption that what happened in the past can shed light on what lies ahead in the future. This is indeed a big assumption: as Knight put it, "the existence of a problem of knowledge depends on the future being different from the past, while the possibility of the solution of the problem depends on the future being like the past" (Knight, 1921, p. 313). As already hinted at in Chapter 2, Taleb (2007) radically dismisses all attempts at forecasting events in the sociopolitical realm: strenuous as they may be, efforts in this sense are simply useless, and insisting that the disastrous track record of human prediction be ignored exposes what the author calls "the scandal of prediction"(p. 138). Should we accept Taleb's view of the sociopolitical world as the realm of 'black swans' – an attitude which has been embraced by other scholars (such as Stevens, 2012) expressing dire skepticism towards quantitative forecasting efforts – and conclude that investing in statistical extrapolation techniques for political forecasting is a waste of time and money? Echoing the views expressed by Farrell (2012) and Ulfelder (2012b), it can be argued that although overconfidence in statistical methods should be avoided for the reasons outlined above, further efforts at spreading a culture of (accountable) political forecasting would help yield better forecasts and, as a positive side-effect, would also strengthen the scientific foundations of political science as a whole.

2.2 *Game theory and simulations*

Game theoretical approaches and simulations are another popular category of techniques applicable to political forecasting. Game theory as a field of inquiry can be defined as "the study of rational behavior in situations of interactive decision making; that is, situations in which two or more individuals make decisions that jointly determine an outcome about which the participants have differing preferences or information" (Calvert, 2011, p. 947). Game theory, whose origins can be traced back to the work of John von Neumann (1928), is a highly valued approach when it comes to predicting strategic behavior: as Hanson et al. (2014) notice, its success is epitomized by the fact that since 1990 eight Nobel Prizes have been conferred to game theorists. This approach has been widely applied to virtually every realm of human knowledge, from psychology to business, from philosophy to biology, not to mention its fruitful and frequent use in the study of conflicts and diplomatic bargaining in international relations (see for instance Avenhaus & Zartman, 2007). Game theory encompasses two main branches: cooperative and non-cooperative games. While the first focuses on situations in which players join coalitions to create value, the second studies the procedures through which players maximize their utility, focusing on the description of the moves and information available to each player (Chatain, 2015). In non-cooperative games, participants act independently, without collaboration or communication with the others (Nash, 1951). In order to exemplify the main mechanisms underpinning the functioning of game theory, it is useful to recall the simplest instance of a strategic game involving two actors, which is the so-called 'prisoner's dilemma', originally proposed in 1950 by Melvin Dresher and Merrill Flood from RAND Corporation, and later famously framed in terms of sentences and payoffs by mathematician Albert Tucker (Geçkil & Anderson, 2009, p. 4). As in every strategic game, the prisoner's dilemma features three elements: a set of participants, a number of strategy sets and a utility function describing each participant's preferences (see Figure 4.1).

The payoff matrix describes a situation in which two 'prisoners', Player A and Player B, are accused of the same crime and placed in separate cells where they cannot communicate. They are offered the choice of either remaining silent (cooperating) or confessing (defecting) according to the following mechanism: if both remain silent (cooperating), they both get a one-year sentence. If Player A remains silent (cooperating) while Player B confesses (defecting), Player B is freed and Player A gets a ten-year sentence. Vice versa, if Player B remains silent (cooperating) while Player A confesses (defecting), Player A is freed and

Player B

	Cooperate	Defect

Figure 4.1 Prisoner's dilemma payoff matrix

Player B gets a ten-year sentence. If both players confess (defecting), they both get a three-year sentence. The intuition behind the prisoner's dilemma is that in pursuing self-interest (that is, aiming to be freed at the expense of the other prisoner) each player will be better off by defecting rather than cooperating, irrespective of the other player's choice: to use game theoretical jargon, defecting is a *dominant* strategy for both players. Yet, if both players defect, the overall result will be worse than if they had chosen to cooperate. Given its focus on rational actors pursuing self-interest, game theory is particularly suited to modeling the strategic interaction between investors and governments, providing useful tools to assess political risks in the form of adverse policy or regulatory change. Analogously, a game theoretical approach can be used to make forecasts about more general issues, such as the selection of a new political leader in the context of party politics.

The main limit of game theoretical approaches is that they are mostly based on the expected utility theory (EUT). According to EUT, there is a limited number of actions that the individual can undertake, each of which leads to a given outcome. The individual also has preferences with respect to the possible outcomes of her or his actions, based on which (and based also on the existing constraints) she or he decides upon a particular course of action. In other words, EUT states that "the decision maker [. . .] chooses between risky or uncertain prospects by comparing their expected utility values, i.e., the weighted sums obtained by adding the utility values of outcomes multiplied by their respective probabilities" (Mongin, 1997, p. 342). In this sense, the decision is the outcome of an activity of calculation. Apparently, EUT is highly normative, as it prescribes what individuals have to do in order to reach their objectives. However, there were also attempts at developing a positive theory of choice based on the conception of the individual as a rational decision-maker and on the assumptions underlying EUT – a prominent example thereof being Friedman (1953), who maintained that those actors who did not 'play by the rules' of rational choice would be gradually excluded thanks to a process of 'natural selection'. Although EUT has met with several criticisms over time (for instance, by Allais, 1953; Schumpeter, 1954), the definitive empirical proof and systematization of its shortcomings as a descriptive theory of decision making under risk was carried out by Kahneman and Tversky (1979, 1986). The rational-choice approach to decision making rests on four main assumptions or rules (Kahneman & Tversky, 1986): (1) cancellation, (2) transitivity, (3) dominance and (4) invariance. Cancellation means that any state of the world which produces the same outcome as the actor's choice is canceled by definition. Transitivity means that when the utility attached to option A is greater than the utility attached to option B, then A is preferred to B (in order for this assumption to hold, the value of each option must not depend on the value of any other available option). Dominance simply means that if option A is equal to option B in all states and better than option B in at least one state, then A must be preferred to B. Finally, according to the invariance rule, different presentations of the identical-choice problem should yield identical preferences. Appealing and logically robust as these axioms may look in normative terms, they are systematically violated when human judgment is required to make decisions under conditions of risk – that is, when we move from the normative to the empirical level. Extensive experiments conducted over time by Kahneman and Tversky showed that the axiom of invariability does not stand the test of reality, and as a consequence EUT theory does not provide a valid description of human decision making under conditions of risk. This and other findings lead the authors to the formulation of the so-called prospect theory, according to which "value is assigned to gains and losses rather than to final assets and in which probabilities are replaced by decision weights" (Kahneman & Tversky, 1979, p. 263). Although behavioral approaches applying the insights of prospect theory to political game theory are becoming more common today, this subfield of inquiry "is still in its infancy" (McCarty & Meirowitz, 2007, p. 51). This means that game theoretical approaches to PRA are useful to the extent that the actors involved in the risk scenario of interest can be reasonably assumed to be rational and their preferences can be mapped accordingly. Political scientist and game theorist Bruce Bueno de Mesquita, for instance, explains how in 1979 at the beginning of his career he used a game-theory-based computer program to predict the outcome of a government crisis in India upon request of the US Department of State. Contrary to what he defines his own 'pundit knowledge', and indeed contrary to the opinion of most State Department pundits on the matter, the model predicted the appointment of the then relatively obscure Charan Singh, a prediction that turned out to be accurate (Bueno de Mesquita, 2009). Just like Bueno de Mesquita's own consulting firm, Mesquita & Roundell LLC, in the last few years many consulting firms have been specializing in the application of game theory to the assessment of business risks – including political risk. Game theory has, for instance, been applied to provide oil and gas companies with intelligence in politically unstable and militarized environments where insurgency was supported by other foreign firms (Open Options, 2013); to successfully predict the evolution of the nuclear energy sector in Canada based on changes in both local and federal government policies (Priiva, 2011); and to predict how foreign governments and competitors reacted when oil giant Chevron embarked on international projects (Rappeport, 2008). Shotts (2015) develops a game theoretical model where political risk is framed as a hold-up problem, in which players' payoffs are the maximization of profits for the firm and, for the host government, tax revenue together with political factors such as reputation, electoral pressure, patronage and external pressure. In sum, it is safe to say that game theory is ideally suited to modeling political risk in terms of strategic inter-action between the firm and the host country's government, provided that their preferences can be defined with precision and their behavior can be assumed to be rational. Simulations based on role playing are an alternative agent-based method that can be used to make forecasts. In fact, simulations in the form of 'political gaming' have been used extensively to this purpose in the context of military and foreign policy. RAND Corporation was a pioneer in this field, developing a stan-dard format for simulations typically involving the operations of two role-playing teams and a control group (see Goldhamer & Speier, 1959; Jones, 1986). One of the advantages of this method is its effectiveness and relative inexpensiveness. The main limitations of this approach are that in order to work effectively, the fol-lowing conditions have to be met: a small number of actors (ideally two) should be involved; the parties involved should be in conflict; and the subject of the pre-diction should involve large changes (Armstrong, 2002, pp. 20–21). An empiri-cal investigation conducted by Green (2002) suggests that, when the conditions outlined above are met, game theorists' forecasts are more accurate than unaided judgment, but not as accurate as forecasts obtained through role-play.

2.3 'Expert' opinion

Practitioners agree in their recognition of expert forecasting being extensively used in PRA (Interview, 2015b, 2015c, 2015d, 2015g). As anticipated in Chap-ter 1, the simplest, least structured forms it can take are the so-called 'grand tour' and 'old hands', but, as further discussed in the rest of this chapter, it is safe to say that expert judgment is truly ubiquitous in political forecasting, even in the case of more sophisticated methods. As already observed in Chapter 2, experts in the context of PRA are individuals with a high level of subject matter knowledge. Typically, they are 'area' or 'country' experts, with an outstanding background either in terms of education or because they possess valuable information about the area or country of interest; in the latter case, they may be employees of com-panies already present in the area or country of interest, government officials, reporters, as well as of course professional consultants, including country nation-als (Howell, 1986). A quick look at the job descriptions for vacancies in political risk consultancies confirms that in general professional political risk consultants today as in the past are mostly subject-matter experts (Interview, 2015c, 2015e). Overall, it can be observed that in spite of claims about the 'death of punditry' made by enthusiasts of highly formal, quantitative forecasting methods (see for instance Ferenstein, 2012), punditry as a source of forecasting still enjoys wide-spread popularity – a symptom of which, Tetlock and Gardner (2015) argue, is the deference shown by the media and the economic and political elites toward the (usually vague) forecasts made by renowned 'experts' such as Tom Friedman. A blatant as well as instructive example of pundit forecasting receiving a tremen-dous amount of public attention is Ravi Batra's (1985) best-selling book entitled *The Great Depression of 1990*. Focusing on the detrimental aspects of capital-ism, the book claimed that a devastating economic crisis would hit the Western world in 1990, a prediction that soon proved to be completely wrong, with the economic expansion of the 1990s representing in fact the longest period of eco-nomic growth in the history of the US. While Batra's prophecy was a predictive failure, it was nonetheless a huge success from a commercial point of view – a circumstance epitomizing the fact that success in the 'punditry industry' is not necessarily dependent on a track record of accurate forecasts. On the contrary, the constant demand for expert opinion seems to be boosted by what Armstrong calls the 'seersucker theory': "No matter how much evidence exists that seers do not exist, suckers will pay for the existence of seers" (Armstrong, 1980, p. 16). Such a constant demand for expert forecasting regardless of track-record accuracy sug-gests widespread resistance to the diffusion of a culture of 'good forecasting' in the sense highlighted by the Forecasting Principles Project (FPP). Starting in the mid-1990s, the FPP brought together the work of internationally known forecast-ing methodologists with the objective of codifying "evidence-based principles, or condition-action statements, in order to provide guidance on which methods to use when" (Armstrong & Green, 2007, p. 998). Before history proved Batra's prediction wrong, Armstrong (1988) had already criticized it on the grounds that the author, among other things, appealed to his own proficiency as an economist as proof of the validity of the book's claims. In sum, even in areas where strict scientific standards should be applied (Armstrong & Green, 2007), a-critical trust in expertise as a source of actionable intelligence and legitimate power[4] seems to be as strong today as in the past. In fact, the concept of 'expertise' in itself con-jures up the idea that if the judge is an 'expert', then his or her forecasts – based on subjective probability calculation[5] – will be more reliable than if the judge were a 'non-expert'. But is that really so? That is, is it truly reasonable to expect forecasts made by subject matter experts to be more accurate than forecasts made by non-experts?

Philip Tetlock's (2006) renowned work on expert political judgment suggests a negative answer to this question. The idea of assessing the accuracy of past forecasts by contrasting them with actual events had already been applied to other studies, such as Klugman (1947) studying predictions made by soldiers about the ending of hostilities between the US and Germany and the US and Japan; the originality in Tetlock's study on expert political judgment is its remarkable extension in terms of time span: building on the results of experiments conducted over twenty years, Tetlock shows how highly educated experts were not able to outperform untrained forecasters in predicting long-term sociopolitical events. Thus, apparently the accuracy of forecasts tested against actual outcomes does not depend on expertise commonly defined as having outstanding knowledge in the subject of interest. In a nutshell, in Tetlock's words, *"What* experts think matters far less than *how* they think" (Tetlock, 2006, p. 2; emphasis original). This recalls the famous 'fox and hedgehog' metaphor coined by Isaiah Berlin (1953) whereby individuals who can be portrayed as 'foxes' – that is, more eclectic and prone to self-criticism – make better forecasters than self-confident 'hedgehogs', who tend to see the world through the analytical lens of one single idea. In 2011, Tetlock and Mellers launched a new research project, sponsored by the US government's Intelligence Advanced Research Projects Activity (IARPA). The Good Judgment Project (GJP) was one of five different teams led by top researchers competing to produce accurate forecasts. The GJP was organized as a tournament, with aspirant forecasters recruited online and asked to answer precise questions on issues such as the "likelihood of an Israeli sneak attack on Iranian nuclear facilities or the departure of Greece from the Eurozone" (Tetlock & Gardner, 2015, p. 17). Over one million individual judgments about the future were collected in a four-year period. Compared to the previous research, the GJP involved a much higher number of participants but relied on shorter time frames for the questions asked. The main finding of the GJP was that a number of individuals, defined 'superforecasters', systematically outperformed control groups in terms of Brier score: a combined measure capturing the extent of calibration and resolution of the forecasts. Interestingly, superforecasters were not subject matter experts: they relied on publicly accessible information to come to their projections. Equally, the positive correlation between higher accuracy in forecasting and higher intelligence in terms of IQ, quantitative skills and the amount of time spent in news updating was only marginal. The GJP basically confirmed the previous findings by Tetlock in the sense that apparently superforecasting skills principally depend on the thinking style of individuals, with commitment to self-improvement being the strongest predictor of good forecasting performance. Another important finding of the GJP was that very simple (and inexpensive) training led to limited but still detectable improvements in accuracy. A further, important result was that forecasts made by groups were more accurate than individual ones. This is in line with a substantial body of literature showing that forecast accuracy can be improved by combining multiple individual forecasts and that simple combination methods often work reasonably well compared to more complex ones (Clemen, 1989; Schneider, 2014; Early Warning Project, 2016). An extremely important contribution of the GJP is that it offers a credible method for developing level playing-field tests of forecast accuracy. Thus, it allows for a tool to hold analysts and models accountable for forecasting failures both in terms of false positives and false negatives (Tetlock & Mellers, 2011). Predictably, the GJP produced a commercial spin-off, Good Judgment Inc., whose application of "proprietary forecasting and training techniques leverage competition and collaboration to produce superior predictions, making individuals and organizations better at risk analysis, probabilistic reasoning and decision making" (Good Judgment Inc., 2015). Such developments, Tetlock and Gardner (2015, p. 23) sustain, augur a new era in expert political forecasting, in which the 'guru' model based on punditry will be increasingly replaced by a blend of computer-based forecasting and subjective judgment. It should be noted that in light of the findings of the GJP, an intriguing question emerges at this point with regard to the future of political subject matter expertise. Is it possible to envisage a scenario in which political knowledge will become increasingly irrelevant when it comes to carrying out political risk analysis and assessment? In its further exploration of the meaning of expert judgment in PRA, Chapter 5 argues in favor of a negative reply to this question.

2.4 The Delphi technique

The Delphi technique can be generally defined as "a method for structuring a group communication process so that the process is effective in allowing a group of individuals, as a whole, to deal with a complex problem" (Linstone & Turoff, 1975, p. 3). Although it can be considered in broader terms as a tool for decision making and problem solving tout-court, this technique has been widely used to forecast trends in multiple fields, from technology to education, from urban planning to policy analysis (Cornish, 1977). The technique owes its suggestive name – recalling the ancient Delphi Oracle – to one of its developers, Kaplan, a scholar working for the RAND Corporation (Woudenberg, 1991, p. 132). Originally, the technique was devised as a means to rationalize "the use of experts for the estimation of bombing requirements" (Dalkey & Helmer, 1951): as happened with many other innovations – the Internet, to name but one – it represents a spillover of military research into the public sphere. In fact, the scholars and practitioners who created the Delphi technique were interested in questions similar to those investigated in Tetlock (2006) and Tetlock and Gardner (2015) – namely, problems of evaluation (that is, how good expert predictions are in areas relevant to policy making); improvement (that is, how it is possible to reach a better predictive performance); and appraisal (that is, how to appraise the accuracy of a prediction beforehand) (Kaplan et al., 1950). As such, the Delphi technique adopts the same epistemological assumptions (Helmer & Rescher, 1959) of expert political forecasting as outlined above, its primary focus however being on collective rather than individual judgment. In this sense, as happens with prediction markets, Delphi assumes that under certain conditions collective intelligence is superior to that of the individual – a concept echoing the idea of 'the wisdom of crowds' (see Sub-section 2.5). The technique is used to generate insights into the future in issue areas for which it is not reasonable or appropriate to extrapolate forecasts from past information or for which empirical data about the past is simply not available. After the declassification of its first experimental applications as a tool for forecasting and future planning, Delphi quickly became very popular. As observed by Linstone and Turoff (1975), between 1969 and 1974 the number of Delphi studies passed from the order of hundreds to the thousands. The main objective of Delphi is therefore to elicit opinion consensus in a group of experts by subjecting them to various rounds of questionnaires, with controlled opinion feedback occurring after each round. Questionnaires must be crafted with an eye to encouraging the participant to expose the reasoning behind the answer of a primary question. Such an answer must be provided by pointing to the elements which are deemed to be relevant, also providing an estimate of those elements and a description of the kind of data that would be necessary to obtain a deeper and more precise understanding of the problem at stake. After such analytical process, the participant is invited to close the loop and go back to the answer to the primary question (Dalkey & Helmer, 1963). Four main aspects come to relevance when it comes to unpacking the function of the Delphi technique: the composition and structure of the panel of experts; the significance of anonymity in the procedure; the time dimension; and the crucial role of moderators administering the questionnaires and governing the feedback process.

2.4.1 Panel of experts

A first element of extreme salience to the outcome of every Delphi exercise is the choice of individuals to be included in the expert panel, as the composition of the panel has an obvious impact on the quality of the outcome of the whole procedure. As far as the number of panelists is concerned, in spite of the wide applicability of the Delphi technique there is no consensus or standard on what constitutes an appropriate number of participants in the panels (Akins et al., 2005). As stressed by Powell (2003), "the Delphi does not call for expert panels to be representative samples for statistical purposes" (p. 378). Mitchell (1991) notes that panels can be as large as the resources available permit but that the ideal number "should be no less than eight to ten members" (p. 342), while Hyndman and Athanaso-poulos (2014) state that "the usual suggestion is somewhere between 5 and 20 experts with diverse expertise" (p. 71). It should thus be noted that the time and resources necessary for the forecasting exercise are a function of the number of individuals involved. In addition, it should be considered that both costs and the amount of time needed are inferior today than in the past, when the various tasks, from the mailing of the questionnaires to research or data retrieval, were carried out manually. In the first experiment described by Dalkey and Helmer (1963), seven experts with quite diverse yet specialized backgrounds were included (four economists, a physical vulnerability specialist and a system analyst). In running a long-term – ten- to fifteen-year – forecasting experiment, RAND produced fore-casts in six areas: scientific breakthrough; population control; automation; space progress; war prevention; and weapon systems (Gordon & Helmer, 1964). Six groups of experts were accordingly formed, one for each area to be investigated, for a total of eighty-two responders. Unsurprisingly, experts were chosen on the basis of subject matter expertise, but there is no account whatsoever of the pro-cedure or the method applied for their selection. In general, it can be said that despite the frequent resort to the Delphi technique, since its very inception the procedure of expert selection has rarely been problematized (Baker et al., 2006) nor has methodological research systematically focused on the style of reasoning (such as 'foxes versus hedgehogs') of the respondents. In this sense, the findings of the GJP discussed above are clearly relevant. Applying them to the Delphi

technique will logically entail a 'division of labor' whereby subject matter expertise is indispensable to crafting the questionnaires, while panelists will be chosen
according to different criteria – namely, for their forecasting skills rather than
solely for their special expertise.

2.4.2 Anonymity

Another feature of Delphi exercises in their original formulation is procedural anonymity – a condition introduced to deliberately avoid direct collision
between experts. According to the proponents of this approach, such a mode
of supervised interaction is aimed at circumventing the undesirable aspects of
more traditional forms of expert consulting, such as unstructured round-table
discussions which are prone to risks such as drawing hasty conclusions, the
infiltration of preconceptions or misconceptions, the tendency to close the panelists' minds to fresh ideas or to defend a given position once it has been taken,
or the predisposition to be swayed by compelling opinions expressed by others,
all to the detriment of genuinely independent thought (Dalkey & Helmer, 1963).
As stressed by Hyndman and Athanasopoulos (2014), anonymity is desirable to
remove possible sources of social or political pressure on the panelists, to guarantee individual accountability and to avoid dominance of more charismatic
individuals over the group – emotional intelligence being associated with the
emergence of a leader in small groups (Côté et al., 2010). Moreover, a study
on planning processes by Buehler Messervey and Griffin (2005) suggests that
forecasts obtained through group discussions are systematically more optimistic
than individual ones. In summary, anonymity in Delphi plays an important role
in 'extracting' quality information from the expert (Rowe, 2007) while avoiding
a number of loopholes that can be associated with 'groupthink'. The concept of
groupthink, as first introduced by psychologist Irving Janis, describes a process
that may lead a group toward poor-quality or irrational decisions when group
pressures lead to a deterioration of "mental efficiency, reality testing, and moral
judgment" (Janis, 1972, p. 9). Groupthink has been extensively used to analyze
important fiascos in political decision-making, from McCarthyism to the escalation of the US military presence in Vietnam, and according to Janis (1982) it
is characterized by eight main symptoms: the illusion of invulnerability (that
is, excessive optimism resulting in extreme risk-taking); a strong belief in the
inherent morality of the group, meaning that the group overlooks the ethical
consequences of its decisions; collective rationalization, resulting in the group
ignoring possible warnings about the poor quality of the decisions taken; ste-
reotyped negative views of group nonmembers; self-censorship (that is, the tendency not to express doubts that may challenge the perceived group consensus);
illusion of unanimity; direct pressure on dissenters; and the presence of self-
appointed 'mindguards' (that is, members of the group who protect the group
from dissonant information that may challenge the illusion of cohesiveness or
intrinsic morality of the group) (p. 244). According to Dalkey (1969), on the
basis of a set of ten experiments conducted by RAND in 1968 and producing

13,000 answers to circa 350 questions from fourteen groups of eleven to thirty respondents each, face-to-face discussion tended to make the group estimates less accurate than the anonymous feedback procedure. Although the groupthink paradigm has been challenged, especially with regard to the extent to which it can be generalized, its core message – that is, the need for a group of decision makers to be open to dissonant information – is a central lesson which is still relevant to group problem-solving research (Aldag & Fuller, 1993) and thus to collective expert political forecasting. In this sense, it is interesting to notice that one of the findings of the GJP is that forecasts produced by teams are more accurate than individual ones, but under certain conditions: in fact, the training of superforecasting teams included warnings against both groupthink and its equally dysfunctional extreme opposite – that is, excessive disagreement and rancor. The bottom-line is that if forecasters manage to continually question themselves as well as their teammates, fostering healthy, robust debate, it will remain possible to take advantage of the positive aspects of group forecasting while avoiding its negative ones without necessarily recurring to anonymity.

2.4.3 Time

Time is a key dimension of Delphi exercises in two senses: first, as a procedural element concerning the time interval elapsing between questionnaire rounds; second, from the substantial point of view, when it comes to defining the time horizon on the basis of which experts make their projections. In the first experiment conducted by RAND in 1951, five questionnaires were administered at one-week intervals (Dalkey & Helmer, 1963), while in the more extensive experiment described by Gordon and Helmer (1964), four questionnaires were administered at intervals of approximately two months, which was recognized as too long a period by the very same researchers conducting the experiment. As may occur with the number of experts to be involved in the panel, the number of questionnaire rounds is not standardized, although a minimum of two rounds is obviously required. Due to its structure involving a number of iterations, the Delphi technique is more time consuming than other techniques such as the Nominal Group Technique (NGT) which uses face-to-face meetings (Rowe & Wright, 1999). In any case, the main challenge is to strike a balance between the time necessary for the moderators to appropriately select and assemble the information to be fed to the panelists after each round, the time necessary for panelists to work out the problems they are presented with, and the need to prevent too much time elapsing between rounds so as to minimize the risk of panelist drop-out. As stressed by Hsu and Sandford (2010), when a Delphi questionnaire includes a large number of items, panelists will need to devote extensive portions of their time to provide accurate answers. Coming to the second point mentioned above, there is also another way in which the time dimension is salient in a broader sense with regard to the time horizons of the forecasts. Long-term forecasts are important because, as discussed in Chapter 2, visions of the future inevitably affect present decisions. However, as also stressed by Tetlock (2006), the accuracy of predictions worsens as the time-horizon lengthens. In this sense, it can be said that long-term political forecasts have seldom shown accuracy beyond the vague prediction of very broad trends. In the 1964 long-term exercise run by RAND described above, the research team openly recognized the limits of long-term Delphi forecasting, admitting that no claims could be made for the accuracy of the forecasts produced; at the same time, it showed some optimism by stressing that, at least in principle, long-term Delphi exercises should lessen the chance of surprise to a larger extent than "purely implicit, unarticulated, intuitive judgments" (Gordon & Helmer, 1964, p. vi).

2.4.4 Moderators

The role of moderators in administering the questionnaires and governing the feedback process is crucial at every stage of the application of the Delphi technique. The information provided to the experts between rounds is usually empirical data requested by other participants, or potentially relevant opinions expressed by other participants – presented in the most 'objective' possible way. Moderators enjoy a high degree of discretion in assembling, communicating and feeding the necessary information to participants. One of the most delicate aspects of these tasks relates to the need to ensure an adequate breadth in the contribution of participants as far as the provision of information is concerned, while at the same time maintaining the necessary degree of efficiency in the communication process (Linstone & Turoff, 1975). Moderators generally play a role in the selection of the panel members, in the analysis of the data collected, as well as in the discrimination of the most relevant information drawn from the questionnaire round. They are also in charge of the formulation of the questionnaires, a key aspect of which is breaking down questions which can be very broad into smaller ones to rationalize the forecasting process. Importantly, this breaking-down process proved to be crucial to forecasting accuracy (Tetlock & Gardner, 2015). This means that moderators need to have both methodological and subject-matter expertise. The most crucial aspect of the moderators' role is perhaps the influence that they may exert with higher or lower levels of awareness on the final result of the Delphi exercise by framing questions. A famous example of the 'framing effect' cognitive bias is the 'Asian Disease' experiment conducted by Kahneman and Tversky (1986). The problem was framed as follows (the numbers between parentheses refer to the percentage of respondents who chose each given option):

> Imagine that the U.S. is preparing for the outbreak of an unusual Asian disease, which is expected to kill 600 people. Two alternative programs to combat the disease have been proposed. Assume that the exact scientific estimates of the consequences of the programs are as follows:
>
> - If Program A is adopted, 200 people will be saved. (72%)
> - If Program B is adopted, there is 1/3 probability that 600 people will be saved, and 2/3 probability that no people will be saved. (28%)
>
> (p. 260)

When a similar sample was presented with exactly the same problem, this time framed in terms of number of casualties rather than of lives saved, the results were completely different:

- If Program C is adopted 400 people will die. (22%)
- If Program D is adopted there is 1/3 probability that nobody will die, and 2/3 probability that 600 people will die. (78%)

(p. 260)

Experiments like these highlight one of the many cognitive biases exposed by the tradition of empirical study of decision-making initiated by Tversky and Kahneman, and leading to the formulation of the so-called prospect theory. As further discussed in Chapter 5, such theory is particularly salient as it sheds light on a number of issues related to PRA. McDermott (1998) for instance extensively used prospect theory to analyze risk-taking by decision-makers in international politics in cases such as the 1956 Suez crisis or the 1979 Iranian hostage rescue mission.

In conclusion, it is possible to highlight a number of advantages and disadvantages of the Delphi technique. In general, Delphi allows for individuals with potentially differing perspectives and cognitive skills to contribute to the solution of complex problems by sharing their knowledge (Turoff & Hiltz, 1996). Delphi could also be the best available option when the amount of historical data is limited, as may occur within a new industry; it can be considered a relatively straightforward and inexpensive alternative to unstructured expert opinion; it has the practical advantage of lending itself to the solution of problems to which precise analytical techniques cannot be applied (Linstone, 1975); it allows for the provision of forecasts based on 'collective wisdom' while avoiding possible bias deriving from face-to-face interaction. As Murray (1979) puts it, Delphi is recommended "for applications involving high levels of uncertainty or that are ill-structured [as it] . . . offers one or more expert opinions when, in fact, nothing better than opinion can be achieved" (p. 157). Overall, as prudently stated in the evaluation of the first Delphi experiment, this technique is useful at least to the extent that it provides preliminary insights into a given subject matter (Dalkey & Helmer, 1963). The list of possible critiques to Delphi – somewhat surprisingly, in light of the widespread use of this technique – is nevertheless long, ranging from the disappointing results it yields when used to produce quantitative estimates (Murray, 1979) to its lack of accountability due to anonymity (Becker & Bakal, 1970). The main problem, however, is that even if through the use of Delphi consensus is reached about a given estimate, this does not necessarily mean that the estimate constitutes an accurate forecast. As highlighted by Tetlock and Gardner (2015) as well as by Taleb (2007), there is a substantial, if under-appreciated, difference between the realm of the *possible* and what is deemed to be *plausible* by a given epistemic community.

2.5 *Opinion polls and prediction markets*

Opinion polls and prediction markets are two different techniques to obtain aggregate forecasts. Although they can both be considered 'judgmental' forecasting methods, they are underpinned by different logic: opinion polls are based on the collection of information about the respondents' *intentions*, defined as "statements that people make about their planned behavior, or about the behavior of things they can control", while prediction markets are based on *opinion*, defined as "forecasts about events over which the judge has little control" (Armstrong, 1985, p. 81). Both opinion polls and prediction markets are particularly salient to PRA as they are extensively used to forecast the results of elections[6] – an obvious object of interest to PRA, considering the impact of political elections in a given country on the domestic as well as the international arena. Elections are also crucial for corporate actors as expectations about electoral outcomes are often incorporated into current decisions (Kou & Sobel, 2004): analyzing the US context Akey and Lewellen (2015) for instance found that firms which are sensitive to changes in economic policy typically hedge against uncertainty in the electoral outcome resorting to donations to more than one candidate.

Opinion polls for electoral forecasting have a long history. Modern polling techniques based on a scientific approach to sampling 'came of age' on the occasion of the 1936 US presidential election, when the traditional *Literary Digest* mail survey (whose base of respondents was skewed toward upper-income strata) wrongly forecast a win for candidate Alf Landon, while Fortune, Gallup and Crossley polls correctly predicted the landslide electoral victory of Franklin D. Roosevelt (Brown, 2004, p. 448). A number of different polling techniques can be applied to electoral forecasting – namely, benchmark surveys usually taken at the beginning of an electoral campaign, trial-heat or 'brushfire' surveys conducted later in the campaign, followed by focus groups and tracking polls which are usually conducted shortly before election day (Brox, 2006, p. 30). Asher (2012) further distinguishes between cross-sectional (different samples surveyed at the same moment) versus panel surveys (the same sample is surveyed at different points in time to map the volatility of voters' preferences over time); focus groups meant to get in-depth qualitative insights into voters' attitudes; deliberative opinion polls in which a representative group of voters is asked to discuss a number of issues and then is interviewed on preferences about those issues; and exit polls, which consist of questioning voters as they leave the polling stations. It is important to remember that all opinion polls are estimates, which means that they are vulnerable to a number of errors. Asher (2012, pp. 188–199) suggests that the forecasting accuracy of opinion polls depends on at least five elements: timing, with the accuracy of forecasts typically improving when they are made closer to the election day; the handling of undecided voters, as the pollsters may interpret the meaning of indecision in different ways as well as choose to include or exclude undecided voters; turnout estimates, which represent a forecasting challenge in their own right;[7] the truthfulness of responses, which is assumed by the pollsters when in fact the interviewees' actual voting behavior may not be consistent with the intentions expressed due for instance to the so-called 'Bradley effect';[8] and possible changes in the political and economic climate with a last-minute impact on voters' preferences. Other sources of possible error in polling forecasts are instructions to interviewers, as well as question wording and order. In spite of the methodological challenges it entails, it can be said that electoral poll accuracy has systematically increased over time (Traugott, 2014), but eventually, in the words of a prominent elections scholar, "beyond the many possible sources of errors in constructing election forecasting models, every election's campaign has effects on the vote that cannot be anticipated" (Campbell, 2012, p. 611).

Prediction markets, sometimes referred to as 'information markets' (see for instance Hahn & Tetlock, 2006), can be defined as "markets that are designed and run for the primary purpose of mining and aggregating information scattered among traders and subsequently using this information in the form of market values in order to make predictions about specific future events" (Tziralis & Tatsiopoulos, 2007, p. 75). Thus, in prediction markets the payoffs of the traded futures contracts depend on the unknown outcome of some uncertain event which is situated at a given point in the future; this means that the current price of a contract expresses the (collective) estimate of the likelihood of that event actually occurring at or by the specified deadline. As anticipated when describing the Delphi technique, prediction markets are based on the idea of 'collective intelligence' or 'the wisdom of crowds', a concept first formalized by the Condorcet jury theorem discussing cases in which collective bodies can outperform individual members in making binary choices (Condorcet, 1785) and popularized by Surowiecki (2004): under certain circumstances, groups can be very intelligent – in fact, even more intelligent than their most intelligent members. The conditions under which crowds can display their 'wisdom' are diversity in the group, independence of each member from the others, and decentralization, meant as "setting a crowd of self-interested independent people to work in a decentralized way on the same problem" (Surowiecki, 2004, p. 70), in the presence of a system that guarantees the aggregation of individual judgments. In the case of prediction markets, which are based on collective assessments made by decentralized judges, the mechanism that guarantees aggregation of individual estimates is evidently constituted by prices. A growing body of literature discusses the remarkable accuracy of prediction markets such as the Iowa Electronic Market (IEM), Intrade and PredictIt in anticipating electoral outcomes (Berg et al., 2008; Boon, 2012; Erikson & Wlezien, 2012). It should be added that in spite of their prevalent application to electoral forecasting, prediction markets can obviously be used to forecast virtually any sort of political events, from the occurrence of terrorist attacks to regime changes worldwide. In fact, in 2001 DARPA launched the so-called Policy Analysis Market (PAM) project, whose aim was to exploit the wisdom of crowds as a possible source of valuable intelligence on matters of national security. Regardless of its promises, the project was abruptly terminated in 2003 amidst a media storm following complaints by several members of the US senate that DARPA was in fact promoting a 'terror market', encouraging people to wager on terrorist attacks (Looney, 2007). Ethical concerns and fears about the alleged risk of manipulations eventually prevailed, regardless of protests by the PAM research team that the decision to terminate the project was taken with the sole purpose of putting an end to a public relations disaster while neglecting the potentialities of PAM as a precious tool for intelligence analysis (Hanson, 2007). In this respect, it should however be noted that although the extant literature converges on the idea that prediction markets are quite robust to manipulation (Wolfers & Leigh 2002; Rhode & Strumpf, 2007), such risk in principle cannot be excluded in the presence of single-minded, well-funded manipulators (Deck et al., 2013). In general, as a further symptom of the success of the 'wisdom of crowds' model, it is possible to observe a trend toward increasingly hybrid forecasting methods combining results by polls and prediction markets to achieve greater accuracy, especially as far as election forecasting is concerned (Rothschild, 2015). Websites such as election.princeton.edu, fivethirtyeight.com, pollyvote.com and realclear-politics.com all constitute examples of this composite approach. In the same vein, Schneider (2014) proposes a mixed approach combining prediction markets and expert judgment to forecast political development in the Middle East with the help of financial markets.

2.6 Scenario analysis

Scenario analysis is one of the most popular and versatile 'foresight' methodologies, whose multiple applications in the business world are generally meant to produce long-term, big-picture projections for which purely quantitative techniques would be inadequate. It is also a transversal methodology, as other techniques among those discussed above – especially Delphi – can be used as ancillary tools to build scenarios. In turn, scenarios are often used to provide the necessary background in gaming and simulations (deLeon, 1973). As Van der Heijden (2005) puts it, while the underlying thinking process and the assumptions made in risk assessment are not always clear in forecasts provided to the decision-maker by experts, scenarios

> specifically address key uncertainties through chains of cause and effect. Because they differ on these key logics scenarios put these on the management agenda. Scenarios let the decision maker look not just at outcomes, but also at the driving forces that could move the business one way or the other.
> (p. 108)

In outlining a history of scenarios as tools for decision making, Bradfield et al. (2005) notice that their use can be traced back to classic utopian and dystopian thinkers, like Plato, Thomas More or George Orwell, but that in their more recent applications they are firmly rooted in military strategic studies, such as the writings of Prussian military strategists von Clausewitz and von Moltke. In the wake of this tradition, just like Delphi, modern scenario analysis was first developed in the context of the Cold War, as a tool for military planning. In the 1960s Herman Kahn, who had previously been involved in the US Air Force effort, refined scenarios for use in business prognostication, while in the 1970s with the work of Pierre Wack at Royal/Dutch Shell they came to the fore as a prominent instrument for long-range political risk assessments (Schwartz, 1991, p. 7). When it started planning new investments in oil fields in the 1970s, Shell performed scenario analysis to generate insights into future trends in oil prices in Western Europe. Among the scenarios Shell built, one explicitly envisaged a crisis of the Organization of Petroleum-Exporting Countries (OPEC), another highlighted that one of the possible consequences of political détente between the Western and the Soviet bloc was an increase in oil exports from Central Asian Republics to Europe, and a third one suggested that environmental concerns combined with high oil prices would result in the emergence of new technologies to exploit alternative sources of energy (Maack, 2001, p. 64). In light of these scenarios, Shell designed a cautious investment strategy thanks to which it managed to avoid the significant losses incurred by its competitors when an OPEC crisis (and its inability to keep oil prices high by limiting supply) actually materialized. As Wack (1985) stresses, although scenarios and classic forecasting techniques share the common purpose of helping the investor navigate increasingly turbulent business environments, scenarios are characterized by a distinctive logic: while most forecasting techniques are ostensibly based on the assumption that the future will – to a reasonable extent – resemble the past, scenario analysis opens the investor up to the possibility of 'thinking the unthinkable' – that is "anticipating major shifts in the business environment that make whole strategies obsolete" (Wack, 1985, p. 73). As argued by Barbieri Masini (1989), the main purpose of studying alternative futures is explorative, and by no means does it entail the accurate prediction of just one future. In this vein, a long-standing debate among practitioners focuses on whether or not likelihood estimates should be included in scenarios, with first-generation scenario specialists such as Shell, SRN International and Global Business Network (GBN) firmly opposing the use of probabilities in scenarios as their objective is to explore the broader realm of the 'possible' rather than the 'likely' (Millet, 2009, p. 61), in light of the view that rather than seeking to produce accurate forecasts, scenario analysis should primarily aim at engaging in an 'imagination challenge' (Manu, 2007).

From the methodological point of view, the distinction between probabilistic and non-probabilistic scenarios is still the most relevant one. Examples of the first are the cited Shell exercise in the 1970s, which set the standard for corporate scenario analysis, or the scenarios developed by the World Economic Forum (WEF) Global Risks Reports. In its 2030 security outlook, the WEF Global Risks Report (2016) proposes three different scenarios ('walled cities', 'strong regions' and 'war and peace') to describe three possible futures in terms of international security challenges, clarifying that they are meant to provide not predictions but rather "plausible trajectories that can usefully challenge current thinking and serve as a call to action for the development of more adaptable and resilient response systems" (WEF, 2016, p. 31). This typology of scenarios which according to Bradfield, Wright and Cairns (2013) are characterized by an 'intuitive logic', is thus "focused on the development of multiple scenarios that explore the 'limits of possibility' for the future, rather than on the development of singular, 'normative' scenarios of some ideal future" (p. 634). On the other hand, probabilistic scenarios start from the extrapolation of past trends to incorporate specific likelihood estimates. By design, they lend themselves to the quantification of risk of impacts, but a relevant drawback is that those estimates heavily depend on the approach used in the analysis (New et al., 2007). Bradfield et al. (2005) distinguish this approach from that of 'intuitive logic', highlighting that it focuses on specific phenomenon and a number of key variables that are deemed to affect future developments of that phenomenon, admitting that in practice, if not in principle, it is more limited than the first category of scenarios because it entails the availability of credible time series data. A classic example of this type of scenario is the famous and debated study by Meadows et al. (1972) on the "Limits to growth", which pioneered the application of computer simulations to calculate alternative trends regarding five major variables: population, food production, industrialization, pollution and consumption of nonrenewable natural resources. As the authors themselves stressed, their scenario-building exercise was meant to uncover "the system behavioral tendencies" (p. 93) rather than making precise predictions, but they did so with the use of time series data. Whether including likelihood estimates or not, from a conceptual standpoint scenario analysis should not be confused with scenario planning, in which not only risk identification and assessments but also elements of risk management are integrated. Thus, in a sense scenario development and analysis constitute the first, preliminary steps in the process of risk management, while scenario planning represents a further step toward developing full-fledged alternative hedging strategies.

Testifying to the difficulty of making sense of the wide-ranging and diverse uses of scenarios, Van Notten et al. (2003) propose a typology of scenarios based on their main goal, which can be explorative or decision-making oriented; the process design, which can be intuitive or formal, also depending on the type of data available; the scenario content, which may be complex or simple, depending on features such as the time horizon and the number and character of the variables considered. Börjeson et al. (2006) instead propose a scenario typology including predictive, explorative and normative scenarios. Predictive scenarios can take the form of simple forecasts or multiple forecasts based on 'what if' questions. Explorative scenarios may be external or strategic, depending on whether they focus on the external environment or on the consequences of distinct courses of action undertaken by the investor. Normative scenarios may serve the different purposes of preserving or transforming a given situation in the presence of various types of environmental constraint. It should be noticed that typologies are useful as heuristic devices to orient both scholars and professional users in the jungle of a fast-changing, practice-driven field. However, it would be difficult and indeed misleading to prefer one specific scenario typology over others as – as is the case with political risks – diverse typologies simply reflect a fast-changing state of the art. What is interesting to notice, however, is that the multiplication of efforts to make sense of a growing literature and of numerous practical applications can certainly be interpreted as a symptom of the frequent resort to scenario analysis by corporate actors willing to commit to long-term investments in a world characterized by 'fat tails' (Bremmer & Keat, 2010) – that is, political events which escape 'thin-tailed' normal statistical distributions and thus are particularly difficult to 'imagine', let alone predict with accuracy, before they occur.

Notes

1 As an in-depth treatise of statistical extrapolation techniques is beyond the scope of this book, this sub-section limits itself to explaining the basic ideas behind the models described. For a systematic account of regression analysis see Lewis-Beck (1983); for time series see Ostrom (1990); for exponential smoothing see Gardner (2006); for ARIMA models see Box and Jenkins (1976). For excellent, in-depth overviews on the subject of statistical forecasting techniques, see Armstrong (Ed.) (2002) and Hyndman and Athanasopoulos (2014).
2 On the impact of technological innovation on PRA, see Chapter 6.
3 The role of human judgment in the operationalization of political variables was already illustrated with reference to PR indexes in Chapter 3 and is further explored in Chapter 5.
4 Examples of the 'legitimizing' power of expertise are so-called 'technical governments' – that is, cabinets whose members are not chosen according to criteria reflecting electoral outcomes but 'appointed' by virtue of their expertise. A recent example is the government formed in Italy in 2011 under the leadership of Mario Monti. On 'epistemic' democracy and the accountability of experts see Holst and Molander (2014).
5 The notion of subjective probability is closely linked to the Bayesian approach to probability, which postulates "a 'prior probability' model that describes a modeler's initial uncertainty about parameters, a likelihood function that describes the distribution of data, given that a parameter holds a specific value, and Bayes' rule, which provides a coherent method of updating beliefs about uncertainty when data becomes available" (Chick, 2006, p. 225).
6 For comparative analyses of these two techniques applied to elections forecasting, see Kou and Soble (2004) and Leigh and Wolfers (2006).
7 An empirical study by Rogers and Aida (2013) for instance reveals that vote self-prediction is misleading because it suggests that there is no participatory bias and that past voting is a better predictor of voting behavior than self-predicted voting.
8 The Bradley effect refers to the case in which interviewees lie to pollsters, and is named after the (black) candidate in the 1982 governor race in California, who lost to his (white) opponent in spite of the fact that opinion polls showed Bradley to be the favorite. Thus, the Bradley effect is often referenced to explain possible discrepancies between declared voting intentions and actual preferences in US presidential elections – for instance, in the context of the 2008 campaign leading to the election of Barack Obama and again in 2016 with reference to a possible 'reverse Bradley effect' against Donald Trump (see for instance Kapur, 2015).

References

Akey, P. & Lewellen, S. (2015). Policy uncertainty, political capital, and firm risk-taking. *University of Exeter Business School Working Paper*. Available at http://business-school.exeter.ac.uk/documents/Seminars_by_visitors/policy_uncertainty.pdf [Accessed on 10 April 2016].

Akins, R.B., Tolson, H. & Cole, B.R. (2005). Stability of response characteristics of a Delphi panel: Application of bootstrap data expansion. *BMC Medical Research Methodology*, 5, 37–49.

Aldag, R.J. & Fuller Riggs, S. (1993). Beyond fiasco: A reappraisal of the groupthink phenomenon and a new model of group decision processes. *Psychological Bulletin*, 113(3), 533–552.

Allais, M. (1953). Le comportement de l'homme rationnel devant le risque: Critique des postulats et axiomes de l'ecole americaine. *Econometrica*, 21(4), 503–546.

Armstrong, I.S. (1980). The seer-sucker theory: The value of experts in forecasting. *Technology Review*, 83, 18–24.

Armstrong, J.S. (1985). *Long-range forecasting: From crystal ball to computer.* New York: John Wiley & Sons Inc.

Armstrong, J.S. (1988). Review of Ravi Batra, The Great Depression of 1990. *International Journal of Forecasting*, 4(3), 493–495.

Armstrong, J.S. (2002). Role playing: A method to forecast decisions. In Armstrong, J.S. (Ed.), *Principles of forecasting: A handbook for researchers and practitioners* (pp. 15–30). New York: Kluwer.

Armstrong, J.S. & Green, K.C. (2007). Global warming: Forecasts by scientists versus scientific forecasts. *Energy & Environment*, 18(7–8), 997–1021.

Asher, H. (2012). *Polling and the public: What every citizen should know.* Washington, DC: CQ Press College.

Asimov, I. (2010). *Foundation trilogy.* London: Everyman.

Avenhaus, R. & Zartman, I.W. (Eds.) (2007). *Diplomacy games: Formal models and international negotiations.* Berlin: Springer.

Baker, J., Lovell, K. & Harris, N. (2006). How expert are the experts? An exploration of the concept of 'expert' within Delphi panel techniques. *Nurseresearcher*, 14(1), 59–70.

Barbieri Masini, E. (1989). The future of futures studies: A European view. *Futures*, 21(2), 152–160.

Batra, R. (1985). *The great depression of 1990.* New York: Dell.

Bauer, J.C. (2014). *Upgrading leadership's crystal ball. Five reasons why forecasting must replace predicting and how to make the strategic change in business and public policy.* Boca Raton, London, New York: CRC Press.

Becker, G. & Bakal, D.A. (1970). Subject anonymity and motivational distortion in self report data. *Journal of Clinic Psychology*, 26(2), 207–209.

Berg, J., Forsythe, R., Nelson, F. & Rietz, T. (2008). Results from a dozen years of election futures markets research. In Plott, C.R. & Smith, V.L. (Eds.), *Handbook of experimental economics results, Volume 1* (pp. 742–751). Amsterdam: North Holland.

Berlin, I. (1953). *The hedgehog and the fox: An essay on Tolstoy's view of history.* London: Weidenfeld & Nicolson.

Bhasin, T. & Gandhi, J. (2013). Timing and targeting of state repression in authoritarian elections. *Electoral Studies*, 32(4), 620–631.

Boon, M. (2012). Predicting elections: A 'wisdom of crowds' approach. *International Journal of Market Research*, 54(4), 465–483.

Börjeson, L., Höjer, M., Dreborg, K., Ekvall, T. & Finnveden, G. (2006). Scenario types and techniques: Towards a user's guide. *Futures*, 38(7), 723–739.

Box, G.E.P. & Jenkins, G.M. (1976). *Time series analysis, forecasting and control.* San Francisco: Holden-Day.

Bradfield, R., Wright, G., Burta, G., Cairns, G. & Van Der Heijden, K. (2005). The origins and evolution of scenario techniques in long range business planning. *Futures*, 37, 795–812.

Bradfield, R., Wright, G. & Cairns, G. (2013). Does the intuitive logics method – and its recent enhancements – produce "effective" scenarios? *Technological Forecasting and Social Change*, 80(4), 631–642.

Bremmer, I. & Keat, P. (2010). *The fat tail: The power of political knowledge in an uncertain world.* New York: Oxford University Press USA.

Brown, C.W., Jr. (2004). Roper, Elmo. In Geer, J.G. (Ed.), *Public opinion and polling around the world: A historical encyclopedia* (pp. 447–451). Santa Barbara: ABC-CLIO.

Brox, B.J. (2006). Benchmark poll. In Sabato, L.J. & Ernst, H.R. (Eds.), *Encyclopedia of American political parties and elections* (pp. 30–31). New York: Facts On File, Inc.

Buehler, R., Messervey, D. & Griffin, D. (2005). Collaborative planning and prediction: Does group discussion affect optimistic biases in time estimation? *Organizational Behavior and Human Decision Processes*, 97(1), 47–63.

Bueno de Mesquita, B. (2009). *The predictioneer's game.* New York: Random House.

Calvert, R. (2011). Game theory. In Badie, B., Berg-Schlosser, D. & Morlino, L. (Eds.), *International encyclopedia of political science* (pp. 947–951). Los Angeles: SAGE Publications Inc.

Campbell, J.E. (2012). Forecasting the 2012 American national elections. *PS: Political Science & Politics*, 45, 610–613.

Chatain, O. (October 2015). *Cooperative and non-cooperative game theory.* Available at http://www.palgraveconnect.com/esm/doifinder/10.1057/9781137294678.0132 [Accessed on 10 April 2016].

Chick, S.E. (2006). Subjective probability and Bayesian methodology. *Handbooks in Operations Research and Management Science*, 13, 225–257.

Cho, Y.H. (1972). A multiple regression model for the measurement of the public policy impact on big city crime. *Policy Sciences*, 3(4), 435–455.

Clemen, R.T. (1989). Combining forecasts: A review and annotated bibliography. *International Journal of Forecasting*, 5, 559–583.

Condorcet, M. (1785). *Essai sur l'application de l'analyse a la probabilité des descisions redues a la pluralité de voix.* Paris: De l'Imprimerie Royale.

Cornish, E. (1977). *The study of the future: An introduction to the art and science of understanding and shaping tomorrow's world.* Washington, DC: The Society.

Côté, S., Lopes, P.N., Salovey, P. & Miners, C.T.H. (2010). Emotional intelligence and leadership emergence in small groups. *The Leadership Quarterly*, 21(3), 496–508.

Cronje, F. (2014). *A time traveller's guide to our next ten years.* Cape Town: Tafelberg.

Dalkey, N.C. (1969). The Delphi method. An experimental study of group opinion. Paper prepared for US air force project RAND. Available at http://www.rand.org/content/dam/rand/pubs/research_memoranda/2005/RM5888.pdf [Accessed on 10 April 2016].

Dalkey, N. & Helmer, O. (1951). The use of experts for the estimation of bombing requirements: A project Delphi experiment. *The RAND Corporation*, RM-727-PR.

Dalkey, N. & Helmer, O. (1963). An experimental application of the Delphi method to the use of experts. *Management Science*, 9(3), 458–467.

Deck, C., Lin, S. & Porter, D. (2013). Affecting policy by manipulating prediction markets: Experimental evidence. *Journal of Economic Behavior & Organization*, 85, 48–62.

DeLeon, P. (1973). Scenario designs: An overview. *DARPA Report.* Available at http://www.rand.org/content/dam/rand/pubs/reports/2006/R1218.pdf [Accessed on 10 April 2016].

Early Warning Project (2016). *Expert opinion pool.* Available at http://www.earlywarning-project.com/opinion_pools [Accessed on 10 April 2016].

Ellis, A.K. (1970). *Teaching and learning elementary social studies.* Boston: Allyn & Bacon.

Erikson, R.S. & Wlezien, C. (2012). Markets vs. polls as election predictors: An historical assessment. *Electoral Studies*, 31, 532–539.

Farrell, H. (2012, June 24). *Why the Stevens op-ed is wrong.* Available at http://themonkeycage.org/2012/06/why-the-stevens-op-ed-is-wrong/ [Accessed on 10 April 2016].

Ferenstein, G. (2012, November 7). *Pundit forecasts all wrong, silver perfectly right: Is punditry dead?* Available at http://techcrunch.com/2012/11/07/pundit-forecasts-all-wrong-silver-perfectly-right-is-punditry-dead/ [Accessed on 10 April 2016].

Franchet, P. (2010, April 3). *The corrupt practices of financial manipulation: The meaning of the Greek economic crisis.* Available at http://www.globalresearch.ca/the-corrupt-practices-of-financial-manipulation-the-meaning-of-the-greek-economic-crisis/18467 [Accessed on 10 April 2016].

Friedman, M. (1953). *Essays in Positive Economics.* Chicago: University of Chicago Press.

Gardner, E.S., Jr. (2006). Exponential smoothing: The state of the art – Part II. *International Journal of Forecasting*, 22(4), 637–666.

Geçkil, I.K. & Anderson, P.L. (2009). *Applied game theory and strategic behavior.* Boca Raton: Chapman and Hall/CRC.

Goldhamer, H. & Speier, H. (1959). Some observations on political gaming. *World Politics*, 12, 71–83.

Goldstone, J., Bates, R., Epstein, D., Gurr, T.R., Lustik, M.B., Marshall, M.G., . . . & Woodward, M. (2010). A global model for forecasting political instability. *American Journal of Political Science*, 50(1), 190–208.

Good Judgment Inc. (2015). *Good Judgment Inc. contact webpage.* Available at http://www.goodjudgment.com/contact.html [Accessed on 10 April 2016].

Gordon, T.J. & Helmer, O. (1964). Report on a long-range forecasting study. *RAND Paper.* Available at http://www.rand.org/content/dam/rand/pubs/papers/2005/P2982.pdf [Accessed on 10 April 2016].

Green, K.C. (2002). Forecasting decisions in conflict situations: A comparison of game theory, role-playing, and unaided judgement. *International Journal of Forecasting*, 18, 321–344.

Hahn, R.W. & Tetlock, P.C. (Eds.) (2006). *Information markets: A new way of making decisions.* Washington, DC: AEI Press.

Hanson, J., Hanson, K. & Hart, M. (2014). Game theory and the law. In Chatterjee, K. & Samuelson, W. (Eds.), *Game theory and business applications* (pp. 233–263). New York: Springer.

Hanson, R. (2007). The policy analysis market: A thwarted experiment in the use of prediction markets for public policy. *Innovations: Technology, Governance, Globalization*, 2(3), 73–88.

Helmer, O. & Rescher, N. (1959). On the epistemology of the inexact sciences. *Management Science*, 6(1), 25–52.

Holst, C. & Molander, A. (2014). Epistemic democracy and the accountability of experts. In Holst, C. (Ed.), *Expertise and democracy* (pp. 13–36). ARENA Report No 1/14. Available at https://www.sv.uio.no/arena/english/research/publications/arena-publications/reports/2014/report-01-14.pdf [Accessed on 10 April 2016].

Howell, L.D. (1986). Area specialists and expert data: The human factor in political risk analysis. In Rogers, J. (Ed.), *Global risk assessments: Issues, concepts & applications Book 2* (pp. 47–84). Riverside: Global Risk Assessments, Inc.

Hsu, C. & Sandford, B.A. (2010). The Delphi technique: Making sense of consensus. *Practical Assessment, Research & Evaluation*, 12(10), 1–8.

Hyndman, R.J. & Athanasopoulos, G. (2014). *Forecasting: Principles and practice.* Melbourne, Australia: OTexts.

Interview (2015b, August 6). Semi-structured face-to-face interview with managing director of political risk analysis consultancy firm.

Interview (2015c, October 1). Semi-structured face-to-face interview with CEO of political risk consultancy firm.

Interview (2015d, October 1). Semi-structured face-to-face interview with security operations manager at global business/financial intelligence firm.

Interview (2015e, October 3). Semi-structured face-to-face interview with senior political risk analyst at global risk forecasting company.

Interview (2015g, December 1). Semi-structured telephone interview with regional head at global risk forecasting company.

Janis, I.L. (1972). *Victims of groupthink*. New York: Houghton Mifflin.

Janis, I.L. (1982). *Groupthink: Psychological studies of policy decisions and fiascoes*. Second Edition. Boston: Houghton Mifflin.

Jones, W.M. (1986). On the adapting of political-military games for various purposes. *RAND Paper*. Available at http://www.rand.org/content/dam/rand/pubs/notes/2009/N2413.pdf [Accessed on 10 April 2016].

Kahneman, D. & Tversky, A. (1979). Prospect theory: An analysis of decision under risk. *Econometrica*, 47(2), 263–291.

Kahneman, D. & Tversky, A. (1986). Rational choice and the framing of decisions. *The Journal of Business*, 59(4, Part 2: The Behavioral Foundations of Economic Theory), S251–S278.

Kaplan, A., Skogstad, A.L. & Girshick, M.A. (1950). The prediction of social and technological events. *The Public Opinion Quarterly*, 14(1), 93–110.

Kapur, S. (2015, December 22). *Trump's big if: Why polls may underestimate his support*. Available at http://www.bloomberg.com/politics/articles/2015-12-22/a-reverse-bradley-effect-polls-may-underestimate-trump-s-support [Accessed on 10 April 2016].

Klugman, S.F. (1947). Group and individual judgments for anticipated events. *Journal of Social Psychology*, 26, 21–28.

Knight, F.H. (1921). *Risk uncertainty and profit*. Mineola, NY: Dover Publications Inc.

Kou, S.G. & Soble, M.E. (2004). Forecasting the vote: A theoretical comparison of election markets and public opinion polls. *Political Analysis*, 12, 277–295.

Leigh, A. & Wolfers, J. (2006). Competing approaches to forecasting elections: Economic models, opinion polling and prediction markets. *NBER Working Paper No. 12053*. Available at http://www.nber.org/papers/w12053 [Accessed on 10 April 2016].

Lewis-Beck, M.S. (1983). *Applied regression: An introduction*. Beverly Hills: SAGE Publications Inc.

Linstone, H.A. (1975). Eight basic pitfalls: A checklist. In Linstone, H.A. & Turoff, M. (Eds.), *The Delphi method: Techniques and applications* (pp. 559–571). Boston: Addison-Wesley Publishing.

Linstone, H.A. & Turoff, M. (1975). Introduction. In Linstone, H.A. & Turoff, M. (Eds.), *The Delphi method: Techniques and applications* (pp. 3–12). Boston: Addison-Wesley Publishing.

Looney, R.E. (2007). DARPA's policy analysis market for intelligence: Outside the box or off the wall? *International Journal of Intelligence and Counter Intelligence*, 17, 405–419.

Lorenz, E.N. (1963). Deterministic nonperiodic flow. *Journal of the Atmospheric Sciences*, 20, 130–141.

Lorenz, E.N. (1972). *Predictability: Does the flap of a butterfly's wings in Brazil set off a tornado in Texas?* Paper prepared for the 139th Annual Meeting of the American Association for the Advancement of Science. Available at http://eaps4.mit.edu/research/Lorenz/Butterfly_1972.pdf [Accessed on 10 April 2016].

Lyons, D. (2012, November 7). *Why Nate Silver won, and why it matters*. Available at http://readwrite.com/2012/11/07/why-nate-silver-won-and-why-it-matters [Accessed on 10 April 2016].

Maack, J. (2001). Scenario analysis: A tool for task managers. In Krueger, R., Casey, M.A., Donner, J., Kirsch, S. & Maack, J. *Social development paper no. 36, Social analysis: Selected tools and techniques* (pp. 62–87). Washington, DC: World Bank.

Makridakis, S.G., Wheelwright, S.C. & Hyndman, R.J. (1998). *Forecasting: Methods and applications*. New York: John Wiley & Sons, Inc.

Manu, A. (2007). *The imagination challenge: Points of departure for strategic creativity and innovation*. Berkeley: Peachpit Press.

Marcovina, M. & Pellero, B. (2015). A mathematical analysis of domestic terrorist activity in the years of lead in Italy. *Peace Economics, Peace Science and Public Policy*, 21(3), 351–389.

McCarty, N. & Meirowitz, A. (2007). *Political game theory: An introduction*. Cambridge: Cambridge University Press.

McDermott, R. (1998). *Risk-Taking in international politics. Prospect theory in American foreign policy*. Ann Arbor: The University of Michigan Press.

Meadows, D.H., Meadows, D.L., Randers, J. & Behrens, W.W., III (1972). *Limits to growth*. New York: New American Library.

Millet, S.M. (2009). Should probabilities be used with scenarios? *Journal of Futures Studies*, 13(4), 61–68.

Minford, J. (2014). *I Ching: The essential translation of the ancient Chinese oracle and book of wisdom*. New York: The Penguin Group.

Mitchell, V.W. (1991). The Delphi technique: An exposition and application. *Technology Analysis & Strategic Management*, 3(4), 333–358.

Mongin, P. (1997). Expected utility theory. In Davis, J., Hands, W. & Maki, U. (Eds.), *Handbook of economic methodology* (pp. 342–350). London: Edward Elgar.

Mun, K.C. (2007). *Chinese leadership wisdom from the book of change*. Hong Kong: The Chinese University Press.

Murray, T.J. (1979). Delphi methodologies: A review and critique. *Urban Systems*, 4(2), 153–158.

Nash, J. (1951). Non-cooperative games. *Annals of Mathematics*, 54(2), 286–295.

New, M., Lopez, A., Dessai, S. & Wilby, R. (2007). Challenges in using probabilistic climate change information for impact assessments: An example from the water sector. *Philosophical Transactions of the Royal Society*, 365, 2117–2131.

Open Options (2013). *Case studies description – civil unrest: "Under attack"*. Available at http://www.openoptions.com/industry-experience/oil-gas-and-energy [Accessed on 10 April 2016].

Ostrom, C.W. (1990). *Time series analysis: Regression techniques*. Beverly Hills: SAGE Publications Inc.

Popper, R., Keenan, M., Miles, I., Butter, M., Sainz, G. *Global foresight outlook 2007*. European Foresight Monitoring Network. Available at http://www.inovasyon.org/pdf/efmn.global.foresight.outlook_Popper.et.al.2007.pdf [Accessed on 10 April 2016].

Powell, C. (2003). The Delphi technique: Myths and realities. *Journal of Advanced Nursing*, 41(4), 376–382.

Priiva (2011). *Case studies: Regulatory affairs*. Available at http://www.priiva.com/case Studies/regulatoryAffairs/ [Accessed on 10 April 2016].

Rabin, M. (2003). Risk aversion and expected-utility theory: A calibration theorem. *Econometrica*, 68(5), 1281–1292.

Rappeport, A. (2008, July 15). Game theory versus practice. *CFO Magazine*. Available at http://ww2.cfo.com/strategy/2008/07/game-theory-versus-practice/ [Accessed on 10 April 2016].

Rhode, P. & Strumpf, K. (2007). Manipulating political stock markets: A field experiment and a century of observational data. *NBER Working Paper*. Available at http://www.unc.edu/~cigar/papers/ManipNBER.pdf [Accessed on 10 April 2016].

Rogers, T. & Aida, M. (2013). Vote self-prediction hardly predicts who will vote, and is (misleadingly) unbiased. *American Politics Research*, 42(3), 503–528.

Rothschild, D. (2015). Combining forecasts for elections: Accurate, relevant, and timely. *International Journal of Forecasting*, 31, 952–964.

Rowe, G. (2007). A guide to Delphi. *Foresight: The International Journal of Applied Forecasting*, 8, 11–16.

Rowe, G. & Wright, G. (1999). The Delphi technique as a forecasting tool: Issues and analysis. *International Journal of Forecasting*, 15, 353–375.

Schneider, G. (2014). Forecasting political events with the help of financial markets. In Wayman, F.W., Williamson, P.R., Bueno de Mesquita, B. & Polachek, S. (Eds.), *Predicting the future in science, economics, and politics* (pp. 213–234). Cheltenham and Northampton: Edward Elgar Publishing.

Schumpeter, J.A. (1954). *History of economic analysis*. New York: Oxford University Press.

Schwartz, P. (1991). *The art of the long view*. New York: Doubleday.

Scott, M. (2014). *Delphi: A history*. Princeton: Princeton University Press.

Sherden, W. (1997). *The fortune sellers: The big business of buying and selling predictions*. New York: John Wiley & Sons Inc.

Shotts, K. (2015). Political risk as a hold-up problem: Implications for integrated strategy. *Stanford Graduate School of Business, Working Paper No. 3254*. Available at https://www.gsb.stanford.edu/faculty-research/working-papers/political-risk-hold-problem-implications-integrated-strategy [Accessed on 10 April 2016].

Simonsohn, U. (2009). Direct risk aversion evidence from risky prospects valued below their worst outcome. *Psychological Science*, 20(6), 686–692.

Stevens, J. (2012, June 23). Political scientists are lousy forecasters. Available at http://www.nytimes.com/2012/06/24/opinion/sunday/political-scientists-are-lousy-forecasters.html?_r=0 [Accessed on 10 April 2016].

Surowiecki, J. (2004). *The wisdom of crowds*. New York: Anchor books.

Taleb, N.N. (2007). *The black swan: The impact of the highly improbable*. New York: Random House.

Tetlock, P.E. (2006). *Expert political judgment: How good is it? How can we know?* Princeton: Princeton University Press.

Tetlock, P. & Gardner, D. (2015). *Superforecasting: The art and science of prediction*. New York: Random House.

Tetlock, P.E. & Mellers, B.A. (2011). Intelligent management of intelligence agencies: Beyond accountability ping-pong. *American Psychologist*, 66(6), 542–554.

The Economist (2012). Don't lie to me, Argentina – Why we are removing a figure from our indicators page. Available at http://www.economist.com/node/21548242 [Accessed on 10 April 2016].

Traugott, M.W. (2014). Public opinion polls and election forecasting. *PS: Political Science & Politics*, 47(2), 342–344.

Turoff, M. & Hiltz, S.R. (1996). Computer based Delphi process. In Adler, M. & Ziglio, E. (Eds.), *Gazing into the oracle: The Delphi method and its application to social policy and public health* (pp. 56–88). London: Jessica Kingsley Publishers.

Tziralis, G. & Tatsiopoulos, I. (2007). Prediction markets: An extended literature review. *Journal of Prediction Markets*, 1(1), 75–91.

Ulfelder, J. (2012a, November 8). Why the world can't have a Nate Silver. *Foreign Policy*. Available at http://foreignpolicy.com/2012/11/08/why-the-world-cant-have-a-nate-silver/ [Accessed on 10 April 2016].

Ulfelder, J. (2012b, June 24). *In defense of political science and forecasting.* Available at https://dartthrowingchimp.wordpress.com/2012/06/24/in-defense-of-political-science-and-forecasting/ [Accessed on 10 April 2016].

Ulfelder, J. (2015, April 5). *A bit more on country-month modeling.* Available at https://dartthrowingchimp.wordpress.com/tag/gdelt/ [Accessed on 10 April 2016].

Van der Heijden, K. (2005). *Scenarios: The art of strategic conversation.* Chichester: John Wiley & Sons, Ltd.

van Notten, P.W.F., Rotmans, J., van Asselt, M.B.A. & Rothman, D.S. (2003). An updated scenario typology. *Futures,* 35, 423–443.

von Neumann, J. (1928). Zur theorie der Gesellschaftsspiele. *Mathematische Annales,* 100, 295–300.

Wack, P. (1985). Scenarios: Uncharted waters ahead. *Harvard Business Review,* 63(5), 73–89.

Ward, M.D. & Metternich, N. (2012, November 16). Predicting the future is easier than it looks. *Foreign Policy.* Available at http://foreignpolicy.com/2012/11/16/predicting-the-future-is-easier-than-it-looks/ [Accessed on 10 April 2016].

Ward, M.D., Metternich, N.W., Carrington, C., Dorff, C., Gallop, M., Hollenbach, F. & Schultz, A. (2012). Geographical models of crises: Evidence from ICEWS. In Schmorrow, D.D. & Nicholson, D.M. (Eds.), *Advances in design for cross cultural activities* (pp. 429–438). Boca Raton: CRC Press LLC.

WEF (2016). *The global risks report 2016.* Available at http://www3.weforum.org/docs/Media/TheGlobalRisksReport2016.pdf [Accessed on 10 April 2016].

Wolfers, J. & Leigh, A. (2002). Three tools for forecasting federal elections: Lessons from 2001. *Australian Journal of Political Science,* 37(2), 223–240.

Woudenberg, F. (1991). An evaluation of Delphi. *Technological Forecasting and Social Change,* 40, 131–150.

5 The cross-cutting role of expert judgment

An expert is someone who knows some of the worst mistakes that can be made in his subject, and how to avoid them.

(W. Heisenberg, 1971, p. 210)

1. The omnipresence of 'subjectivity' in PRA

As argued throughout the book, any operation of political risk assessment begins with an appraisal of the past and present situation but eventually hinges on the projection of the investor's activities in the future. In particular, as stressed in the previous chapters, modeling political risk on the basis of such conjectural knowledge to deliver forecasts always entails more or less explicit appeals to 'human judgment' or, as often repeated in the literature, 'expert judgment'(Howell, 1986; Tetlock, 1992, 2006). Even a superficial glance at the various techniques explored in Chapter 4 is sufficient to reveal that when it comes to forecasting political events human judgment is indeed omnipresent – although in varying degrees. References to the prevalence of 'subjective estimates' in PRA also abound in the literature (Lax, 1983; Solberg, 1992; Bouchet et al., 2003; Bremmer, 2005). Moreover, a precise definition of what is 'subjective' as opposed to 'objective' is seldom provided, although there is a tendency to equate objective with 'quantitative' and subjective with 'qualitative' methods. Nevertheless, as clearly stated by Armstrong (1985), both objective (also referred to as explicit, statistical or formal) and subjective (also referred to as implicit, intuitive or informal) forecasting techniques can in fact indiscriminately rely on (and be used to produce) quantitative as well as qualitative data. Ultimately, the essential difference between subjective and objective would be that in the first case "the inputs are translated into forecasts in the researcher's head . . . [while in the second] . . . the inputs are translated into forecasts using a process that can be exactly replicated by other researchers" (Armstrong, 1985, p. 73). In fact, as already stressed above, virtually no method for PRA can be classified as purely quantitative. Similarly, as illustrated in Table 5.1 below, subjective aspects can be found in all of the forecasting techniques discussed in Chapter 4, including those which are normally considered to be extremely objective. This 'hybrid' nature is typical of risk analysis in general. In all stages of risk assessment "there is uncertainty, the need for judgement,

Table 5.1 'Subjective' aspects in PR forecasting techniques

Technique	'Subjective' Aspects
Statistical Extrapolations	• Model design: choice of independent/dependent variables • Assumptions about causal relationships • Possible use of qualitative input
Game Theoretical Approaches	• Assumptions about the rationality of the players • Assumptions about the preferences of the players
Expert Opinion	• 'Subjective' input processing • Possible use of qualitative input • Individual judgment • Non-reproducible
Delphi	• 'Subjective' input processing • Possible use of qualitative input • Collective judgment • Framing of questions • Selection and dissemination of information by moderators • Non-reproducible
Opinion Polls	• Framing of questions • Handling of undecided voters • Assumptions about the truthfulness of responses
Prediction Markets	• Framing of questions • Collective judgment
Scenarios	• 'Subjective' input processing • Possible use of qualitative input

considerable scope for human bias, and inaccuracy . . . [so that] . . . [t]he results obtained by one risk analyst are unlikely to be obtained by others starting with the same information" (Redmill, 2002, p. 91). In this sense, it should be noted that even the most sophisticated statistical extrapolations need to use inputs which are at least partially subjective when they are used to forecast political events: while automated coding of political events data is on the rise and seems to be incredibly promising vis-à-vis time consuming and error-prone 'human' coding (Schrodt & Van Brackle, 2013), it is unthinkable to totally oust expert judgment from the process at least when defining the basic conceptual aspects of the automated procedure – for instance, with respect to the categories of events or actors on the basis of which the coding takes place.

Equally, even formal game theoretical models rely on assumptions being made about the preferences of the players, while Delphi and prediction markets are self-evident instances of collective judgment, the accuracy of which also depends on the way in which questions are framed, an aspect they share with opinion polls, and it is safe to say that both expert opinion and scenario analysis are based on subjective processing of data. In this vein, it can be argued that the role of expert judgment is cross-cutting – after all, its importance as a source of political intelligence has regularly emerged in the literature, as explained in the previous chapters. In addition, as already suggested by Bunn and Wright (1991) and confirmed by Tetlock and Gardner (2015), interaction between judgmental and statistical forecasting methods is desirable and fruitful. Thus, in view of its relevance with respect to the whole body of knowledge related to PRA, the subject deserves specific attention. The rest of the chapter unfolds as follows: Section 2 explores the diverse meanings attached to the concept of expertise, focusing on references to 'experts' in the political risk and forecasting literatures, drawing a clear-cut distinction between expert judgment in the sense of forecasting accuracy on the one hand and expert judgment based on political knowledge needed for the framing and modeling of political risks on the other. To better illustrate how these two concepts can and indeed should be kept separate, Section 3 discusses the role of political knowledge in a realm which is distinct from forecasting yet very salient to PRA (that, is the operationalization of political variables), while Section 4 discusses the most critical aspects in 'human' – that is, not depending on specific knowledge – judgment, which have to do with forecasting skills irrespective of (political) knowledge. Section 5 concludes arguing in favor of a reappraisal of the concept of political expertise based on enhanced accountability of the expert.

2. Political versus forecasting expertise

Given their widespread and manifold use in today's world, it is somewhat surprising to notice how rarely the recourse to experts to assess risks in the public as well as in the corporate sphere is accompanied by a clear definition of the exact content of the invoked 'expertise'. As a matter of fact, due to its public character and its more manifest impact, the status of expertise in domestic and international policy-making has received a fair amount of academic attention over time (see for instance Nowotny, 1980; Bäckstrand, 2003; Tickner & Wright, 2003; Bollard, 2013; Ambrus et al., 2014). Yet, until quite recently – with the work of Tetlock in particular – the meaning of expertise in less exposed realms like intelligence and political risk analysis has been problematized only to a limited extent. In order to substantiate this claim, it is interesting to look at how the question of expertise – as well as the closely linked problem of how to select experts for political analysis – has been tackled over time. Returning to the famous work by Dalkey and Helmer (1963) already quoted in Chapter 4 and documenting the results of the first experiment applying the Delphi technique to the use of experts conducted at the RAND Corporation, references to expertise are ubiquitous. The seven experts participating in the study were presumably recruited on the basis of their extensive knowledge of various subjects: namely, 'economics', 'system analysis' and 'physical vulnerability'; yet there was no strict consistency between their expertise so defined and the subject about which they were asked to provide their forecasts – that is, "the selection, from the viewpoint of a Soviet strategic planner, of an optimal US industrial target system and [. . .] the estimation of the number of A-bombs required to reduce the munitions output by a prescribed amount" (Dalkey & Helmer, 1963, p. 458). The subsequent success and diffusion of the Delphi technique spurred a methodological debate in which the meaning of expertise was also called into question: Mitroff and Turoff (1975) warned against the belief that the expert's view is the only one pertinent to the decision, and lamented the increasing confusion surrounding the role of the expert, criticizing in particular systems analysts, efficiency experts and operation researchers for their great influence – justified in light of their special training – yet narrow focus, as specialization would make them blind to the broader scope of the problems that the decision-maker resorting to their expertise typically has to tackle (p. 29). Goodman (1987) noted how the title of expert is potentially misleading, while Baker et al. (2006) denounced the paucity of the literature on the definition of expertise and on the selection of experts for Delphi panels, noting that in the current usage of this term, notions of expertise stretch from the mastery of specific knowledge – also, but not exclusively, deriving from experience – to the ownership of 'policy influence'. This kind of critique notwithstanding, subject matter experts have retained a central role as providers of assessments, forecasts and projections in the public and in the private sphere.

As already hinted at in Chapter 4, and as testified by the enduring appetite of the media for punditry, the idea of exceptional knowledge as a source of legitimacy and intelligence in dealing with complex situations is still widespread. In suggesting how to pragmatically overcome the 'availability bias'[1] in scenario construction, Wright, Bradfield and Cairns (2013), for instance, suggest that one idea is to involve in the process 'remarkable people' – individuals "who hold a mixture of expertise and viewpoints on issues that the scenario team has identified as either pre-determined trends or critical uncertainties within the scenarios" (p. 635). Interestingly, while in this instance expertise and 'remarkability' seem to overlap, in the original distinction drawn by Van der Heijden (2005) 'remarkable people' differed from experts in that their expertise was more related to their out-of-the-box style of thinking than to subject knowledge. An important remark has to be made at this point: one key assumption almost universally made about experts is that they are better than laypersons at assessing risks. In a nutshell, "the assumption underlying forecasting is that some people can be more expert than others in predicting what will happen, and the best we can do is ask them for their considered opinion on what might be in store" (Van der Heijden, 2005, p. 25). A good example from the international public policy sphere is the Intergovernmental Panel on Climate Change (IPCC), in whose framework climate 'experts' have been entrusted since 1988 with the task of assessing "projections of future climate change and the resultant projected impacts and risks" (IPCC, 2014, p. 36) – that is, of providing intelligence on a problem whose economic, social and political ramifications are potentially gargantuan. The case of IPCC epitomizes the tendency to assume that subject matter knowledge automatically equates to the capability of producing accurate risk assessments and forecasting. Yet, this is far from being unproblematic. Armstrong and Green (2007, 2015) thoroughly analyzed the results of the activity of the IPCC and came to the conclusion that the projections provided by the Panel constituted 'forecasts by scientists' but not 'scientific forecasts', as their *modus operandi* systematically violated the most basic principles of 'good forecasting', including that of prescribing a conservative approach to estimations. In this sense, although given their qualifications and reputation the participants in the IPCC could certainly be considered subject matter experts, they seemed not to display the same level of 'expertise' if by that one means the ability to provide accurate forecasting. This is precisely the same message emerging from the long-term research conducted by Tetlock (2006) and already discussed in Chapter 4. The basic research question of that study, further developed in the following years with the DARPA-sponsored GJP, was whether or not it was possible to find empirical data underpinning the association normally – and intuitively – made between subject knowledge and the ability to provide accurate forecasts. As already stressed, the results of the study were largely negative in this sense, and the claim made by Tetlock (2006) that political experts were no better forecasters than "dart-throwing chimps" (p. 20) immediately became a successful catchphrase among political forecasting skeptics. In a sense, it could be argued that the GJP dealt a fatal blow to the prestige attached to the title of 'political expert'. If superforecasting skills, as already discussed in Chapter 4, essentially depend on a style of thinking rather than on political knowledge, what is the point of political subject matter expertise? To answer this question, it is necessary to make a further distinction between expert judgment and forecasting skills. Unsurprisingly – as they are closely related – the concepts of 'forecasting' and 'expert judgment' have often been used interchangeably. This overlapping of meanings is also evident in Tetlock's landmark study entitled *Expert political judgment: How good is it? How can we know?* which pursued the ambitious goal of setting rigorous standards to 'judge the quality of judgment'. However, in spite of the emphasis given to expert judgment in the very title of the book, the research design and the focus of the analysis actually hinged on forecasting rather than on expert judgment proper: the performance of experts was assessed in terms of *forecasting* skills, as experts were eventually 'judged' on the basis of a two-decade-long study of their performance in predicting political outcomes.

The point is that, intimately linked as they may be, forecasting skills and expert judgment are to be kept separate to better single out the role of each within PRA. Forecasting requires judgment, but there are acts of judgment – based on subject matter knowledge – which do not necessarily call for probabilistic thinking. In other words, while every act of political forecasting entails an element of human judgment, the opposite is not necessarily true – that is, expert judgment in PRA is not used solely to the purpose of forecasting tasks. To illustrate this point, it is timely to provide an example. Superforecasters, according to Tetlock and Gardner (2015), are people who have special cognitive skills and personality traits: they are typically lifelong learners committed to continuous self-improvement, a feature that the authors call the 'perpetual Beta factor'. In this sense, the concept of 'superforecasters' echoes the one of 'remarkable people' as defined by Van der Heijden (2005). When asked questions such as "whether a foreign military would carry out operations within Syria before December 1, 2014" (Tetlock and Gardner, 2015, p. 156), the superforecasters participating in the GJP were able to provide remarkably accurate assessments without necessarily having specific knowledge of the subject of their forecasts. However, an aspect that has received little attention is precisely how the questions asked were formulated and by whom: as was the case with the main focus of the GJP – which was to investigate the features and abilities of the respondents – the role of those who drafted the questions was mentioned only cursorily in the book divulgating the results of the project. Yet, it is precisely in this sense that political expertise could and should be brought back into the picture. An example that could illustrate this point well would be for instance a question asking the respondent to forecast the outcome of the referendum held in Greece in 2015 to decide on the bailout of the country – as is well known, such a bailout by the EU was going to come with many strings attached in the form of further structural reforms and austerity measures. In that instance, it would have been relatively easy for a superforecaster to provide an estimate reflecting the prevalence of the 'No' camp, yet the assessment of the meaning of that outcome, as well as its consequences[2] – which some feared could even stretch to a 'Grexit' from the European Union – at a time of great uncertainty would have inevitably required some contextual knowledge of Greek and European politics. Moreover, as already hinted at in Chapter 4, the 'framing' effect can have a major impact on how the respondent reacts to questions in a situation of uncertainty. As a consequence, asking questions which are not adequately formulated may produce forecasts which are accurate but not pertinent. If we recall another episode in the Greek debt crisis, we see that a 90 percent positive probability proposed in response to a question asking to forecast whether or not Alexis Tsipras would resign by August 25, 2015, would have produced an accurate forecast, but such a framing of the issue could have conjured the idea of a discontinuity in Greek politics that actually did not materialize.[3] In sum, PRA requires not only forecasting skills but also the ability to model problems in ways which are relevant to the specific industry or even the individual investor. Those who provide probabilistic answers should preferably be 'superforecasters', but those who formulate the questions need to have a broader understanding of the issues at stake. After all, the assessment of future scenarios also depends on knowing the present and including the right questions. As Simmonds (1977) warns, "the most revealing and pertinent questions on the topic may never be asked" (p. 24).

Thus, as in the case of Delphi where the role of the moderators is crucial (see Chapter 4), the specific role of political expertise clearly emerges in relation to the selection of relevant information and the framing of questions forecasters are to be asked: as one senior analyst put it, "most of my job is asking the right questions" (Interview, 2015g). As recognized by Tetlock and Gardner (2015) – and as already pointed out by the first proponents of Delphi at RAND – the division of labor in the production of intelligence is of crucial relevance, as the breaking down of broad, complex issues into simpler ones allows for a better appreciation of causal mechanisms, thus facilitating thorough reflection and double-checks in the process of attaching probabilities in risk assessments. As Raiffa (1968, p. 271) famously stated, "The spirit of decision analysis is to divide and conquer: Decompose a complex problem into simpler problems." Moreover, as noted by Gallo (2013), a check of the causal claims made by the analyst in each and every step of PRA exercises is useful both to the analyst and to the consumer of political risk intelligence in assessing the persuasiveness of the arguments put forward when modeling political risk. When we look at the distinct yet complementary roles of political knowledge and (political) forecasting, it is possible to detect an analogy with the process of modeling political risk to create indexes such as those described in Chapter 3. On the one hand lies the design of the model – that is, the type and number of variables included, as well as the relative weighting they are assigned; the task of 'engineering' the model in this sense can be executed only by relying on political expertise. On the other hand, there is the task of feeding data into the models by transforming the ever-increasing amount of information into intelligence by interpreting indicators and assigning probability estimates – which necessitates forecasting skills.

3. Expert political knowledge without probability estimation

The previous section sketched out a clear-cut distinction between expert political judgment meant as subject matter knowledge and the ability to provide accurate forecasts, which as suggested by Tetlock (2006) apparently cannot be acquired simply through study or experience – although it can be somewhat improved through training. The track record of subject matter experts in terms of forecasting accuracy is poor, yet it is a fact that public and corporate actors still resort to 'punditry' for policy advice. A corollary of what has been argued above is that although criticism against punditry applied to political forecasting is well-grounded in theory and in practice, this should not translate into a total dismissal of subject matter knowledge to the purpose of forecasting risks; rather, a 'division of labor' perspective is preferable, in light of the fact that providing forecasts and framing the issues about which forecasts are provided are complementary activities that could not possibly be carried out efficiently by the same category of actors. In sum, both subject matter knowledge and forecasting skills are essential to successful PRA. Although they are bad forecasters, subject matter experts may indeed be very good at what Camerer and Johnson (1991, p. 210) call 'non-predictive functions of expertise', such as measuring variables and discovering new ones. As a senior analyst put it, sometimes the analyst's work rather than on forecasting is focused on the collection and assessment of information on a given event, based on which the investor can subsequently proceed to risk estimation (Interview, 2015i). As a first instance, expert knowledge is key in one of the situations described in Section 1 – that is, when it comes to assessing the preferences of relevant actors in a given political context. The application of spatial models to political controversies illustrates how judgment based on expert political knowledge is essential to producing data which at a later stage can be used to provide forecasts. Bueno de Mesquita and Stockman (1994) for instance looked to expert interviews to map the positions of EU member states on contested policy measures. Tracing out the preferences of the member states can be extremely complex if only for the fact that not all the actors receive the same amount of media attention – hence the need to resort to experts with specific information about both domestic politics and the negotiating process. The positions, which according to the spatial approach adopted were represented as different points in a bi-dimensional space, were subsequently used to test bargaining models studying the outcomes of the relevant EU decision-making processes. The same approach was followed by Thomson et al. (2012) introducing "[a] new dataset on decision-making in the European Union before and after the 2004 and 2007 enlargements (DEUII)". The dataset covers 331 contested issues raised by 125 legislative proposals, identifying the policy options preferred by member states individually as well as by the EU Parliament and Commission. As the authors stress, the policy alternatives and the relative positions of the various actors were determined "by key informants' judgements of the political distances between the alternatives" (Thomson et al., 2012, p. 606). Moreover, according to Junge and König (2007), one key aspect influencing the success of spatial analysis is the specification of preferences – thus, in a sense judgment based on political knowledge is crucial not only to identify the positions of the actors considered but also in the specification of the model (for instance, whether the policy space is assumed to be continuous or discrete or whether or not specific actors' saliences are included in the analysis). It should be underscored that the importance of exercises such as that described above have once again come to the fore on occasion of the recent European sovereign debt crisis – a crisis which has jeopardized the very existence of the common currency and generated widespread concerns among investors on a worldwide scale: understanding the preferences of each and every EU member state became key to grasping the possible outcomes of the complex decision-making mechanisms within the EU arena.

A further example of nonpredictive expert political judgment is the operationalization of political variables: contrary to what happens in the natural world, scholars of social sciences often have to confront the problem of how to operationalize extremely abstract concepts, which lack a concrete counterpart in the physical world.

It is definitely difficult to translate abstract ideas such as political stability, political violence or rule of law into a measurable 'substance', and to do so in a rigorous and convincing manner. Yet, as already hinted at in Chapter 1, when trying to measure 'soft' variables, relying on expert judgment is often the only viable option. This typically happens in the production of data on the quality of democratic institutions – data whose use is widespread in PRA. Also in this case, expert political judgment plays a role both in the selection of indicators and in actual measurement. Both operations present problematic aspects. As far as the choice of indicators is concerned, it can be subject to ideological bias. Munck (2009) for instance draws attention to the fact that the World Bank's rule of law index consists of many indicators on the protection of private property and contract enforcement while disregarding other aspects such as labor rights (p. 10). As far as the actual measurement is concerned, the difficulties encountered in 'assessing assessments' by political experts are well illustrated by a study by Bollen and Paxton (2000), which builds on previous work by Bollen (1993) and Bollen and Grandjean (1981). The authors examine judge-specific errors of measurement by looking at the work of three judges assessing democracy over a period of seventeen years (1972–88). According to their findings, error in judgment-based measurement (which they summarize as 'method factor') can be ascribed to three possible sources: (a) the information available for rating; (b) the judges' processing of this information; and (c) the method by which a judge's processing decisions are translated into a rating (Bollen & Paxton, 2000, p. 62). In focusing on the second aspect – namely, on the way in which judges process information – Bollen and Paxton regress the standardized scores assigned to various countries by three experts measuring the quality of democracy in 1980 on three sets of variables (situational closeness, defensive attribution, and information) in order to assess the impact of various features of countries on the judge's method factors. The authors interpret the results obtained along the lines that, for instance, the first judge tends to underrate Marxist-Leninist countries and to overrate Catholic countries, while the second shows a 'positive bias' towards Marxist-Leninist countries. The third judge's results are similar to the first, and according to the authors this can be partially explained by the fact that the two experts worked for a while for the same institution (namely, the Freedom House). The analysis conducted by Bollen and Paxton is certainly sophisticated and compelling from the statistical point of view, and its results are in line with the literature on expert judgment in the sense that they confirm the existence of a 'human factor' in expert-produced political data. Yet, they could be subject to criticism in at least one respect: what if the first judge was right in deeming as he does the countries classified as 'Catholic' to be more democratic than those that are dubbed 'Marxist-Leninist'? While the regression coefficients in the statistical model built by the authors are quite telling with respect to the assessment style of the judges considered, in absence of an 'objective' measure of democracy we cannot determine whether the judge was right or not. In sum, expert judgment based on political knowledge is relevant to PRA in many different ways including in the identification of political actors' preferences and the measurement of complex concepts such as 'democracy' or 'rule of law'. As such, simplistically equating it with forecasting is limiting and potentially misleading.

4. Probability estimation without expert political knowledge

A conclusion that can certainly be drawn from what has been said so far is that the human mind is not equipped to think statistically,[4] an aspect that becomes particularly salient when the mission of the judge is to estimate the likelihood of events. Thus, irrespective of her knowledge in the relevant field of analysis, it is not possible for a judge to make decisions based on a framework of objective probability, meant as long-term relative frequency of a given outcome in an experimental context (the typical and most banal example of which is tossing a coin N times), or, to recall a mathematical definition, meant as a "limiting relative frequency: the long-run behavior of a nondeterministic outcome or just an observed proportion in a population" (Gill, 2006, p. 285). Evidently, what comes to the fore in PR analysis is not objective probability, but rather subjective probability, which denotes "any estimate of the probability of an event, which is given by a subject, or inferred from his behavior. These estimates are not assumed to satisfy any axioms or consistency requirements" (Kahneman & Tversky, 1972, p. 431). When making judgments, the human mind is inevitably exposed to a number of biases (see Table 5.2 below). In fact, resorting to a consolidated taxonomy in clinical psychology, its functioning can be described as "a tale of two systems" (Kahneman, 2011). System 1 configures an intuitive mode in which judgments and decisions are made in a fast and automatic fashion, while System 2 constitutes a controlled mode, in which decisions are taken deliberately and slowly. While the intuitive System 1 carries out most operations successfully, it is subject to biases which most of the time are impossible to avoid, even if the more 'controlling' System 2 is activated to perform this task.

There are two main approaches to the assessment of intuition and expertise in psychology: naturalistic decision making (NDM) and heuristics and biases (HB). The first approach hinges on the successes of expert intuition vis-à-vis formalized algorithms. It frames expertise in terms of "history of successful outcomes . . . [rather than of] . . . quantitative performance measures" (Kahneman & Klein, 2009, p. 519). The second approach instead focuses on the biases and shortcomings of judges (some instances of which were illustrated above). Its understanding of expertise is based

Table 5.2 Heuristics and biases in human decision making

Heuristics	Description	Biases
Representativeness	"Probabilities are evaluated by the degree to which A resembles B" – e.g., when A is highly representative of B, the probability that A originates from B is judged to be high" (p. 1124).	• Insensitivity to prior probability of outcomes • Insensitivity to sample size • Misconception of chance • Insensitivity to predictability • The illusion of validity • Misconceptions of regression
Availability	"There are situations in which people assess the frequency of a class or the probability of an event by the ease with which instances or occurrences can be brought to mind" (p. 1127).	• Biases due to the retrievability of instances • Biases due to the effectiveness of a search set • Biases of imaginability • Illusory correlation
Adjustment and Anchoring	"In many situations, people make estimates by starting from an initial value that is adjusted to yield the final answer [. . .] different starting points yield different estimates, which are biased toward the initial values" (p. 1128).	• Insufficient adjustment • Biases in the evaluation of conjunctive and disjunctive events • Anchoring in the assessment of subjective probability distributions

Source: Author's elaboration based on Tversky and Kahneman (1974).

on the comparison between the accuracy of experts' decisions and the performance of "optimal linear combinations" (Kahneman & Klein, 2009, p. 519). The work on expert political judgment by Tetlock (2006) is a prominent example of this approach, but, as already noted by Armstrong (1985), many studies from various disciplines operationalize expertise in various ways including education, experience and reputation, and they show that above a relatively low level of expertise, expertise and accuracy in forecasting are "almost unrelated" (p. 92). Although they differ in many aspects (from the advantage point chosen to the very vocabulary they adopt), the two approaches described converge in at least three respects: first, in pointing out that the validity of experts' judgments can be easily hindered by 'subjective (over)confidence' which is not necessarily substantiated by facts; second, in acknowledging that the reliability of intuitive judgment largely depends on the type of environment in which the judgment itself is made (while clinical sciences can be considered 'high-validity' environments, the political world as already hinted at above is considered to the contrary a 'low-validity' environment); third, in recognizing the potential benefits of mixed or semi-formal strategies in coping with overconfidence and improving the outcome of decision-making processes (Kahneman & Klein, 2009, p. 524). An example of semi-formal strategy is the 'premortem method' (Klein, 2007, p. 18) based on a simple yet effective stratagem – that of structuring the analysis of a certain crisis scenario assuming that it has already taken place and the analysts have to list the reasons why it has happened. One of the main conclusions drawn by Kahneman and Klein (2009) is that neither the HB nor the NDM approach can be claimed to provide 'the' correct reading of intuitive expertise. Thus, a mix of the two, where applicable, might yield better results in the realm of political events forecasting, which is universally acknowledged to have low validity, since, as already stated, the quality of intuitive judgment depends on the level of predictability of the environment in the context of which the judgment is made. After all, whether the output is a score as in the case of the construction of PR indices or a report as in the case of qualitative PR assessment, expert intuition entails the successful identification of cause-effect mechanisms. If this is the case, then there are some intermediate objectives to be reached in the quest for 'good' expert judgment, such as developing a shared language, structuring reasoning clearly and doing so in a transparent fashion so that it will be easier to trace the logic foundations – or lack thereof – of judgments made, consequently allowing them to be subject to scrutiny. In conclusion, what is important to underscore is that as suggested by the latest developments in forecasting based on human judgment (Tetlock & Gardner, 2015), accurate political forecasting and political knowledge could and should be decoupled both in theory and in practice.

5. The quest for accountability in PRA

After acknowledging its cross-cutting role in PRA, two essentially distinct perspectives on expert judgment in PRA have been discussed in this chapter: in a first sense, expertise was equated with subject knowledge, while in a second sense expertise was associated with the capability to provide accurate probability estimations of the possible occurrence of political events. In particular, it has been stressed that (a) both subject matter expertise and 'superforecasting' skills are necessary to yield accurate forecasts and (b) expert (political) judgment cannot be reduced to probability estimation but has a broader role: for forecasts to be made, questions and problems must first be modeled. As a consequence, it should be clear at this point that expert judgment cannot simply be equated with forecasting. Another important issue has periodically emerged above, and, since it is particularly salient to the role of expert judgment in PRA, it should be mentioned at this point: the scarce transparency and accountability in PRA methods, be they indexes such as those analyzed in Chapter 3 or expert assessments – which can include one or more of the techniques analyzed in Chapter 4. It is interesting to notice once again that the recent proliferation of political risk indexes and maps in the practice of PRA is not matched by a serious methodological reflection on the way they are constructed, the causal relationships they posit, and last but not least their predictive power. This is in spite of the fact that increased accountability is essential to overcome the theoretical underdevelopment of political risk lamented by virtually every scholar in the field. After all, one of the reasons why punditry is still 'alive' and marketable today is the ability of putative experts to provide vague analyses whose validity can scarcely be put to the test against actual developments in the sociopolitical world (Silver, 2012; Tetlock & Gardner, 2015). Promoting accountability in PRA however is not an easy task. The PRA industry tends to be secretive as quite understandably most PR consultancies are unwilling to disclose their methodologies for reasons of strategy and competition. As one practitioner (Interview, 2015c) noted, there are no incentives in the industry to promote external accountability, especially by consultancies with an established reputation: it is reasonable to expect that they would not welcome any form of public score-keeping. On the other hand, as another senior practitioner observed, it could be argued that the accountability of major PR consultancies – at least towards their clients – is testified to by their very survival in a competitive market over time in the sense that, if the assessments produced turn out to be inaccurate, the analyst will still be obliged to explain why this was so, even if this happens behind closed doors (Interview, 2015g). In fact, there are consultancies specializing precisely in providing 'second opinions' on political risk issues, which suggests that there is indeed a demand for accountability within the PR industry, although perhaps in a diminished, 'confidential' form (Interview, 2015b).

Notes

1　For a definition of 'availability bias' as illustrated by Tversky and Kahneman (1974), see Table 5.2.
2　The problem of how to interpret the results of the Greek 2015 referendum received extensive media coverage. See for instance "Greece referendum: 'No' to what?" (2015) and Lowen (2015).
3　Tsipras resigned on August 20, 2015, but was subsequently reelected in a snap general election one month later.
4　As Tversky and Kahneman showed in their first work together, systematic errors were present also in causal judgments made by statistically trained researchers.

References

Ambrus, M., Arts, K., Hey, E. & Raulus, H. (Eds.) (2014). *The role of 'experts' in international and European decision-making processes*. Cambridge: Cambridge University Press.

Armstrong, J.S. (1985). *Long range forecasting: From crystal ball to computer*. New York: John Wiley & Sons, Inc.

Armstrong, J.S. & Green, K.C. (2015). Forecasting global climate change. In Moran, A. (Ed.), *Climate change: The facts* (pp. 170–186). Melbourne: Institute of Public Affairs.

Bäckstrand, K. (2003). Civic science for sustainability: Reframing the role of experts, policy-makers and citizens in environmental governance. *Global Environmental Politics*, 3(4), 24–41.

Baker, J., Lovell, K., Harris, N. (2006). How expert are the experts? An exploration of the concept of 'expert' within Delphi panel techniques. *Nurse Research*, 14(1), 59–70.

Bollard, R. (2013, June 26–28). *Who knows? The construction of expertise in assisted reproductive technology policy making*. Paper presented at the International Conference on Policy Making, Grenoble.

Bollen, K.A. (1993). Liberal democracy: Validity and method factors in cross-national measures. *American Journal of Political Science*, 37(4), 1207–1230.

Bollen, K.A. & Grandjean, B. (1981). The dimension(s) of democracy: Further issues in the measurement and effects of political democracy. *American Sociological Review*, 46(5), 651–659.

Bollen, K.A. & Paxton, P. (2000). Subjective measures of liberal democracy. *Comparative Political Studies*, 33(1), 58–86.

Bouchet, M.H., Clark, E. & Groslambert, B. (2003). *Country risk assessment: A guide to global investment strategy*. London: John Wiley & Sons Ltd.

Bremmer, I. (2005, June). Managing risk in an unstable world. *Harvard Business Review*. Available at https://hbr.org/2005/06/managing-risk-in-an-unstable-world [Accessed on 10 April 2016].

Bueno de Mesquita, B. & Stockman, F.N. (Eds.) (1994). *European community decision making: Models, applications and comparison*. New Haven, CT: Yale University Press.

Bunn, D. & Wright, G. (1991). Interaction of judgmental and statistical forecasting methods: Issues and analysis. *Management Science*, 37, 501–518.

Camerer, C.F. & Johnson, E.J. (1991). The process-performance paradox in expert judgment – How can experts know so much and predict so badly? In Ericsson, K.A. & Smith, J. (Eds.), *Toward a general theory of expertise: Prospects and limits* (pp. 195–217). Cambridge: Cambridge University Press.

Dalkey, N.C. & Helmer, O. (1963). An experimental application of the Delphi method to the user of experts. *Management science*, 9(3), 458–467.

Gallo, C. (2013, September 13). *Expert judgement in the assessment of political risk*. Paper presented at the Italian Association of Political Science Annual Conference, Florence.

Gill, J. (2006). *Essential mathematics for political and social research*. Cambridge: Cambridge University Press.

Goodman, C. (1987). The Delphi technique: A critique. *Journal of Advanced Nursing*, 12, 729–734.

Greece referendum: 'No' to what? (2015, July 5). *The Economist*. Available at http://www.economist.com/news/europe/21657003-greek-voters-have-rejected-austerity-eu-may-think-they-have-rejected-europe-no-what [Accessed on 10 April 2016].

Heisenberg, W. (1971). *Physics and beyond: Encounters and conversations*. London: HarperCollins Publishers Ltd.

Howell, L.D. (1986). Area specialists and expert data: The human factor in political risk analysis. In Rogers, J. (Ed.), *Global Risk Assessments: Issues, Concepts & Applications, Book 2*, pp. 47–84. Riverside, CA: Global Risk Assessments, Inc.

Interview (2015b, August 6). Semi-structured face-to-face interview with managing director of political risk analysis consultancy firm.

Interview (2015c, October 1). Semi-structured face-to-face interview with CEO of political risk consultancy firm.

Interview (2015g, December 1). Semi-structured telephone interview with regional head at global risk forecasting company.

Interview (2015i, December 23). Semi-structured written interview with senior analyst at international risk and due diligence consulting firm.

IPCC (2014). *Climate change 2014: Synthesis report. Contribution of working groups I, II and III to the fifth assessment report of the intergovernmental panel on climate change.* Geneva: IPCC.

Junge, D. & König, T. (2007). What's wrong with EU spatial analysis? The accuracy and robustness of empirical applications to the interpretation of the legislative process and the specification of preferences. *Journal of Theoretical Politics*, 19(4), 465–487.

Kahneman, D. (2011). *Thinking, fast and slow*. New York: Farrar, Straus and Giroux.

Kahneman, D. & Klein, G. (2009). Conditions for intuitive expertise: A failure to disagree. *American Psychologist*, 64(6), 515–526.

Kahneman, D. & Tversky, A. (1972). Subjective probability: A judgment of representativeness. *Cognitive Psychology*, 3, 430–454.

Klein, G. (2007, September). Performing a project premortem. *Harvard Business Review*. Available at https://hbr.org/2007/09/performing-a-project-premortem [Accessed on 10 April 2016].

Lax, H.L. (1983). *Political risk in the international oil and gas industry*. Boston: IHRDC.

Lowen, M. (2015, July 11). Greek debt crisis: What was the point of the referendum? *BBC News*. Available at http://www.bbc.com/news/world-europe-33492387 [Accessed on 10 April 2016].

Mitroff, I.I. & Turoff, M. (1975). Philosophical and methodological foundations of Delphi. In Linstone, H.A. & Turoff, M. (Eds.), *The Delphi method: Techniques and applications* (pp. 559–571). Boston: Addison-Wesley Publishing.

Munck, G. (2009). *Measuring democracy: A bridge between scholarship and politics*. Baltimore: Johns Hopkins University Press.

Nowotny, H. (1980). The role of the experts in developing public policy: The Austrian debate on nuclear power. *Science, Technology, & Human Values*, 5(32), 10–18.

Raiffa, H. (1968). *Decision analysis*. Reading, MA: Addison-Wesley.

Redmill, F. (2002). Risk analysis: A subjective process. *Engineering Management Journal*, 12(2), 91–96.

Schrodt, P.A. & Van Brackle, D. (2013). Automated coding of political event data. In Subrahmanian, V.S. (Ed.), *Handbook of computational approaches to counterterrorism* (pp. 23–49). New York: Springer.

Silver, N. (2012). *The signal and the noise: Why so many predictions fail while other don't*. New York: The Penguin Press.

Simmonds, W.H.C. (1977). The nature of futures problems. In Linstone, H.A. & Simmonds, W.H.C. (Eds.), *Futures research: New directions* (pp. 13–26). London: Addison Wesley.

Solberg, R.L. (1992). *Country risk analysis: A handbook*. London: Routledge.

Tetlock, P.E. (1992). Good judgment in international politics: Three psychological perspectives. *Political Psychology*, 13(3), 517–539.

Tetlock, P.E. (2006). *Expert political judgment: How good is it? How can we know?* Princeton: Princeton University Press.

Tetlock, P. & Gardner, D. (2015). *Superforecasting: The art and science of prediction*. New York: Random House.

Thomson, R., Arregui, J., Leuffen, D., Costello, R., Cross, J., Hertz, R. & Jensen, T. (2012). A new dataset on decision-making in the European Union before and after the 2004 and 2007 enlargements (DEUII). *Journal of European Public Policy*, 19(4), 604–622.

Tickner, J.A. & Wright, S. (2003). The precautionary principle and democratizing expertise: A US perspective. *Science and Public Policy*, 30(3), 213–218.

Tversky, A. & Kahneman, D. (1974). Judgment under uncertainty: Heuristics and biases. *Science*, 185(4157), 1124–1131.

Van der Heijden, K. (2005). *Scenarios: The art of strategic conversation*. Chichester: John Wiley & Sons, Ltd.

Wright, G., Bradfield, R., & Cairns, G. (2013). Does the intuitive logics method – and its recent enhancements – produce "effective" scenarios? *Technological Forecasting and Social Change*, 80(4), 631–642.

6 The impact of the digital revolution on political risk analysis and assessment

The Internet is the first thing that humanity has built that humanity doesn't understand, the largest experiment in anarchy we've ever had.

(E. Schmidt, quoted by Taylor, 2010)

1. ICTs and political risk

Technological change, particularly as far as progress in hardware, software and communication networks is concerned, has had an obvious bearing on virtually every aspect of any FDI endeavor of the last few decades. Considering their increasing ubiquity and influence, it is safe to say that digital technologies are indeed major driving forces in today's globalized economy, shaping industrial relations through their obvious impact on productivity and employment (Brynjolfsson & McAfee, 2011) and, more generally, exerting a significant influence on the ways in which states design and implement economic policies (Papacostantinou, 2003). The roots of the digital revolution – that is, the shift from analog to digital technologies which paved the way for the creation of the World Wide Web – can be traced back to the ARPANET project developed in the 1960s by the US Advanced Research Projects Agency (ARPA), DARPA's progenitor. The digital revolution has completely changed the way business is done, but has also generated a plethora of unprecedented risks. Thus, while benefiting from unparalleled business opportunities created by the digital revolution, in recent times MNEs worldwide have also become progressively more aware of the numerous hazards connected to reliance on new information and communication technologies (ICTs). In the era of 'big data', information has become both a tradable commodity and a strategic asset for companies, raising concerns about the protection of intangibles such as personal and financial information, intellectual property, and reputation. Buzzwords such as 'cybersecurity', 'cyber risks' or 'cybercrime' have quickly become part of today's business jargon and practice. In addition to the 'classic' political and business risks, a vast array of seemingly new threats have materialized as a by-product of the hyper-connectivity characterizing today's global markets. Considering that the analysis and assessment of political risk is based on the collection, processing and evaluation of information, the digital revolution which has paved the way for the start of the 'information age' has obviously had a pervasive, cross-cutting impact on the way PRA is conducted. For one thing, virtually all the forecasting techniques discussed in Chapter 4 have evolved and are still evolving by riding the wave of technological innovation: the increased processing power of computing machines along with the proliferation of software for statistical elaboration and increased data exchange due to ubiquitous availability of network connections has notably furthered the possibilities of quantitative PR modeling, including complex simulations; opinion markets and polls heavily rely on the web, as – obviously – do the websites aggregating opinion markets and poll data to forecast electoral outcomes.

The advent of the digital revolution has also dramatically changed the way in which the most traditional form of PRA – that is, the elicitation of expert opinion – takes place. Researchers from RAND Corporation for instance recently developed ExpertLens, an online system – grounded in the literature on Delphi and NGT techniques – that gathers and analyzes expert opinion (Dalal et al., 2011) – the innovative aspect of such system being that it reduces the costs traditionally associated with the use of expert panels by exploiting through its functionalities the wisdom of a 'selected crowd' made of non-collocated experts. To provide another example, the GJP described in Chapter 4 was also based on a web platform designed to produce crowd-sourced forecasts: by relying on such a platform, the project was able to show how talented individuals without specialized subject-matter knowledge could provide calibrated and accurate probability estimations about political events by drawing information from the web, while 'superforecaster' teams were formed and worked together online without meeting in person. In summary, it is safe to say that the digital revolution had a twofold effect on political risks, in the sense that it had an impact both from the substantial and from the methodological standpoint: on the one hand, as further illustrated in Section 2, it created new risks and magnified some that already existed; on the other hand, as shown in Section 3, with the emergence of 'big data' analysis and new techniques connected to the diffusion of social networks, such as sentiment analysis, the digital revolution also enriched the PR analyst's toolkit with new instruments and solutions for the identification and assessment of sociopolitical hazards.

2. The digital revolution as a source of new (political) threats

The digitalization of the world economy is much more than the mere flourishing of e-business and e-commerce. As Zekos (2005) put it, "The digital economy has brought about tools for thought, tools that transform every sector of the economy and there is a shift in the very terms and dynamics of market competition" (p. 62). In spite of warnings of a persistent digital divide both within and across countries worldwide (WEF, 2015), the number of individuals connected to the Internet has been growing steadily in the last few years (see Figure 6.1), passing from 8 percent of the world population in 2001 to an estimated 43.4 percent in 2015. In sum, the number of 'connected' individuals joining up in cyberspace grows day by day.

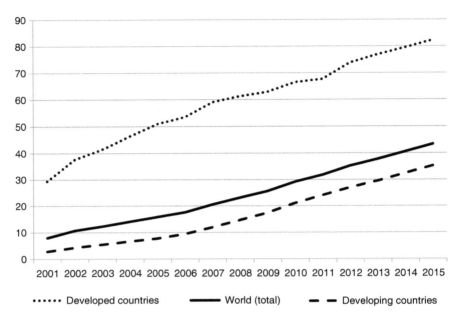

Figure 6.1 Individuals using the Internet per 100 inhabitants (2001–15)

Source: ITU (2015).

Note: Data referring to year 2015 is an estimate.

The challenges faced by policy-makers in governing the political economy of this global, multilevel interconnectivity range from how to overcome the digital divide to how to regulate the new media, from fostering innovation to guaranteeing data privacy and safety (Vogelsang, 2010). The capillary penetration of information technologies has conveyed a competitive advantage to the businesses which have managed to seize the new opportunities on offer; however, at the same time it has also become a source of unprecedented vulnerability. 'Cybersecurity' – which can be broadly defined as "the organization and collection of resources, processes, and structures used to protect cyberspace and cyberspace-enabled systems from occurrences that misalign *de jure* from *de facto* property rights" (Craigen et al., 2014, p. 17) – has turned into a top concern for business executives regardless of the industry in which they operate. IT services giant IBM[1] reported an average number of over 12,000 cyberattacks against its clients in 2014, targeting in particular – but not exclusively – companies from industries as diverse as finance and insurance, information and communication, and manufacturing (IBM, 2015).

In identifying the possible sources of risks that may threaten the cybersecurity of an investment, Touhill and Touhill (2014, p. 12) point to five categories thereof: (1) nation-states; (2) organized crime and hackers; (3) hacktivists; (4) insider threats; and (5) substandard products and services. Out of these five categories of cyber risks, two can immediately be identified as overlapping (at least partially) with traditional sources of *political* risk: governmental actors – that is, entire nation-states – and nongovernmental actors, the so-called 'hacktivists'. Another prominent source of 'cyber political threats' can be added to this list – cyberterrorism.

2.1 Governmental actors and 'patriotic hackers'

As far as governmental actors are concerned, it should be noted that in the information age they can be both victims and instigators of politically motivated cyberattacks. In recent years, countries such as Iran, Israel, North and South Korea, Russia and Turkey have been investing heavily in developing cyberwarfare capabilities and have been involved to various degrees in political hacking (Applegate, 2011) – although the same can also be said for the US. China has attracted the attention of analysts and policy makers for its focus on the theory and practice of cyberwarfare as an ancillary tactic to underpin national security. In a popular work on military strategy, senior colonels Liang Qiao and Wang Xiang-sui point to the reliance of the US military on ITCs as a potential soft spot that could be exploited by weaker countries adopting asymmetrical combat methods (Qiao & Wang, 1999). Instances of cyberattacks as acts of retaliation in situations of political friction include the distributed denial of service (DDoS) attacks against US government websites launched in May 1999 after US bombs hit the Chinese embassy in Belgrade during the NATO bombing of Yugoslavia,[2] and in 2001 after the collision between a US EP-3 spy plane with a Chinese naval F-8 fighter (Lindsay, 2015, p. 18). Large-scale, international incidents in the last few years include the case of Estonia, which in 2007 experienced a massive wave of cyberattacks linked to tensions between Estonia and Russia following the removal of a Soviet-era memorial from downtown Tallin; the 2012 attack against the Saudi state-owned oil company Saudi Aramco, subsequently vindicated by a group of hackers blaming Saudi Arabia for misdeeds on Syrian and Bahraini soil; the 2012 attack – believed to have originated from Iran – against six leading banks in the US; the 2013 attack against three leading banks and three national TV stations in South Korea, for which nobody claimed responsibility, although it was thought to have originated from North Korea; and the 2014 attack against Sony Pictures Entertainment, attributed by the US government to North Korea, just as Sony was about to release a movie portraying the assassination of North Korea's 'dear leader' Kim Jong-Un (van der Meer, 2015).

Although it may be reasonable to assume governmental support – owing to the fact that considerable resources are needed to carry out a successful large-scale attack – proving the direct involvement of national governments in cyberattacks such as those described above is not easy, especially in light of the proliferation of groups describing themselves as 'patriotic hackers': hackers aiming to defend national pride by launching attacks or reprisals against targets which are usually depicted as foes of their country of origin, at times presenting themselves as a 'cyber militia' replacing state forces when the government cannot or does not want to act (Dahan, 2013, p. 51).

2.2 Hacktivists

Compared to patriotic hackers, hacktivists typically pursue a broader political agenda. Hacktivism can be described as a new form of political activism which does not resort to physical violence but rather blends grassroots sociopolitical movements and computer hacking (Jordan & Taylor, 2004, p. 1). The concept of hacktivism is epitomized by Anonymous, the well-known global collective of hacktivists whose origins can be traced back to online communities that emerged in the mid-2000s and that initially was mostly focused on 'trolling' – "an activity that seeks to ruin the reputations of individuals and organizations and reveal embarrassing and personal information" (Coleman, 2014, p. 4) – but also committed to free speech and to the freedom of the web in particular. In 2008, Anonymous took a political turn marked by a wave of 'cyber guerrilla' warfare against the Church of Scientology, which it accused of violating human rights and suppressing free speech through lawsuits and the use of copyright and trademark laws (Barkham, 2008). The anti-Scientology campaign was based on a number of tactics including DDoS attacks, leaks of sensitive information such as email addresses and passwords, but also 'real' street protests. With language imbued with dark humor and its use of highly recognizable symbols such as the Guy Fawkes mask inspired by the comic strip *V for Vendetta*[3] – an emblem of faceless rebellion and insurgency – Anonymous has carried out spectacular operations over the last few years. Actions undertaken range from the so-called 'Operation Payback' – coordinated attacks conducted against anti-piracy companies – to exposing widespread abuses and suppression of citizens' freedoms by the Tunisian government in early 2011 and generally supporting the cause of democracy in the Middle East and Africa through cyberattacks against the governments of Libya, Egypt, Zimbabwe, Jordan and Bahrain (Olson, 2012). Anonymous is also famous for conducting retaliatory attacks on PayPal, MasterCard and Visa after they blocked transfers to WikiLeaks in 2010 in the wake of the major whistleblowing scandal that the organization founded by Australian hacktivist Julian Assange had recently triggered. The WikiLeaks 'cablegate' scandal materialized when the website published hundreds of thousands of classified diplomatic cables and other compromising documents, including video footage showing abuses by the US military overseas and files relating to Guantanamo Bay detainees, leaked by US soldier Bradley Manning. As a matter of fact, the cablegate not only proved a short-term sensation but also produced a number of longer-term consequences on multiple levels, for governments, businesses and society as a whole; it raised questions about the relationship between secrecy and democracy,[4] as well as about the future of freedom of expression on the Internet: according to some, in the wake of the WikiLeaks scandals the very business models developed by social media companies may end up undermining such freedom, as they are aimed at increased concentration and as such are becoming easier to regulate and control (Winseck, 2013). Obviously, WikiLeaks also contributed to further drawing the attention of the business world towards the disruptive effects of poor cybersecurity management. In this respect, it is worth noting that somehow the PRA industry also ended up in the eye of the 'hacktivism hurricane' when the computer systems of consultancy Stratfor were hacked by Anonymous in December 2011 (Palmer, 2012), with WikiLeaks subsequently releasing over five million emails under the banner of 'global intelligence files' (WikiLeaks, 2012).

2.3 Cyberterrorism

Cyberterrorism is another buzzword provoking widespread concern among business executives today. As is the case with the concept of terrorism proper, the notion of cyberterrorism is a highly contested one. There are a number of different interpretations of cyberterrorism, ranging from narrower definitions referring to activities that pertain to the digital domain only – that is, digital attacks on digital targets – to broader definitions also including 'mixed' activities taking place when 'traditional' terrorist groups resort to digital means for propaganda or fundraising (Jarvis et al., 2014). According to some, even the Anonymous coordinated attacks against MasterCard, PayPal and Visa mentioned above may qualify as acts of terrorism, the syllogism behind the attribution of this 'label' being that DDoS attacks are considered crimes, while terrorism can be defined as crime perpetrated to achieve an ideological end; thus, DDoS attacks carried out for ideological reasons could be considered acts of cyberterrorism (Brenner, 2012, p. 210). Yet, this is highly controversial, considering that the traditional tactics of hacktivists undoubtedly encompass harassing and mocking their targets as a means of voicing political protest, but they definitely do not include killing anyone, as stressed by anthropologist Coleman when she was questioned about the possibility of Anonymous attacks on power grids (Coleman, 2014, p. 14). In this sense, it should be noticed that in spite of the remarkable amount of attention that this concept has received in recent time, if we stick to a narrow notion of cyberterrorism, the number of people physically harmed by means of cyberterrorist acts is actually 'zero' (Singer & Friedman, 2014, p. 96). This is not a call to play down the vulnerabilities of critical infrastructures – such as dams, pipelines, communications, power grids and also military systems or nuclear power plants – whose management today inevitably entails reliance on complex IT systems; the point is to simply acknowledge that for the time being 'traditional' terrorist attacks are still cheaper, easier to conduct and more disruptive than cyberterrorist acts in terms of a hypothetical cost-benefits ratio. Thus, although undeniably emotionally charged due to the widespread sense of vulnerability engendered by the current prevalence of both cyberattacks and acts of terrorism, until now the idea of cyberterrorists wreaking havoc on a whole nation by unleashing 'digital Armageddon' has generally been considered too far-fetched to represent an actual, imminent threat, also because, as some noted, the capabilities of nations in terms of restoring systems are improving thanks to advances in disaster management by the authorities (Weimann, 2004). Another argument usually put forward to scale down the likelihood of cyberterrorist attacks is that – while they have certainly used the web to plan and coordinate physical attacks – so far terrorist organizations such as al-Qaeda or ISIS have never staged large-scale acts of cyberterrorism, for the simple reason that doing so requires extremely advanced skills and a large amount of resources. It is not by chance that Stuxnet – to date the only malware which went close to constituting an actual 'digital weapon', used to sabotage the centrifuges of the Natanz nuclear plant in Iran in 2009 – was reportedly developed thanks to the joint efforts of two governmental agencies – that is, the United States' NSA and Israel's Unit 8200 (Broad et al., 2011). As Sanger (2012) puts it, thanks to this unparalleled cyberweapon, the US has apparently "[achieved] with computer code, what until then could be accomplished only by bombing a country or sending in agents to plant explosives". This of course represents an important precedent: even if we concede that the likelihood of full-fledged, physically disruptive cyberterrorist attacks carried out by non-state entities is currently low, we cannot however rule out the possibility that, as suggested by Zetter (2014), the development of Stuxnet has ushered in a new era of cyberwarfare in which digital weapons will be able to produce tangible damage on an unprecedented scale. One of the possible consequences of this is a generalized 'digital' arms race.[5]

The implications of what has been said so far in terms of PRA are manifold. The bottom line however is that, as further illustrated below, damages to a given company can either derive from direct aggressions or spring from other sources such as interstate tensions resulting in the use of cyberwarfare. In any case, considerable losses loom over businesses. The above-mentioned attack on Saudi oil company Aramco damaged 30,000 computers and was thought to be aimed against productive processes, not just IT systems (Reuters, 2012); similarly, the 2012 offensive against American financial institutions reportedly cost millions of dollars, as did the 2013 attacks on South Korean banks and television networks which wrecked 32,000 computers (Perlroth & Sanger, 2013). In sum, whether they are directly targeted or they end up being 'collateral' victims of attacks directed against other corporate or governmental actors, there is no doubt that MNEs today are exposed to cyber risks on multiple fronts. It is equally indisputable that this exposure can be partly explained by the fact that today – when it comes to regulating and governing the uses and abuses of cyberspace – there is an evident gap between what is *known* by the 'IT crowd' and what is genuinely *understood* by managers and policy-makers alike (Singer & Friedman, 2014).

The key aspect that should be highlighted here however is the pervasive and continuous interaction between cyber and political risks. The intimate relationship between these two apparently heterogeneous categories of risks is often overlooked if not completely misunderstood by consumers of PRA. As a PR practitioner noticed, investors today are increasingly anxious about cybercrime and cyber risks in general, as opposed to political risks (Interview, 2015d); in a sense, it can be said that due to their elusive, ubiquitous nature, cyber risks are perceived as a distinctive, separate category vis-à-vis geopolitical risks. Yet, such a vision is shortsighted because it fails to recognize that cyberspace is in fact a new political arena which can also serve as a catalyst for new, 'hybrid' forms of political risk. It is beyond doubt that cybercrime in all its forms – including fraud and data theft – constitutes a genuinely new threat; yet bundling together all risks connected to cyberspace under the label of 'cyber risks' while overlooking their actual source (which may happen to be purely political) may result in confusion between actual causes and instrumental tactics. For instance, in the case of the 2007 DDoS attacks against Estonia discussed above, the battlefield was evidently in cyberspace; however, if we look at its root causes, the dispute triggering the episode was quintessentially political, regarding – as already stressed – problems in the past and present relationship between Estonia and Russia. Equally, the above-mentioned cyberattacks against Aramco or those against Bank of America, JPMorgan Chase, Citigroup, U.S. Bank, Wells Fargo and PNC – which also imposed losses on the targeted organizations in reputational terms – at a superficial glance may be dismissed as cyber incidents; yet doing so would be misleading because their implications are indeed far-reaching beyond the technical shortcomings they exposed: even if – as happens with 'mere' cyberattacks qualifying as common crime – the aggressors certainly took advantage of the digital vulnerabilities of their targets, they were in fact launching *politically* motivated attacks. Thus, it can be argued that not only technical but also political challenges have definitely arisen in the last few years as a result of the digital revolution: while cyberspace certainly represents a new frontier for investors, it constitutes at the same time a new arena for organized crime and geopolitical conflict.

A recent example of the interaction of cyber and political risks – whose consequences are still unfolding as this book goes to press – is the so-called 'Panama Papers' data leak[6] – that is, the acquisition by German newspaper *Süddeutsche Zeitung* of encrypted internal documents from Panamanian law firm Mossack Fonseca, specialized in selling anonymous offshore companies that allow owners to cover up their business operations, in many cases to the purpose of evading taxes (Obermaier et al., 2016). In cooperation with the International Consortium of Investigative Journalists (ICIJ), the *Süddeutsche Zeitung* researched, organized and eventually released documents which cover a time span from the 1970s to the spring of 2016. The political impact of the leak is potentially formidable, considering that, among others, a number of top politicians and high-ranking officials from all over the world appear to be involved in the scandal, including French politician Marine Le Pen, Chinese President Xi's brother-in-law along with eight Politburo members past and present, Saudi Arabia's King Salman, Pakistani Prime Minister Nawaz Sharif, Ukrainian President Poroshenko, Argentinian President Macri and, last but not least, Icelandic Prime Minister Arnar Gunnlaugsson, who announced his intention to step down among massive street protests in the immediate aftermath of the Panama Papers disclosure (Bremmer, 2016b). It should be noticed that leaks such as the Panama Papers can have a media and political fallout even when there is no proof of actual rule-breaking, as shown by the protests targeting British Prime Minister David Cameron, whose father's name was included in the list of Mossack Fonseca's clients (The Economist, 2016).

In some respects, the digital revolution has empowered states, providing governments with new tools to meet their security needs. As Deibert (2015) effectively stated, "The aims of the Internet economy and those of state security converge around the same functional needs: collecting, monitoring, and analyzing as much data as possible" (p. 9). Yet, at the same time, reliance on technology is a double-edged sword that can also weaken governments – especially those characterized by limited legitimacy and responsiveness vis-à-vis their citizens – by fostering social instability (Bremmer, 2016a). The diffusion of social media certainly played an important role as the Arab uprisings began to mount in December 2010, with Internet connectivity catalyzing social mobilization in Tunisia, Egypt and Libya, and also triggering cyber responses by governments struggling to remain in power, as happened when Mubarak's regime shut off the Internet in an attempt to suppress the direct release of information about the protests taking place in Egypt (Scott-Railton, 2013). In this vein, it should be added that the game-changing effects of the digital revolution are not limited to autocratic regimes: suffice it to mention the case of the Italian web-based 'Five Star Movement', which was founded in 2009 by a comedian and in less than four years managed to abruptly reshape the Italian political landscape at the 2013 general elections by turning into the second-largest party in the country (Natale & Ballatore, 2014).

3. PRA in the age of 'big data'

As anticipated in Section 1, 'big data' is another recurrent buzzword in today's business world as well as in many other domains. But what is it exactly, and how is it relevant to PRA? Put simply, big data can be described as the ever-increasing amount of information that individuals more or less voluntarily and with varying degrees of awareness share every day with third parties – usually privately held companies – through web-browsing and the use of social media, mobile connectivity and cloud – that is, Internet-based – computing (Deibert, 2015). The information thus gathered also includes 'metadata' – that is, data about the data: examples of metadata include the personal details of a smartphone user as well as her geospatial coordinates and other information items which are usually embedded in, say, text messages or social media posts and inevitably end up being "stored on a server somewhere, or in multiple places – on 'clouds' of computers – spread out across the physical infrastructure of cyberspace" (Deibert, 2013, p. 60). An increasingly relevant source of big data accumulation is the so-called 'Internet of Things' (IoT): not just the number of people, but also the number of devices which are connected to the Internet is constantly increasing. Connectable 'things' encompass not only objects such as smartphones, e-book readers and digital TV sets but also millions of other devices, from cars to coffeemakers, that can send information and meta-information gathered from sensors to servers which are able to process information.[7]

The IoT is in fact auguring a new wave of technological change whose disruptive and transformative effects on the global economy – and ultimately also on everyday life – are potentially huge (Höller et al., 2015), at least if the current trend continues: according to an IT analysis firm over twenty billion connected things will be in use by 2020 (Gartner, 2015), while the Mckinsey Global Institute (2015) estimated that the IoT could have an economic impact of up to $11.1 trillion a year by 2025 (Mckinsey & Company, 2015). The insurance industry was obviously one of the first movers towards an intensive use of big data analytics, considering that the diffusion of the IoT has huge potential to improve the significance of risk assessments thanks to the possibility to collect real-time data (Reiss, 2016). Advancements in data-gathering are of course matched by the constant development of new data-mining computing frameworks that go beyond conventional statistical data analysis (Japkowicz & Stefanowski, 2015): after all, the proliferation of big data would be meaningless in itself without the parallel evolution of the algorithmic calculative devices needed to make data tractable, which is an indispensable passage on the way to transforming information into actionable intelligence (Amoore & Piotukh, 2016). As the world enters this new stage of the digital revolution, however, the implications of this booming hyper-connectivity begin to unfold, raising a number of crucial issues of enormous practical, ethical and political import. As noticed by Howard (2015), while adopting an optimistic outlook the roll-out of the IoT may constitute a tool for active civic participation and political engagement ushering in a truly open society, in the worst-case scenario it may instead turn into the most effective system of mass surveillance ever built. The booming 'commodification' of data (Werbin, 2012) and of privacy (Sevignani, 2013) are further relevant trends, also intertwining with the privatization of security and surveillance, a process whereby the control of critical technologies such as satellite surveillance systems is shifting into the hands of private actors (Interview, 2015h). As a result, governments increasingly resort to private contractors to outsource activities and functions that traditionally fell within their direct control. The problematic triangulation between governments, private actors and the control of key technologies clearly emerged in the context of a recent controversy involving hi-tech giant Apple and the US government. The FBI sought the collaboration of Apple to access the encrypted iPhone of one of the perpetrators of the San Bernardino mass shooting, carried out in December 2015 by a married couple of Islamic extremists. Apple's refusal to create – as the FBI requested – a 'backdoor' to unlock the iPhone, made public via an open letter written by Apple CEO Tim Cook (2016), spurred a heated debate over privacy and security in the digital age. This was further ignited by the subsequent introduction of end-to-end encryption – meant to protect the privacy of users from any intrusion – by WhatsApp, an online messaging service owned by Facebook and currently used by over a billion people worldwide (Metz, 2016). Another recent, controversial episode raising concerns over the relationship between democracy and the use of technology for surveillance regards Italian hackers-for-hire company Hacking Team, which in 2015 was subject to a cyberattack resulting in the leak of 400 gigabytes of internal data, including customer invoices, emails and even source code (Greenberg, 2015). The leaked data proved that Hacking Team had been ruthlessly selling spyware to governments, including those of authoritarian regimes such as the United Arab Emirates and Sudan, currently one of the most strictly embargoed countries in the world.

Against this fluid backdrop of growing complexity and clashing values, where the sociopolitical reality is to an increasing extent shaped by the virtually endless applications of ICTs, a vast array of new tools for PRA is emerging. The common thread is the use of data science to devise early warning methods for disruptive events relying on open-source intelligence extracted from the Internet. An expanding niche of consulting firms within the PRA industry has started to deploy big data analytics as a tool to ensure real-time detection of critical events, including strikes, protests, terroristic attacks or air strikes in war zones. Recorded Future, a pioneer in this field, relies on a patented web intelligence engine that is able to scan hundreds of thousands of open content media sources to collect data – including data drawn from the 'deep' and 'dark' web[8] – which resorting to computing techniques such as natural language processing[9] can be used to turn 'unstructured' data into structured forecasts and risk assessments. An example of how such data can be used is the Ethnographic Edge crisis forecast project, which relies on sentiment data produced by Recorded Future to analyze the positive or negative sentiment expressed in media sources about specific issues and provide forecasts and risk assessments for organizations operating in the framework of international crises in Asia and the Middle East (Chemier & Milosevic, 2013). Along the same line, Kallus (2014) employs data from Recorded Future to show how web intelligence can be effectively used to study and anticipate 'real' socio-political events, focusing in particular on two categories of event: mass unrest in a specific location and politically motivated cyberattacks perpetrated by/against specific actors. Looking at the case of the 2013 coup which lead to the ousting of President Morsi in Egypt, the author finds that it is possible to produce fine-grained forecasts about when and where mass protest is likely to occur by monitoring sentiment trends on Twitter. A recent report released by the Big Data Lab of the research department of Chinese search engine Baidu describes a new approach to anticipate the occurrence of potential crowd events with one to three hours of notice by leveraging on big data generated by users of the Baidu mobile map app, the most popular mobile map app in China (Zhou et al., 2016). While the report stresses the beneficial impact of such an early warning system in avoiding calamitous events such as the Shanghai 2014 New Year's Eve stampede during which thirty-six people died and forty-nine were injured (Jiang, 2015), the ambiguity of this type of technology as a tool for mass surveillance is manifest. It should be added that in order to provide accurate estimates of the number of people in restricted areas it is not necessary to rely on data provided by mobile phone apps, as the availability of meta data about the volume of texts and voice calls supplied by mobile phone services providers is in itself a valid proxy (Botta et al., 2015).

In recent years, a growing number of companies have started to invest in the development of proprietary event-detection engines to capitalize on the potential of Twitter and other social media as a source of data and meta data, such as US company Dataminr, which can process 500 million tweets a day in order to spot 'black swan' events before the markets react (Wieczner, 2015), or Ban.jo, whose event-detection engine performs linguistic and topic analysis and geospatial analysis, as well as the classification of images and videos, based on the mapping and monitoring of the whole globe surface with a grid of 35 billion squares of the approximate size of a football field (MacMillan, 2015). Cytora, another company using data science to provide analysis merging geopolitical and web intelligence, used open source data to fill an information gap regarding the tactics of terrorist group Boko Haram operating in Nigeria (Wallace, 2014), relying on data from the Armed Conflict Location & Event Dataset (ACLED), an open source collection of data on political violence and protest in the developing world whose event-focused approach is similar to that of the GDELT and ICEWS databases described in Chapter 4 (Raleigh et al., 2010).

In sum, the advent of the age of big data has afforded PRA with a number of new sources of data and of techniques for data-crunching. What is important to stress, however, is a relevant constraint on the applicability of the early warning and monitoring techniques discussed in this chapter, specifically, their short-term temporal scope: while they can relay immediate updates when conditions in the target area change, their current applicability to long-term projections is much more limited.

4. Understanding the interaction between cyber and political risks

Evidently, the digital revolution and its ramifications are having an extraordinary sociopolitical impact on a global level. The ubiquity and accessibility of ICTs – which are both a byproduct and a catalyst of such a revolution – have dramatically changed the technical tools and conceptual categories available for the analysis of sociopolitical realities. Today, cyber risks understandably sit at the top of the security agenda of international investors across industries, from the banking sector to telecommunications, from the extraction of natural resources to tourism and entertainment. However, it is crucial to understand that cyber risks do not stand alone as an isolated category of hazards, but on the contrary they should be analyzed through the holistic prism of their dynamic interaction with political risks. Politically motivated cyberattacks by patriotic hackers or hacktivists, far-reaching scandals and political storms triggered by leaks of confidential documents, and dystopian scenarios of large-scale disruption caused by cyberwar or cyberterrorism which until a few decades ago all seemed impossibly futuristic have now come to the fore as key sources of concern for MNEs of all sizes. While transforming the nature of the challenges ahead, fast-paced technological change has at the same time enriched the toolkit of the political risk analyst with new instruments, including high-resolution event data sets and sophisticated real-time early warning systems which are often developed and maintained by private actors.

The ambiguities intrinsic to the functioning of the booming surveillance industry are fostering a heated debate about the relationship between users, producers and targets of surveillance systems, primarily hinging on the problematic trade-off between privacy and security. Also in light of these complex dilemmas, the advent of the digital age has forced MNEs to confront further challenges posed by the constant overflow of information and by the need to find effective ways to navigate it, especially when it comes to risks which content-wise are not closely related to their business activity but rather pertain to the political and geopolitical sphere. In the end, the role of the analyst and in a broader sense of 'expert judgment' as discussed in Chapter 5 above maintains its centrality (Interview, 2015e). As one senior analyst put it,

> in recent years the surge in availability of social media has provided another stream of information for companies such as ourselves. For specialists like ourselves this is an advantage and a good thing but our challenge and the business model upon which we are based is to make sense of that information and to provide the client with a structured view of all the sources that are now available.
>
> (Interview, 2015l)

Notes

1 By Information Technologies or IT, here it is meant the whole industry related to networks, hardware, software and any other 'equipment' (including software) necessary to manage information.
2 In the case of the 1999 NATO operations in Serbia, it should be noted that the US had been targeted by pro-Serbian hackers even before the Chinese Embassy bombing (Messmer, 1999).
3 The mask was inspired by David Lloyds illustrations for Alan Moore's original graphic novel *V for Vendetta*, which was made into a film in 2006 ("The Economist explains", 2014).
4 In 2013, such debate was further ignited by another major whistleblowing scandal set in motion by former CIA employee Edward Snowden, who leaked documents relating to the operations of mass surveillance put in place in previous years by the NSA.
5 References to a 'new digital arms race' abound in the media. See for instance Brewster, 2014; Appelbaum et al., 2015; Paletta et al., 2015.
6 The Panama Papers apparently constitute the biggest data leak to date, with 2.6 terabytes of leaked documents vis-à-vis the 1.7 gigabytes leaked at the time of the cited WikiLeaks cablegate,
7 The 'IoT revolution' became possible thanks to the fact that sensors which act as data collectors have become extremely cheap.
8 As opposed to the 'surface web' whose contents are available to anyone through ordinary search engines, the 'deep web' – which accounts for about 90 percent of total Internet content – refers to the corpus of all websites which cannot be reached via search engines (Greenberg, 2014). The 'dark web' refers to the portion of the deep web which, thanks to anonymity guaranteed (among other things) by IP-concealing software Tor, is suitable for use by criminal and terrorist organizations, political dissidents or whistleblowers (for a thorough discussion of the dark web as a tool for international terrorist groups see Chen, 2012).
9 Natural language processing is a field within computer science studying how computational techniques can be used to process natural language text or speech to make it suitable for various tasks such as translation or the creation of data sets that can be employed to perform sentiment analysis; thus, it can essentially be described as a manipulative process meant to extract information from unstructured natural language documents (Rodrigues & Teixeira, 2015).

References

Amoore, L. & Piotukh, V. (2016). Introduction. In Amoore, L. & Piotukh, V. (Eds.), *Algorithmic life: Calculative devices in the age of big data* (pp. 1–18). London & New York: Routledge.

Appelbaum, J., Gibson, A., Guarnieri, C., Müller-Maguhn, A., Poitras, L., Rosenbach, M., . . . & Sohnteimer, M. (2015, January 17). The digital arms race: NSA preps America for future battle. *Der Spiegel*. Available at http://www.spiegel.de/international/world/new-snowden-docs-indicate-scope-of-nsa-preparations-for-cyber-battle-a-1013409.html [Accessed on 10 April 2016].

Applegate, S.D. (2011). Cybermilitias and political hackers – Use of irregular forces in cyberwarfare. *IEEE Security & Privacy*, 9(5), 16–22.

Barkham, P. (2008, February 4). Hackers declare war on scientologists amid claims of heavy-handed cruise control. *The Guardian*. Available at http://www.theguardian.com/technology/2008/feb/04/news [Accessed on 10 April 2016].

Botta, F., Moat, H.S. & Preis, T. (2015). Quantifying crowd size with mobile phone and Twitter data. *Royal Society Open Science*, 2(150162). Available at http://rsos.royalsocietypublishing.org/content/royopensci/2/5/150162.full.pdf [Accessed on 10 April 2016].

Bremmer, I. (2016a, March 21). *How technology creates 21st-century political risk*. Available at https://www.linkedin.com/pulse/how-technology-creates-21st-century-political-risk-ian-bremmer?trk=prof-post [Accessed on 10 April 2016].

Bremmer, I. (2016b, April 6). These 5 facts explain the massive political fallout from the Panama papers. *Time*. Available at http://time.com/4283587/these-5-facts-explain-the-massive-political-fallout-from-the-panama-papers/ [Accessed on 10 April 2016].

Brenner, S.W. (2012). *Cybercrime and the law: Challenges, issues, and outcomes*. Boston: Northeastern.

Brewster, T. (2014, June 17). The digital arms race – and what is being done to fight it. *The Guardian*. Available at http://www.theguardian.com/technology/2014/jun/17/the-digital-arms-race-and-what-is-being-done-to-fight-it [Accessed on 10 April 2016].

Broad, W.J., Markoff, J. & Sanger, D.E. (2011, January 15). Israeli test on worm called crucial in Iran nuclear delay. *The New York Times*. Available at http://www.nytimes.com/2011/01/16/world/middleeast/16stuxnet.html?pagewanted=all&_r=0 [Accessed on 10 April 2016].

Brynjolfsson, E. & McAfee, A. (2011). *Race against the machine: How the digital revolution is accelerating innovation, driving productivity, and irreversibly transforming employment and the economy*. Lexington: Digital Frontier Press.

Chemier, B. & Milosevic, T. (2013, December 16). Recorded future used to predict crises. *International Policy Digest*. Available at http://intpolicydigest.org/2013/12/16/recorded-future-used-predict-crises/ [Accessed on 10 April 2016].

Chen, H. (2012). *Dark web: Exploring and data mining the dark side of the web*. New York: Springer.

Coleman, G. (2014). *Hacker, hoaxer, whistleblower, spy: The many faces of Anonymous*. London & New York: Verso.

Cook, T. (2016, February 16). *A message to our customers*. Available at http://www.apple.com/customer-letter/ [Accessed on 10 April 2016].

Craigen, D., Diakun-Thibault, N. & Purse, R. (2014). Defining cybersecurity. *Technology Innovation Management Review*, 4(10). Available at http://timreview.ca/article/835 [Accessed on 10 April 2016].

Dahan, M. (2013). Hacking for the homeland: Patriotic hackers versus hacktivists. In Hart, D. (Ed.), *International conference on information warfare and security: 51-VII* (pp. 51–63). Reading: Academic Conferences International Limited.

Dalal, S., Khodyakov, D., Srinivasan, R., Straus, S. & Adams, J. (2011). ExpertLens: A system for eliciting opinions from a large pool of non-collocated experts with diverse knowledge. *Technological Forecasting and Social Change*, 78(8), 1426–1444.

Deibert, R. (2013). *Black code: Inside the battle for cyberspace.* Toronto: McClelland & Stewart.

Deibert, R. (2015). The geopolitics of cyberspace after Snowden. *Current History*, 114(68), 9–15.

The Economist explains: How Guy Fawkes became the face of post-modern protest. (2014, November 4). *The Economist.* Available at http://www.economist.com/blogs/economist-explains/2014/11/economist-explains-3 [Accessed on 10 April 2016].

Gartner (2015, November 10). *Gartner says 6.4 billion connected "things" will be in use in 2016, up 30 percent from 2015.* Available at http://www.gartner.com/newsroom/id/3165317 [Accessed on 10 April 2016].

Greenberg, A. (2014, November 19). Hacker lexicon: What is the dark web? *Wired.* Available at http://www.wired.com/2014/11/hacker-lexicon-whats-dark-web/ [Accessed on 10 April 2016].

Greenberg, A. (2015, July 5). Hacking team breach shows a global spying firm run amok. *Wired.* Available at http://www.wired.com/2015/07/hacking-team-breach-shows-global-spying-firm-run-amok/ [Accessed on 10 April 2016].

Höller, J., Tsiatsis, V., Mulligan, C., Karnouskos, S., Avesand, S. & Boyle, D. (2015). *From machine-to-machine to the internet of things: Introduction to a new age of intelligence.* Oxford: Academic Press.

Howard, P.N. (2015). *Pax technica: How the internet of things may set us free or lock us up.* New Haven, CT & London: Yale University Press.

IBM (2015). *Cyber security intelligence index.* Available at http://public.dhe.ibm.com/common/ssi/ecm/se/en/sew03073usen/SEW03073USEN.PDF [Accessed on 10 April 2016].

Interview (2015d, October 1). Semi-structured face-to-face interview with security operations manager at global business/financial intelligence firm.

Interview (2015e, October 3). Semi-structured face-to-face interview with political risk analyst at global risk forecasting company.

Interview (2015h, December 13). Semi-structured face-to-face interview with policy analyst at a think tank specializing in the privatization of security.

Interview (2015l, December 28). Semi-structured written interview with managing director of international risk and due diligence consulting firm.

ITU (2015). *World telecommunication/ICT indicators database 2015 (19th edition).* Available at http://www.itu.int/en/ITU-D/Statistics/Pages/publications/wtid.aspx [Accessed on 10 April 2016].

Japkowicz, N. & Stefanowski, J. (2015). A machine learning perspective on big data analysis. In Japkowicz, N. & Stefanowski, J. (Eds.), *Big data analysis: New algorithms for a new society* (pp. 1–31). New York: Springer.

Jarvis, L., Nouri, L. & Whiting, A. (2014). Understanding, locating and constructing cyberterrorism. In Chen, T., Jarvis, L. & Macdonald, S. (Eds.), *Cyberterrorism: Understanding, assessment and response* (pp. 25–41). New York: Springer.

Jiang, S. (2015, January 21). Shanghai new year's eve stampede 'totally preventable'. *CNN.* Available at http://edition.cnn.com/2015/01/21/world/china-shanghai-stampede/ [Accessed on 10 April 2016].

Jordan, T. & Taylor, A. (2004). *Hacktivism and cyberwars: Rebels with a cause?* London & New York: Routledge.

Kallus, N. (2014). On the predictive power of web intelligence and social media: The best way to predict the future is to tweet it. In Atzmueller, M., Chin, A., Janssen, F., Schweizer, I. & Trattner, C. (Eds.), *Big data analytics in the social and ubiquitous context* (pp. 26–45). Geneva: Springer Lecture Notes in Artificial Intelligence 9546.

Lindsay, J.R. (2015). Introduction – China and cybersecurity: Controversy and context. In Lindsay, J.R., Cheung, T.M. & Reveron, D.S. (Eds.), *China and cybersecurity: Espionage, strategy, and politics in the digital domain* (pp. 1–26). Oxford: Oxford University Press.

MacMillan, D. (2015, May 6). Banjo raises $100 million to detect world events in real time. *The Wall Street Journal.* Available at http://blogs.wsj.com/digits/2015/05/06/banjo-raises-100-million-to-detect-world-events-in-real-time/ [Accessed on 10 April 2016].

Mckinsey & Company (2015, June). *Unlocking the potential of the Internet of Things.* Mckinsey Global Institute Report. Available at http://www.mckinsey.com/business-functions/business-technology/our-insights/the-internet-of-things-the-value-of-digitizing-the-physical-world [Accessed on 10 April 2016].

Mckinsey Global Institute (2015). *The internet of things: Mapping the value beyond the hype.* Available at http://www.mckinsey.com/business-functions/business-technology/our-insights/the-internet-of-things-the-value-of-digitizing-the-physical-world [Accessed on 10 April 2016].

Messmer, E. (1999, April 6). Serb supporters sock it to NATO, U.S. web sites. *CNN.* Available at http://edition.cnn.com/TECH/computing/9904/06/serbnato.idg/index.html [Accessed on 10 April 2016].

Metz, C. (2016, April 5). Forget Apple vs. the FBI: Whatsapp just switched on encryption for a billion people. *Wired.* Available at http://www.wired.com/2016/04/forget-apple-vs-fbi-whatsapp-just-switched-on-encryption-billion-people/ [Accessed on 10 April 2016].

Natale, S. & Ballatore, A. (2014). The web will kill them all: New media, digital utopia, and political struggle in the Italian 5-Star movement. *Media Culture Society*, 36(1), 105–121.

Obermaier, F., Obermayer, B., Wormer, V. & Jaschensky, W. (2016). About the Panama papers. *Süddeutsche Zeitung.* Available at http://panamapapers.sueddeutsche.de/articles/56febff0a1bb8d3c3495adf4/ [Accessed on 10 April 2016].

Olson, P. (2012). *We are Anonymous: Inside the hacker world of Lulzsec, Anonymous, and the global cyber insurgency.* New York: Little, Brown & Company.

Paletta, D., Yadron, D. & Valentino-Devries, J. (2015, October 11). Cyberwar ignites a new arms race. *The Wall Street Journal.* Available at http://www.wsj.com/articles/cyberwar-ignites-a-new-arms-race-1444611128 [Accessed on 10 April 2016].

Palmer, M. (2012, February 27). WikiLeaks releases 5m intelligence emails. *The Financial Times.* Available at http://www.ft.com/intl/cms/s/0/2b933f26-613d-11e1-a738-00144fe-abdc0.html#axzz44aukuNXb [Accessed on 10 April 2016].

Papacostantinou, G. (2003). E-Policy: The impact and political economy of the digital revolution. In Doukidis, G.I., Mylonopoulos, N. & Pouloudi, N. (Eds.), *Social and economic transformation in the digital era* (pp. 19–30). Hershey: IGI Global.

Perlroth, N. & Sanger, D.E. (2013, March 28). Cyberattacks seem meant to destroy, not just disrupt. *The New York Times.* Available at http://www.nytimes.com/2013/03/29/technology/corporate-cyberattackers-possibly-state-backed-now-seek-to-destroy-data.html [Accessed on 10 April 2016].

Qiao, L. & Wang, X. (1999). *Unrestricted warfare.* Beijing: PLA Literature and Arts Publishing House.

Raleigh, C., Linke, A., Hegre, H. & Karlsen, J. (2010). Introducing ACLED: An armed conflict location and event dataset. *Journal of Peace Research*, 47(5), 651–660.

Reiss, R. (2016, February 1). 5 ways the IoT will transform the insurance industry. *Forbes.* Available at http://www.forbes.com/sites/robertreiss/2016/02/01/5-ways-the-iot-will-transform-the-insurance-industry/#c7d3ee672cb9 [Accessed on 10 April 2016].

Reuters (2012, December 9). Aramco says cyberattack was aimed at production. *The New York Times*. Available at http://www.nytimes.com/2012/12/10/business/global/saudi-aramco-says-hackers-took-aim-at-its-production.html [Accessed on 10 April 2016].

Rodrigues, M. & Teixeira, A. (2015). *Advanced applications of natural language processing for performing information extraction*. New York: Springer.

Sanger, D.E. (2012, June 1). Obama order sped up wave of cyberattacks against Iran. *The New York Times*. Available at http://www.nytimes.com/2012/06/01/world/middleeast/obama-ordered-wave-of-cyberattacks-against-iran.html?pagewanted=4&_r=1&hp [Accessed on 10 April 2016].

Scott-Railton, J. (2013). *Revolutionary risks: Cyber technology and threats in the 2011 Libyan revolution*. Newport, RI: US Naval War College, Center on Irregular Warfare and Armed Groups.

Sevignani, S. (2013). The commodification of privacy on the Internet. *Science and Public Policy*, 40(6), 733–739.

Singer, P.W. & Friedman, A. (2014). *Cybersecurity and cyberwar: What everybody needs to know*. Oxford: Oxford University Press.

Taylor, J. (2010, August 18). Google chief: My fears for generation Facebook. *The Independent*. Available at http://www.independent.co.uk/life-style/gadgets-and-tech/news/google-chief-my-fears-for-generation-facebook-2055390.html [Accessed on 10 April 2016].

The Economist (2016, April 10). What the Panama papers really reveal about David Cameron. Available at http://www.economist.com/blogs/bagehot/2016/04/david-cameron-s-taxes [Accessed on 10 April 2016].

Touhill, G.J. & Touhill, C.J. (2014). *Cybersecurity for executives: A practical guide*. Hoboken: John Wiley & Sons, Inc.

van der Meer, S. (2015, September). Foreign policy responses to international cyber-attacks: Some lessons learned. *Clingendael-Netherland Institute of International Relation Policy Brief*. Available at http://www.clingendael.nl/sites/default/files/Clingendael_Policy_Brief_Foreign%20Policy%20Responses_September2015.pdf [Accessed on 10 April 2016].

Vogelsang, M. (2010). *Digitalization in open economies: Theory and policy implications*. Heidelberg: Springer.

Wallace, J. (2014, July 30). Using open source intelligence to track Boko Haram tactics. *The Huffington Post*. Available at http://www.huffingtonpost.com/joshua-wallace/using-open-source-intelli_b_5404051.html [Accessed on 10 April 2016].

WEF (2015). *The global information technology report 2015: ICTs for inclusive growth*. Geneva: WEF. Available at http://www3.weforum.org/docs/WEF_Global_IT_Report_2015.pdf [Accessed on 10 April 2016].

Weimann, G. (2004). Cyberterrorism: How real is the threat? *United States Institute for Peace Special Report*. Available at http://www.usip.org/sites/default/files/sr119.pdf [Accessed on 10 April 2016].

Werbin, K.C. (2012). Auto-biography: On the immanent commodification of personal information. *International Review of Information Ethics*, 17, 46–53.

Wieczner, J. (2015, December 7). How investors are using social media to make money. *Fortune*. Available at http://fortune.com/2015/12/07/dataminr-hedge-funds-twitter-data/ [Accessed on 10 April 2016].

WikiLeaks (2012, February 12). *The global intelligence files*. Available at https://wikileaks.org/the-gifiles.html [Accessed on 10 April 2016].

Winseck, D. (2013). Weak links and WikiLeaks: How control of critical internet resources and social media companies' business models undermine the networked free press. In Brevini, B., Hintz, A. & McCurdy, P. (Eds.), *Beyond Wikileaks: Implications for the future of communications, journalism and society* (pp. 166–177). London: Palgrave Macmillan.

Zekos, G. (2005). Foreign direct investment in a digital economy. *European Business Review*, 17(1), 52–68.

Zetter, K. (2014). *Countdown to zero day: Stuxnet and the launch of the world's first digital weapon*. New York: Crown Pub.

Zhou, J., Pei, H. & Wu, H. (2016, March 22). Early warning of human crowds based on query data from Baidu map: Analysis based on Shanghai stampede. *Baidu research –* Big Data Lab, Beijing. Available at http://arxiv.org/pdf/1603.06780v1.pdf [Accessed on 10 April 2016].

Concluding remarks

To date, political risk analysis remains a practice-driven field of inquiry. To borrow the words of a renowned PR scholar:

> Political risk analysis is a field replete with competition and demands as the world becomes an increasingly complex mosaic of political entities, cultures, tribes, racial configurations, and religions. Political risk analysis has been around as a field of study and a service to foreign investors for 50 years but we still don't have consensus on what it actually is.
>
> (Howell, 2013, p. 3)

The overarching objective of this work was to call for a reappraisal of the conceptualization and measurement of political risk from an academic point of view, showing how theory and practice are inextricably intertwined and stressing that even the most pragmatic approaches to risk analysis cannot escape the necessity of relying on epistemological assumptions – which in turn inevitably have a bearing on operationalization, assessment and eventually also management.

Chapter 1 went through the vast plethora of alternative – sometimes even conflicting – meanings attached to the catch-all term 'political risk', recalling the traditional distinction between 'micro' and 'macro' political risk and showing that for operationalization purposes PR can in fact be treated as a social science concept, more specifically as a latent variable to measure which it is necessary to resort to carefully selected proxy variables. Chapter 2 explored some crucial epistemological and heuristic issues raised by PRA. In particular, it showed how 'prediction' has traditionally been downplayed by social scientists in favor of 'explanation', as if they were heterogeneous rather than essentially analogous tasks; it subsequently argued in favor of a more clear-cut distinction between 'prediction' and 'forecast', describing the first as an apodictic statement and the second as a probabilistic one; and finally it proposed a matrix that, acknowledging the dyadic nature of political risk, intersects different levels of analysis for both political risk sources and impacts, essentially proposing a more nuanced and accurate way to categorize risks and impacts vis-à-vis the old 'micro' versus 'macro' distinction. Chapter 3 started with a discussion of the quantitative-qualitative divide in PRA methods, warning the reader against the intrinsic 'persuasiveness' of numbers and the 'overselling' of quantitative indicators. Subsequently, in an attempt to shed some light on the under-explored question of PR meta-analysis, Chapter 3 proposed a comparison between five different PR indexes by looking at their performance in forecasting the Arab uprisings. While such performance was – indeed predictably – mediocre, as after all such a large-scale event was certainly difficult to predict accurately, the meta-analysis conducted showed that the shortcomings of the existing approaches to PR assessment can be attributed at least partially to the way in which PR indexes are built. In contrast to the 'pragmatic turn' taking place in PRA in the last few years, throughout this work it has been argued that choices regarding the dimensions to be incorporated in PR indexes when the concept is operationalized are inevitably theory-laden. It has also been argued that, once epistemological and heuristic problems have been settled, by borrowing from the existing theories, the analyst can avoid the conceptual loopholes implicit in the complex task of forecasting social and political events while combining them with the cultural, geographical, strategic specificities of the relevant corporate actor. In discussing some of the most used techniques to provide political forecasts, Chapter 4 further delved into the quantitative-qualitative methods divide, showing that clear-cut distinctions in this sense are neither possible nor desirable, and that in general it does not make much sense to argue in favor of one approach rather than another: in fact, the convenience of the various methods available can be assessed in a comparative fashion only by first specifying the type of question that the analyst wants to answer. For instance, while the use of statistical extrapolation of past trends may be the most suitable choice when it is reasonable to assume that the future will resemble the past, in order to gauge the occurrence of rare events – the so-called 'black swans' – other techniques such as the Delphi or scenario analysis may be preferable. Chapter 5 started off by highlighting the ubiquity of human judgment in PRA techniques. Consequently, the chapter outlined a distinction between subject-matter expertise and cognitive and forecasting skills, showing how these two aspects, although they can both be brought back to 'human judgment', in fact refer to distinct and complementary operations in PRA. In particular, the chapter confuted the equation of 'judgment' with 'forecast', providing examples of 'nonpredictive' expert political judgment. Chapter 6 offered an overview of the formidable sociopolitical impacts of the digital revolution on a global scale. First, the chapter stressed the importance of understanding that cyber and political risks are intimately intertwined, an aspect that is often overlooked by consumers of PRA who tend to perceive cyber risks as a separate category vis-à-vis geo-political risks. Second, the chapter discussed some of the most promising, cutting-edge techniques developed to provide real-time intelligence forecasts based on big data analysis, showing that their main limitation at the present time is that they cannot convey long-term insights. While the author acknowledged their extraordinary potential as a source of sociopolitical intelligence – including beneficial applications for early warning in cases of possible conflict or calamity – the ambiguous nature of such techniques was also emphasized, stressing how based on the same premises tools for mass surveillance may also be developed and deployed.

To conclude, it can be said that while some of the questions raised at the beginning of the book found an answer, much room is left for further inquiry in the realm of political risk analysis in order to effectively bridge the hiatus between academia and practitioners. After all, as already stressed, a further central objective of this book was to reorganize the research agenda on PRA. In this sense, it can be said that future research could shed further light on issues concerning the relationship between certain types of institutional settings (such as 'hybrid' regimes) and particular forms of political risks (such as 'creeping expropriation' or the outbreak of low-intensity conflict); it could focus on modeling the 'external' dimension of 'systemic' political risk, by looking at the regional and/or the global level; or it could explore the promises of computational social science (Cioffi-Revilla, 2014) in terms of analysis of complex systems for predictive purposes while in parallel delving more in depth into the epistemological foundations of future-oriented political risk assessments.

References

Cioffi-Revilla, C. (2014). *Introduction to computational social science: Principles and applications*. London: Springer.

Howell, L.D. (2013). Country and political risk analyses: "What are they?". In Howell, L.D. (Ed.), *The handbook of country and political risk analysis* (pp. 3–24). East Syracuse: PRS Group Inc.

Index

For Product Safety Concerns and Information please contact our EU
representative GPSR@taylorandfrancis.com
Taylor & Francis Verlag GmbH, Kaufingerstraße 24, 80331 München, Germany

www.ingramcontent.com/pod-product-compliance
Ingram Content Group UK Ltd.
Pitfield, Milton Keynes, MK11 3LW, UK
UKHW020948180425
457613UK00019B/582